IN OVER
MY HEAD

*The Adventures of a Brooklyn Bad Boy Who Became a
Madison Avenue Prince*

Henry Holtzman

ISBN: 1979767769
ISBN 13: 9781979767767
Library of Congress Control Number: 2017917836
CreateSpace Independent Publishing Platform
North Charleston, South Carolina

DEDICATION

For my wife, Cheryl, who gave this book its happy ending

CONTENTS

1

OFF TO A BAD START

SEPTEMBER 12, 1942

My mother cried when I was born, and they weren't tears of joy. Years later I was told that I was covered all over in black hair, and she thought I looked like a monkey. My mother was always one for appearances.

This was one thing that she couldn't blame on my father. His side of the family were all pale-skinned, fair-haired Ashkenazi Jews. Her people were the dark gypsy types with dangerous looks.

After that inglorious beginning, much to my mother's dismay, I made it a point to take after the old man in every way I could. That hairy entrance into the world was just my first message of defiance, telling everyone out there that I refused to accommodate anyone's expectations but my own.

2

THE LITTLE KINGDOM ON THE HILL

Approximately twenty-two thousand years ago, the glaciers of the last Ice Age reached their farthest point south and stopped. In Brooklyn, the glacial retreat left a long ridge overlooking the plain that was to become the central and southern parts of the borough. It was atop that lofty ridge that I was brought to live a few days after my birth: to the tiny kingdom of Union Street.

The one-block street had the bustle and energy of a European village, filled with people minding each other's business, conspiring, clashing, and getting along. It was a place filled with color and brashness and optimism despite its location in Brownsville, Brooklyn, a neighborhood that had just clawed its way up from bottom drawer to lower middle class.

Brownsville had been home to Murder Incorporated, the gang that did the hits for the Mafia, and when I arrived, it was still filled with gangsters, racketeers, scam artists, street gangs, bookie joints, and chop shops. To be fair, the greater population was composed of garment workers, truckers, shopkeepers, tradesmen, and salespeople. They were for the most part honest people, but not unwilling to take advantage of some edge, if it was there for the taking.

There was common ground for the people on both sides of the criminal divide: they had all come up the hard way, from the shtetls of Eastern Europe, with its inequities, humiliations, and murderous pogroms, and through the teeming tenements of the Lower East Side. But even given its low socioeconomic status, Union Street had a special splendor.

Our little block was seemingly cut off from the rest of the world, coming to a T on both ends. To the west, it ended at the cobblestones of Portal Street and the wall of the elevated subway tracks that shot out from under the ground. The trains came roaring out, gasping for air, happily returned from their subterranean journey to the city, their iron wheels screaming. Every twelve minutes one of those metal monsters would send shudders through our tiny one-bedroom apartment as it galloped past our windows.

Beyond the tracks was Lincoln Terrace Park, with its trees, meadows, and playing fields. North of us, a block away, was Eastern Parkway, six lanes of traffic rushing like a two-way river, bound on both sides by tree-lined promenades—a Parisian boulevard surrounded by a Brooklyn slum.

At the bottom of the block where our hill sloped down was a large empty lot, a place for kids to make fires, play war games, and hide behind bushes while spying on the outside world.

In the 1940s my friends and I would launch patrols to hunt down Adolf Hitler in the event he was still alive and hiding in America. We knew that we wouldn't have to look far, because if he was there, he was undoubtedly hiding in the cellar of my apartment building, cowering behind the mountain of coal in the furnace room.

We never caught him, but if we had, we would have dragged him out into the street and beaten him mercilessly to avenge the six million Jews he had murdered. Only then would we hand him over to J. Edgar Hoover and his G-men.

Later, in the early 1950s, we were prepared to defend America and beat back the Communist Chinese hordes, if they somehow swept ashore at Coney Island. Perched at my sixth-floor living-room window, I was diligently on the watch for any sign of the Yellow Peril, ready to alert the guys on the block and spring into action, leading a counterattack that would start on Union Street and end up in Beijing.

On our block there were three six-story apartment buildings and a row of four-family brick houses—spawning grounds for scores of children and adults of various ages, who filled the street and the stoops and lined the front of the buildings with folding chairs. These people were loud, tough, and funny. They had nicknames like Woo-Woo, Cha-Cha, Mister Clean, Simian, Snot Rag, and Piss-Head.

Around the corner on Eastern Parkway, there was only a small, motley group of kids, whom we looked down upon like Romans viewing the outlying barbarians. Every so often someone would shout out, "Let's go have a rock fight with the Easterns," and we would gather handfuls of stones and go marching around the corner, where we would bombard that hapless crew.

This would continue until one of our gang would holler, "Here comes Leon and Junior!" Two black brothers, just a bit older than we were, would come streaking out of their apartment to defend the honor of Eastern Parkway. They would come at us like silent avenging wraiths. We'd drop our rocks and run for our lives.

Around the other corner, past the elevated tracks on East New York Avenue, was a narrow dirt path, just wide enough for a car to pass through. It led down into a gully and disappeared into high grasses littered with mountains of automobile tires. Anyone who walked down the path a little would catch sight of a run-down wooden house. Very few people dared to venture down that path, and then only for a few yards, because in that house lived the Cummings family.

There were always about seven of them running in a pack; they all looked alike, and they seemed to be constantly replenished as they grew older. They would appear out of nowhere, all seven of them, running at full speed and screaming like banshees. They were like a human tornado, sudden and violent. Any kid they swooped down on would be knocked to the ground, beaten, and kicked before the Cummings kids raced on to wherever it was they were going.

I could survey all of this from our apartment where I could see all the way to Coney Island and the ocean. 6-H was on the sixth and top floor, making us the pinnacle of the pinnacle under a crenelated roof that gave the building an appropriately castle-like appearance. From our windows, I would spend endless hours watching the subway trains hurrying past or the trolleys flashing sparks as they changed direction. I could spy on the buses, police cars, ambulances, and fire trucks forcing their way through the busy traffic of East New York Avenue. I would study the roof-scape of wooden water towers and later the growing congestion of television aerials. I could pretend that I could actually see the ocean on the horizon. At night, I would be hypnotized by the large, multicolored and constantly changing neon signs on the roofs of the two clothing factories across the way. With my cheek resting against the window, and the stale, dead, and dirty smell of the glass filling my nostrils, I watched and made up stories about the people out there in the world down below.

3

FEAR AND THE FELDMANS

1944

At the beginning, there was only my family adoring me and anointing me prince of the universe, and I must humbly admit, after I shed my hair I was a beautiful baby. Soon, even strangers eyeing me in my carriage or my stroller would agree. It was obviously true; a thousand Brooklynites couldn't possibly be wrong. Armed with this knowledge, I was prepared for my first real encounter with the outside world. Enter the Feldmans.

There were four Feldmans. Fay, the mother, was constantly in our house. Her appearance lacked any clear definition: a shapeless body in a formless housecoat, a lumpy smudge of blunt features topped by a shaggy tangle of gray steel-wool hair. She walked into our unlocked apartment several times a day, announcing herself with a loud: "Knock, knock, come in", then "Hello, Holtzman?" Invariably followed by an explosive five-syllable belch and the words, "Oy, I've got gas."

Leon, the father, diminutive, mousy and bald, had the least to say in the Feldman household. He was a tailor, and could usually be found sitting at a sewing machine, tucked into a corner of the foyer, working on garments that he'd brought home.

On the other hand, Barbara Feldman, three years older than I, was glamorous and knowing. I intuitively knew that she held the keys to unimaginable secrets.

Then there was Sheila Feldman, who was my very own age. A cute, dimpled face crowned by a shock of springy, sawdust-colored Shirley Temple curls. Sheila laughed easily, a winning trait that charmed me for almost a year, until I realized that she laughed at everything, whether it was funny or not. It then occurred to me that maybe Sheila just wasn't very bright.

Sheila and I were a constant couple, sitting side by side in our strollers or bumping into each other as we walked along on our still-shaky legs. Her mother started referring to me as her future son-in-law. Here I was, only two years old, and I was already getting married off to the first and only girl I'd ever met. I knew there had to be other choices for a prince.

Then one day, my mother brought me down to meet Gerry Post, a boy my age who lived on the third floor. Playing with Gerry made me realize that boys did different things than girls. Things like wildly running through an apartment, knocking things over, jumping on couches, and making fart noises. It seemed to have a purpose beyond just standing around giggling. While I still had regular visits with Sheila, I was now clearly differentiated from her. I was a boy.

Soon I met other boys my age. Our gang of four-year-olds stayed close to the stoop, where we could speak of manly things like baseball and cowboy movies, and take up masculine pursuits like hide-and-go-seek or ring-a-lievo.

This was the time in our young lives when pecking orders were established; I figured my innate intelligence would be apparent to all the other kids and they would naturally look to me for leadership. This strategy suited me and worked well enough to satisfy my need for recognition, but it all came tumbling down when Larry and Corky appeared.

Larry and Corky were bigger, stronger, and fiercer—but not smarter—than the rest of us. They took offense if they felt that one of the other kids was trying to put them down by showing off his own smarts. Unfortunately, that other kid was usually me. However, no matter how many times I got the crap beaten out of me, I wasn't going to stop broadcasting my opinions or wisecracking about some ridiculous claim being made by one of my tormentors. My wit was my weapon, and I wouldn't allow myself to be disarmed. To do so would be to give up my identity.

Still, I learned that I had entered into a new arena where brute force and cunning, rather than intelligence and good looks, would be required to compete. I also learned about the smell of the concrete sidewalk and of the dirty glass windows of cars parked on the street, as I was repeatedly smashed into those surfaces, my head held against them by one or both of the bullies.

I knew that I couldn't retreat to my life with Sheila Feldman. If I was going to get out of being endlessly beaten up by Larry and Corky, I was going to have to fight my way out. My first thought was that there was strength in numbers. The other kids were also being victimized by the two bullies, so we all shared a righteous cause. I pitched my idea to about a half-dozen other kids, and they all agreed to stand together, but when the time came, nobody made a move. Maybe the others harbored the same resentment toward me as Larry and Corky did. Maybe they thought I was getting my just deserts, and maybe they were right.

One thing was clear: something was out of place between myself and the rest of the world; the pieces just didn't fit. It couldn't have been me, because I was perfect. It had to be the world that wasn't right.

Reading and drawing were my great escape into a private world of my own. I guess I got the reading bug from my father. Although he never got out of high school, his library contained many of the great authors, from classical times down to the time of his adulthood.

Reading didn't help me much in dealing with Larry and Corky. It only served to make me feel more superior to them, and it gave me more opportunities to correct their erroneous comments, which, of course, always led to a beating. Even when I kept my mouth shut, I would incur their wrath. I discovered that something about the way I looked communicated intelligence and skepticism, and that if I just listened and watched while others spoke, they thought that I was casting judgment on them. They were right.

Throughout these early years, Fay Feldman continued her habit of barging into our apartment unannounced. She began to make nutty remarks about my mother's housekeeping, complaining that it was too good. After my mother cleaned the house and scrubbed the floors, she always polished up our doorknob and doorbell with its brass nameplate. Mrs. Feldman told her that she was shaming all the neighbors because our door was the only one with gleaming hardware.

My mother had other things to worry about: mainly feeding a family of four on the twenty-five dollars that my father's meager earnings allowed for food. Soon my mother started locking our front door, which seemed to insult Mrs. Feldman, and a coolness developed between them.

That would have seemed to be the end of the Feldman chapter of my life, but there was still one major event that was to be played out. By the second grade, I had somehow decided that it was better to be bad than to be good. Being only six years old at the time, I didn't have a real handle on the causes of this phenomenon. It might have been part of a toughening process to help me deal with Larry and Corky. Or it might well have been payback for my parents' constant bickering; or resentment of my mother's expectations for me to succeed in a way that my father hadn't; or just my fierce desire for self-determination. I'm pretty sure that boredom and an overactive mind had a lot to do with it, as did my need to establish my macho credibility.

I made faces and wisecracks in class. I spoke back to my teachers and made jokes behind their backs. I got into fights and played pranks on the local shopkeepers. In the neighborhood parlance, I was a regular hooligan. One of my favorite pieces of mischief was the water-bag drop, which I usually executed with at least one accomplice. We'd take a brown paper shopping bag and a bucket of water up to the roof. We'd wait for a car to turn onto the block, then fill the bag with water, and drop it, so that it landed just a few feet in front of the moving car. The bag would land with an explosive bang. The car and most of the street would be awash with water. The driver, scared shitless, would slam on the brakes, and we'd laugh hysterically as we ran downstairs and hid out in my apartment. That accomplishment, however, was eventually eclipsed, when Richie Wood started tossing shopping bags filled with live cats off the roof, in a rigorous scientific investigation of the nine-lives myth.

Unfortunately for me, my bad behavior infuriated my father. Normally, he was a very affectionate man who readily showed his love, but when it came to my misbehavior, my father became explosively violent. Maybe it was his way of venting his frustrations with marriage and money; maybe it was his disappointment in the way I seemed to be developing; maybe he thought that it was the best way to straighten me out; maybe it was all those things. Whatever the reason, if he came home from work and my mother told him that I'd been bad, he whaled the shit out of me.

Sometimes he'd hit me with his hands, but usually he'd use "the strap." He had a worn-out belt that hung like a limp noodle from a hook in the broom closet, and he'd give my ass a good lashing with it. Sometimes, if I could get away, I'd escape to the bathroom and lock myself in there. My father would bang on the door, demanding that I open up, which I'd refuse to do unless he'd promise not to hit me. His next move was usually to threaten to call the police or the fire department to come and break the door down. This always got me, and I'd reluctantly unlock the door and take my medicine.

One day I must have done something particularly bad. I don't remember what it was, but it must have been something that was guaranteed to get me a serious licking. My father was as good as a clock. No matter how hard I wished for him to be late, he came home at the same time every evening, giving the downstairs buzzer two quick hits to let us know he was on the way up. A few minutes later, I heard his key in the lock, and my mother went to the door to greet him and tell him what I had done.

He glared at me as he quickly hung up his coat and put his hat on the closet shelf. Then he went for me. I managed to squirm out of his grasp and pushed myself into the wall that separated our apartment from the Feldmans'. Then I screamed bloody murder as loud and long as I could. I screamed louder than I had thought myself capable of.

My father recoiled, but that only put him off for a second. That second, however, gave me enough time to duck under his hands and race into the bedroom and around to the far side of the bed. He strode into the room, sizing up the situation.

That's when the pounding on the front door began. My mother quickly opened the door, and in flew Mrs. Feldman. "Holtzman, what's happening? It sounded like someone was being murdered in here."

Fay Feldman to the rescue! Maybe it was embarrassing for me to hide behind this woman's skirt and shameful to use her in this way. It certainly wasn't what a real tough guy would have done, but I didn't care. My hide was saved, at least for that day. That day Fay Feldman was the most beautiful woman in the world.

4

PACKING HEAT

1953

I was packing heat. There was no way any self-respecting sixth grader was going without a piece during water-gun season. Certainly, I wasn't.

Everything in my neighborhood had a season. There was punch-ball season, stick-ball season, ring-a-lievo season, you name it, we had a season for it, and now it was water-gun season, and I wasn't going to be cornered by my enemies without being able to give as good as I got. If anyone wanted a piece of me, I was ready.

It was a perfect blue-sky, white-cloud morning. The spring weather was still cool enough to call for a light jacket, and as I entered the hulking red brick bruise of a prison that they called a school, I kept my gun hidden in the side pocket. My classroom was on the fourth and top floor of the building, and I trudged up the wide metal staircase along with hundreds of other fellow students. We moved with slow and heavy steps, as if we were a prison gang on our way to the rock pile. The stairwell was filled with a muffled column of murmurs and footfalls, changing yet unchanging. There was something about this depressed beginning of a day that demanded a rebellious response.

Looking up, I spotted one of the most hated jailers, Mrs. Baxter, a large-boned woman with messy brown hair, thick glasses, and an angry red face. She had the reputation of a tyrant, and my friend Philly, who was in her class, told me that he had to throw up every time she walked past his desk.

That was enough for me. Now I was going to exact revenge on her. The mob on the staircase was the perfect cover. She'd never know what hit her, and I'd fade into the crowd. She was directly above me, and I could see way up her dress, as far as her thick legs would allow. I took out my water gun, squeezed the trigger, and shot a hard, cold stream right up there.

I quickly slipped the gun back into my pocket as she screamed loud enough for the whole building to shake. "Who did that? Who did that?"

I had my most innocent face on, as if I had no idea what she was talking about.

"He did it!" said Ellen Moss, pointing at me. Ellen Moss was a tall, pretty girl in my grade. Bright too. I kind of liked her but didn't know what to do about that. But now that she was ratting me out, I knew exactly what to do; I ran up to where she was standing, next to the outraged Mrs. Baxter, and started to choke her.

It took about two seconds for Mrs. Baxter to pull me off her.

"I don't know what you're talking about. I didn't do anything," I proclaimed. But before I knew it, Mrs. Baxter had me against a wall and had taken my gun away. She took me into her classroom and made me sit there while she went to report me.

She came back about ten minutes later and told me to go to my own classroom. I was confused. I had figured she would be sending me down to the principal's office. I thought maybe I was getting off the hook.

When I walked into my class, everyone was already seated. Our teacher, Mr. Willen, called me over to his desk. He opened a drawer and pulled out my water gun.

"Is this yours?" he asked.

"No," I replied.

"This isn't yours?"

"No. Lots of kids have water guns. It's water-gun season." I figured that I'd tough it out. I was probably pretending to be James Cagney or Humphrey Bogart. They never spilled the beans about anything.

Mr. Willen sent me down to the principal's office, where I sat most of the day before being sent back to class. There wasn't any grilling, nor was there any corporal punishment. I'd served short time and gotten off easy.

But I still had to deal with Ellen Moss. She had squealed, and now she had to pay. I rejected the idea of bringing my friends along. This was my issue to deal with, and besides, she was a girl.

When the bell rang at three o'clock, I raced down the stairs and out of the building. It was perfect weather for playing ball or just hanging out on the stoop, but I had unfinished business to take care of. I wanted to make sure I was outside when Ellen Moss came out the door. Sure enough, she emerged about ten minutes later. I stayed back in the milling crowd and followed her at a safe distance.

She crossed over to the park on the other side of the street and walked toward the better part of the neighborhood, where there were mostly private and two-family houses. This was perfect, much better than jumping her on a street; here in the park, there were only a few people passing through.

I made my move when she was midway through the park. There was no one else around at that moment. I ran to catch up with her and spun her around. Now, stark reality began to take hold. Ellen Moss was a girl and a squealer, but she was as big as I was, maybe even bigger. This wasn't a movie, where the squealer would cower on the ground and beg forgiveness. In her mind, she had done the right thing, and had no intention of being blamed for it; she certainly had no intention of being pushed around by me.

I shoved her, and she shoved me right back. I tried to wrestle her down, but she was as quick and as strong as I was. We wound up trying to kick each other in the shins, without either of us landing a clean shot. It was a draw, but for me it was a total humiliation. How could I ever face Cagney or Bogart again? I could feel them looking down on me and shaking their heads in disgust. Fortunately, they were the only ones I brought along with me for this job, and they weren't going to rat me out to the guys on the block.

5

HIGH NOON AT PS 189

1954

The movie *High Noon* was a big hit at the box office in 1952, two years later the impression it had made on me was still stuck in my mind. It was what was then called a "psychological western." Gary Cooper, by then approaching middle age, was the sheriff of a small town. He was retiring from his job and marrying Grace Kelly, who was a young, beautiful practicing Quaker. As the newlyweds were about to depart on their honeymoon, word came that three men were on their way to kill Cooper.

The townspeople wanted no part of this trouble. They wanted Cooper to leave town. His new wife, a pacifist by religion, agreed with them. Cooper, however, knew in his heart that running away was just plain wrong. It went against everything that he had stood for.

I was struck by the similarity between Gary Cooper's situation and my own. But while his problem was solved after a cinematic gunfight, my problem was ongoing. I was getting beaten up by the two block bullies, while my supposed friends looked on, letting me stand alone, like a carpet on a clothesline waiting to get whacked.

Next year I was going on to junior high school, and a totally new and unknown universe. It was frightening, but it was also a chance for a new beginning. But all that was a good three months away. On this particular morning there was nothing for me to do except to have a good time, which meant getting out of the house and down to the street as soon as possible.

The only one of my gang there was Herbie from across the street. Herbie was one of the good guys. He was smart and had a sly sense of humor. His older brother, Stan, was a good athlete; his father, a ladies' hat manufacturer, went to Vegas twice a year and, rumor had it, played in the big floating crap game in Manhattan. All those things combined to make Herbie a valuable friend.

With no one else around, we decided to go to the park and try to get into a pickup basketball game.

We shot hoops until well past midday. Herbie and I were the only ones waiting for a turn, and we picked up three terrific players from the losing team. From there, we went on a winning tear that seemed as if it would never end. I was on a roll. I loved playing this game. I could get myself into a trancelike state, moving fluidly, always knowing where my teammates were, when to pass the ball, and when to shoot it. It was what in later years was called "being in the zone."

The weather was hot and muggy, but we were young and tireless, so when someone mentioned that it was nearly two o'clock, we were surprised. We finished off our game and headed home.

I wanted to make a quick detour into the schoolyard across the street. I'm not sure why. Maybe it was a last farewell. At any rate, we went in at the entrance farthest from our block with the intention of walking through to the opposite gate. Only things didn't work out quite that smoothly.

Sauntering into the schoolyard, I noticed a group of about ten kids hanging out against the fence. They lived on the school block. Some of them were my age, some a little older, some a little younger. I wasn't particularly friendly with any of them. I knew that some of them didn't like me at all.

During the winter, the kids on my block had wiped them out in a monumental and heroic snowball fight.

That was winter, long ago; now it was spring, time for old vendettas to thaw out and bloom. Time to go to war again. It seemed that the schoolyard gang was still nursing a grudge, and it seemed to be mostly directed at me.

"There's Holtzman," one of them shouted. "Let's get him!"

I hadn't realized that they disliked me *that* much. Maybe it was just that they thought we were trespassing on their turf, but on the other hand, I didn't hear anyone shouting, "Let's get Herbie."

Before I clearly understood their intentions, they had me cut off from the two gates to the street and were quickly closing in. I looked over to Herbie and noticed a distance growing between us. Then the gang of ten was right in my face, ready to rumble. I turned on my heels and ran, with them right on my back. I was pretty fast, but there was no place to run. I dodged, and ducked, and juked, and jived, but all to no avail, as I found myself with my back to the handball courts, facing a semicircle of kids who seemed intent on doing some serious damage.

Two of them came at me from either side. I wrestled and twisted, but the others piled on, and I was soon pinned down on the ground. Two of the larger kids sat on my arms and shoulders, and two others sat on my legs so that I couldn't kick out at them.

"You think you're such hot shit. Now you're gonna get yours," said one of the kids who just a few weeks ago had been my classmate.

My first panic-stricken thought was, "Don't hit me in the glasses!" I was petrified of being blinded by broken glass. But after a few shots to the side of my head, and a couple of kicks, they let up. Instead they did something worse. They had one of the younger kids stand over me and spit on my face; then they all took their turns before walking away and letting me pick myself up to slump home in a state of total humiliation.

Herbie was waiting for me on the other side of the street. I didn't blame him for not jumping in. He wouldn't have accomplished anything and would undoubtedly have taken a beating for his efforts. I certainly didn't expect the kids on my block to join me in a war on the schoolyard gang. But I was seething with rage. I wanted revenge, and I was determined to get it.

I stewed on it the rest of the day and all that night. I couldn't let them get away with it. I wasn't going to let them make the schoolyard off-limits to me, and I certainly wasn't going to let their insult go unanswered. But what could I do? There were just too many of them. It didn't make sense for me to get into a fight that I couldn't win. Why not just move on to the next phase of my life? I never had to go back to that playground again, and I most likely never would; but that was all beside the point.

No, I wasn't going to run away from this. Gary Cooper didn't run away from the killers who wanted to gun him down in *High Noon*. He easily could have left that town behind with a clear conscience and a beautiful bride, but two strong beliefs held him there: his sense of right and wrong, and his pride. He wasn't going to be chased away. He told his new bride, "Once you start running, you can never stop."

Those guys in the schoolyard weren't going to make me run. I fell asleep with the theme song from the movie running through my head and with my plan for the next day racing through my mind.

The next day was almost a carbon copy of the day before: the same hot, humid weather, and Herbie again the only other kid in the street. Once again, we trooped off to the park to play basketball. There wasn't much action at the courts, and my game was off, probably because I had other things on my mind. After a couple of hours, we called it quits.

I told Herbie that I wanted to go back to the schoolyard. He was surprised, but since it wasn't his ass on the line, he came along. I could see that he was wondering whether or not I'd lost my mind. Maybe I had.

We entered the schoolyard the same way we had the day before. This time, however, I was scanning the yard for the kids who had attacked me, and my body was tensed for action.

There they were, pretty much in the same spot as they had been the day before, pretty much doing the same thing, which was *nothing*.

I took the same route, walking straight to the gate on the other side of the yard—a path that would take me right past their field of vision.

A moment later I heard, "Hey, there's Holtzman again." Then the shuffling sound of bodies getting to their feet and running toward me.

I let them get closer before I turned around. Then I started to run, and they took off after me. Again, I wound up trapped at the handball courts. Again, Herbie was nowhere to be seen, which, today, was all for the better.

As the group closed in on me, I looked at the leering faces, wondering which one of them was going to make the first move. I was hoping it would be one of the leaders, but I didn't really care. I crouched into a fighting stance, and I could see that this event was becoming more interesting to them. They hadn't realized that I had slipped a clasp knife out of my pocket and opened it up behind my back.

This was my little surprise, my way of evening out the odds. The knife had been lying in one of the kitchen drawers, along with a mess of miscellaneous junk. It had a smallish blade, maybe only three inches, but it looked like it meant business. Suddenly my mind went blank, and a feeling of panic burst in, replacing all semblance of lucid thought. I had only figured this plan out up to this very point. Now I was flying blind. I didn't have a clue what I'd do next. The only thoughts in my head were screaming out to God and my mother to get me the hell out of there. But there I was, and there was no turning back. I'd just have to improvise.

The circle closed in tighter. In one more step they'd be able to lay hands on me. It was now or never. I whipped the knife out from behind my back. I knew how to hold it from watching movies about juvenile delinquents, so at least I looked like I knew what I was doing.

"Open knife!" shouted one of the kids, and the whole group froze in their tracks. What came next was a blur of roaring, slashing, and running for my life, as the circle parted before me. I threw the knife away as I flew out of the schoolyard, and I didn't stop running until

I was home in my apartment and the door was locked. I was safe, at least for the moment.

That evening during dinner in the kitchen with my parents and younger brother, I couldn't hear a word of their conversation. This was normally okay, as I usually tuned out the constant bickering that went on between my parents. But *that night* was different. *That* night I was waiting for a knock on the door. And then the dreaded knock came. I cringed and sank down into my chair as my father went to answer it. I was expecting him to come back into the kitchen accompanied by a couple of cops, but instead he came back with Herbie, who had something important to talk to me about.

The two of us huddled in the living room. Herbie had watched everything from outside the schoolyard. After I raced out of there, the schoolyard gang had come out and confronted him. Two of them had been slashed on their arms. All of them were pissed off. I guess that they hadn't appreciated my cinematic flair. Fortunately, the wounds were superficial. Even better, they didn't want to get the cops involved. Nobody in my neighborhood liked the police, who regularly kicked us off the streets we lived on, and smacked around anyone who was slow to move.

No, they didn't want the cops, but they did want my father. They had my knife, and they wanted my father and me to show up at the schoolyard at noon the next day. They would give back the knife in return for an apology. If we didn't show, then they would call the law.

My father! What inquisitor had devised this torture? It was the lesser of two evils, but it was still a miserable outcome to what I had hoped would be a significant act of courage. My valiant big-screen adventure of manhood was becoming a television sitcom, in which father knew best.

My father had lightning-quick hands and an equally fast temper. In his youth, he had been an amateur boxer, which old photographs and his hand speed attested to. This was going to be bad. I was going to get both beaten up and beaten down.

The next day my father and I trudged over to the schoolyard. I could see that he was seething, although he hadn't hit me or even yelled at me.

The meeting itself was brief and fairly uneventful. There were some older brothers involved on the other side, and I guess they were interested in keeping the peace. I apologized to the kids who had attacked me, hating every word that came out of my mouth, but it had to be done. They gave my father the knife, and we turned around and went home.

My father looked at me with anger and disappointment, but he didn't say a word. I guess he was worried about what was going on in my mind, what ill-advised path I was going down, and what he could possibly do about it. For my part, I was figuring how I could get another knife to carry around. It would be an important accessory in my new identity at my new school with the new friends I was going to meet.

6

A LONG DAY AT THE COURT

1955

I t was a great day for basketball, although for me every day was a great day for basketball, no matter what the season or time of day. Basketball was my parallel universe, and from the ages of twelve to twenty-one, I turned to it for comfort, escape, and a knowledge that was available to me only on the court.

The game was my great escape from a one-bedroom apartment that was way too small to hide the constant backbiting, nagging, and carping that had become the common mode of communication between my parents. It was endless, and it drove me nuts. I wasn't worried about my parents breaking up; that didn't enter the picture back in those days. I was worried about my ability to stay sane in that toxic atmosphere. At fourteen, my life was turbulent enough without the addition of permanent parental warfare.

To be in the park, three whole blocks away, totally immersed in a game of basketball, was also an escape from the often brutal and boring intercourse of so-called normal, everyday life—a life that involved too many rules, too much school, and too many times that I had to face the bullies.

Playground basketball is a lot like jazz. There are no preconceived positions; everyone is equal and constantly in the stream of play. It's possible to become oblivious to the personalities of the players, as the game is about finding the right positions in a constantly changing matrix, and instantaneously making the necessary adjustments. Obviously, it's about getting the ball in the basket, making passes, and getting rebounds. But since the game is a nonstop back and forth, none of those momentary achievements seemed that important to me.

At the age of fourteen, I thought the game was about form and flow. When I first started playing, at ten, it was an accomplishment to dribble the ball without bouncing it off my foot, or to reach the hoop with a two-handed heave. Now, after four years of playing and growing, I knew about the beauty of moving without the ball, anticipating where a rebound would bounce off the rim, knowing when to switch off when playing defense, and lots of other things that made sense out of the confusing weave of interaction that made up the game.

Needless to say, the game wasn't always played that way. There were always the chuckers, who would throw up a shot any time they got their hands on the ball; the ball hogs, who would dribble all over the court and refuse to pass the ball off even if someone was wide open under the basket; the schlubs, who would stand in one place, waiting for the ball to magically come to them; and the hackers, who played dirty on defense and went after the player rather than the ball. For my part, I had my own shortcomings, although they were of a different nature. I couldn't jump very high, my shot had only mediocre accuracy, and I could only dribble with my left hand. None of those failures took away my joy or enthusiasm for the game. On the right day, I was ready to run from morning to nightfall.

This was one of those days. It was Sunday, and there was a soft, warm breeze flowing through the streets. It wasn't too hot or too humid. Small puffy white clouds dotted the royal-blue sky. In the morning, my gang gathered around the stoop of my apartment building.

Everyone agreed that it was a basketball kind of day, so off to the park we went.

There were five half courts set on the concrete of a long, fenced-in triangle near the entrance to the park. We started shooting around on one of the empty courts and were soon joined by other kids, some around our age and some older. Before long we chose up sides and started playing. We played until one o'clock, when it was time to go home for lunch. I was reluctant to leave because I was having a really good day. My shots were going in, and I was making a lot of good passes and grabbing a lot of rebounds, but it was time to go, and I figured that I'd return later.

In the afternoon, I went back alone and took my own ball, a pebble-surfaced Wilson that I had bought for twenty-five dollars as an anniversary gift for my parents. The year before I'd bought them a left-handed fielder's mitt that was also about twenty-five bucks. The fact was that I couldn't afford those precious items and gifts for my parents as well, and my folks seemed to be unable to buy me the gear that I felt I needed.

A few years earlier my old man had brought home a baseball glove for me. It looked like he had found it in a garbage can. It was flat as a pancake, without any kind of pocket, and the leather was covered with a cobweb of cracks. It was so shapeless it could be worn on either hand. I only showed up at a game once with that glove, and the kids teased me unmercifully.

I ran all the way to the park, but when I got to the courts, they were practically empty, with just a few guys shooting around, not enough for a game. I went up to the kiddy park, where there was a single court; this was the primo court where the best players went at each other. This was the place where skin color ceased to count and ability was everything.

Since the mid-1950s, the black migration from the South had been filling up more and more of Bedford-Stuyvesant, the neighborhood directly to the north of us. By the 1950s Eastern Parkway had become the racial border. There were frequent battles between the black and white gangs, and it had become dangerous to step onto the wrong block, but the big court in the kiddy park was only about the game.

I sized up the game going on; the players were good, but not the best, so I decided to stick around.

The game on the court ended, and my turn came up. I started out a little stiff with nervousness about being on the big court, but that quickly wore off as I got into the flow of the game. To my pleasant surprise, my team won the game, and I got to stay on the court. In fact, we kept on winning, and I soon found myself entering the zone. I was just doing it, passing, shooting, blocking out, switching off, knowing where the players were on the court, and anticipating where they would be next. It was jazz, with the whole band playing together and individuals taking solos at the right time, intuitively knowing when to give it up to the next player. I was banging bodies with guys much larger and stronger than I was and not feeling anything but good. I knew that my body was tired, but the play felt effortless. It was basketball heaven.

I only realized that it was getting late because the crowd of guys waiting for their turn was beginning to thin out, but I was having too good a time to care what the hour was. As more of the players began to leave, the size of the sides became reduced, as did the quality of the players.

There was a small group of five black kids about my age who looked out of place. That they were wearing shoes instead of sneakers was a clue. They didn't have much of a game and didn't seem to be too into it. In fact, they looked like trouble.

Then a large group of players left, and it was just the five black kids and me, three on a side. I suddenly felt alone and vulnerable. It was my ball we were playing with, so if I left, the game would be over. I didn't want to look as if I was afraid, so I played on, even though my instincts told me it was a mistake.

The sky started to darken, and the playground attendant start-ed to lock up the kiddy things. I knew that I had to make my move, so I announced that this would be the last game. While we played, the park attendant left, and I had a sinking feeling that my best hopes were leaving with him. The game ended, and I asked for my ball, but the guys protested that they wanted to play *just one more game.* Their attitude as well as their play made it obvious that what they wanted wasn't just a game. I had a choice: to stick around and hope they were just going to give me a hard time and not a beat-ing, or to let them have the ball and make a run for it. I wasn't happy with either choice.

"Come on, guys, I have to go. Let me have the ball," I said.

"Let's play!" shouted one of the kids, and they started passing the ball around and doing awkward lay-ups. I looked over toward the exit to size up my chances of grabbing the ball and getting away from them, and there, walking toward the court, was my father. I was saved! My old man, amateur boxer in his youth, would take this situ-ation in hand.

I had seen photographs of him in his boxing trunks and gloves, standing in a fighting crouch. He looked dangerous, although my aunt Dora said that the one time she went to see him fight, he got knocked out in the first round. Still, whenever we fooled around sparring, his hands were so quick that I never even saw his shots coming.

Now he walked up to the fence and stood there, taking in the scene. I walked over to him.

"What's going on?" he asked.

"They won't give me back the ball."

He didn't say anything. He just stood there watching the five kids horsing around with my ball. After a while, I realized that he wasn't going to do anything about getting the ball back. There was nothing he could do. There were five of them, and only two of us. I wasn't a fighter, and he was old, and these were five tough street kids. The startling and disappointing truth about my old man came to me in a flash. He was just that: an old man whose prime was far behind him.

That was when Richie Kaminsky showed up with two of his side-kicks. Crazy Richie Kaminsky from around the corner on Eastern Parkway. Richie never made any pretense about who he was. He was bad to the bone. His older brother Teddy was reputed to be a member of the Snake Pit Dukes, one of the most feared gangs in Brooklyn. Richie never bothered studying anything in school. His only concern was making as much trouble as he could. Because of that, he was constantly left back, which didn't seem to bother him at all.

As crazy and tough as he was, Richie was never belligerent to any of the kids his age. His entire animosity seemed to be aimed at any authority he was faced with. He always maintained an insane grin on his face, as if to say that life was a joke, so he might as well be crazy.

That day Richie was dressed in his usual leather motorcycle jacket, T-shirt, dungaree bell-bottoms, garrison belt, and engineer boots. His two pals were in the same uniform. They had seemed to come out of nowhere, piling onto the court and joining in the pseudo-game being played by the five black kids. Only it was obvious that Richie and his friends not only were not dressed for the game but had no clue about how to play it. They just ran around the court, grabbing the ball when they could, tossing it around. Finally, Richie got his hands on the ball and, pretending to take a shot, flung it over the fence to where my father and I were standing.

I quickly gathered it in, and we walked just as quickly out of the kiddy park. Before we left, I took one look back over my shoulder and saw Richie and his two partners lining up opposite the five black kids.

I never found out what happened on that court after we left. I never knew what Richie's unexpected appearance was about. Did he see someone in trouble and decide to come to the rescue? Or were he and his pals just out looking for a fight? Were they packing weapons? Was there a fight, or did everyone just go home? The only thing I do know is that crazy Richie Kaminsky, whom I had always thought to be a joke, showed up in the nick of time and pulled my fat out of the fire, and my father, whom I had idealized, had come up short.

7

ACROSS THE RIVER

1957

" **I** hate Jews."
"What!" I was stunned, stuck to my seat in my new home-room. It was the morning of my first day at my new school: the School of Industrial Art, or SIA.

His words took me by surprise. Where I came from, almost everyone was Jewish—tough Jews too, Jews who wouldn't take those words without a fight. But this guy was six feet two, quite a bit larger than I was, and he seemed to be made of hard, sinewy muscle. Worst of all, he was German—not of German descent, but the real thing, with an accent and the look to go with it—from the same stock that had wiped out over six million children of Israel. His name was John Gebhardt, and I had absolutely no idea what to do about him.

Gebhardt's declaration came after he recited a litany of complaints to me about his Hassidic Jewish landlords: how they would never do repairs on a Saturday, and how dirty and smelly they were. Having no love for the weirdly dressed and oddly behaved Hassids myself, I kind of drifted along with Gebhardt's diatribe. My father had made similar comments himself whenever we drove through Williamsburg, then a Hassidic stronghold. But when Gebhardt spat out that last hateful invective, it was as if I had been hit by a steel rod.

"I'm a Jew!" I proclaimed, trying to keep my rage contained.

"I know that," he responded.

At that point, our homeroom teacher took charge and started to tell the class what we had to know. There was nothing for me to do but to shut up and stew.

That day was my first real stay in the city, which was what everyone on Union Street called Manhattan. The other times were just day-trip excursions to see the Thanksgiving Day Parade, or to go to the Planetarium or to Radio City Music Hall for a movie and the Rockettes. This time I was in the city to do something real.

SIA was one of the city's vocational schools, the schools that taught kids how to become auto mechanics, printers, machine workers, and the like. SIA was for art, and all I had to do to get in was to take a drawing test. Easy.

The school had two buildings, both on the East Side of Manhattan, both crumbling brick structures built in the mid-nineteenth century. The Annex, which housed the freshman and sophomore classes, was on Fifty-First Street between Lexington and Third Avenues. Rumor had it that it was built in 1864 as an infirmary for wounded Civil War soldiers. The main building, which housed the junior and senior classes, was on Seventy-Seventh Street between Third and Second. The buildings were small, corresponding with the student body, which had only about a hundred students in each grade.

And what a funny, raucous student body it was! The school was divided into three departments: Art, Fashion, and, inexplicably, Engineering. The Art Department was a rebellious lot of creative delinquents with large chips on our shoulders, always looking for trouble to get into.

The Fashion Department was mostly female and guys who tended to be effeminate, sometimes flamboyantly so. There was always an excited, high-strung clatter and chatter about this group, who were by far the most glamorous and sophisticated in the school.

Sadly, the male fashion students were also the most maligned, being the object of scornful jibes and sometimes physical abuse from the more thuggish Art Department kids. But, then again, what could a young man expect if he came to school wearing a jeweled turban and a long purple robe, with his face made up in a nice rust-red color, and his eye shadow a stunning emerald green?

The Engineering Department students were the smallest group in the school. They carried slide rules in leather sheaths that hung from their belts. They tended toward corduroy pants that rode too high on their waists and flannel shirts. A few of the more socialized future engineers mingled with the general population, but for the most part, they were content to be invisible, avoiding any potential abuse.

The black kids hung together in a group, as did the Latinos and the Asians. For the most part, the white kids didn't break themselves down by ethnicity. Italians, Jews, Irish, Greeks, Germans, and the occasional WASP all mashed themselves together in a polyglot pink lump. There were some crossovers who ignored the color lines, and there were the loners like Gebhardt who were too creepy to belong to any group.

We were all basically immigrants in the midst of the squeaky-clean buttoned-down white shirt and tie, gray flannel suit, shirtwaist dress, midcentury world of commerce that swarmed all around us. We were mostly kids from working-class neighborhoods trying to figure out how to have a life.

This was the vibe I felt when I first arrived at the building, then milled around the entrance and the hallways as I found my way to my homeroom. That's why I was so taken aback by John Gebhardt's declaration of undying hatred. I had already felt accepted, and now I wasn't so sure of myself.

There was a break, and I had five minutes before our first class. I wandered over to a group of guys who looked and acted as if they came from a neighborhood similar to my own. We mumbled our names and where we came from, which was as close as we could come to formal introductions.

Anxious to get my brush with the Third Reich off my chest, I told the group what Gebhardt had said to me. A few of the kids shook their heads, and one of them said, "What an asshole." But in general, I had the feeling that it wasn't that big a deal to them. Maybe I was expecting a bigger, more righteous reaction. Something like, "Let's kick that motherfucker's ass!" But it wasn't going to come from this group. I quickly glanced around and deduced that I was probably the only Jew in the huddle, and I wasn't going to organize a posse from this group. It was *High Noon* all over again. If I was going to take on John Gebhardt, I was on my own.

After a few weeks, it became clear what SIA was about. We could learn the basic skills necessary to land a worker-bee job in one of New York City's creative trades. Tradecraft, rather than creativity, was the requirement. Even in the cartooning class, which I was in, workmanship was valued over humor.

In general, the classes were a humdrum affair. Besides misbehaving in class, the only outlet for all that pent-up creative energy was at lunchtime on the ground floor.

The ground floor looked more like a finished basement than anything else. At lunchtime, a record player was set up to spin all the latest Top 40 songs. There were a lot of good, smooth dancers who filled the floor, gliding, juking, and bopping along with the music. It was great to watch, but the sexual tension that it oozed made a shy, inexperienced, two-left-footed introvert like myself nervous.

Out the side door was a small courtyard. Sometimes a small group of the toughest kids would play a game I'd never seen before. It involved one of the guys throwing a ball high in the air, and when the ball landed, everyone jumped on one of the players and beat the shit out of him. I never knew what determined who would catch the beating, because I never wanted to get close enough to find out.

Most of the time, however, the yard was used as a handball court. I liked handball, I liked it a lot, and I was good at it, very good. It was the perfect relief from the tedium of my classes and the perfect outlet for my anxieties.

Handball is the physical equivalent of a video game. The action is instantaneous, and if you screw up, there's no chance of a recovery. You have about an eighth of a second to anticipate what's coming at you and a quarter of a second to react. There's no coasting; either you're all in or you're out.

And guess who else loved to play handball? My old pal John Gebhardt, the National Socialist Party's representative at SIA.

Handball was my opportunity to kick his Nazi ass. To make him feel the wrath of the Maccabees, the avenging blows of the Hebrew hammer, the victorious roar of the Lion of Judah.

This was new for me as far as sports were concerned. In the past, I had never felt bad after losing a game in which I had played well. Of course, I wanted to win, but it was the game, not the victory, that was paramount to me. This was different. This was about justice. There were six million dead souls waiting for me to bring home a victory.

I'd played the game from time to time on the courts of Lincoln Terrace Park, which always seemed to be filled with grown men wearing four-knotted handkerchiefs on their heads. They also wore leather handball gloves if they were going to play with the official small black ball that was as hard as iron.

My game was pink-ball, played with a Spalding and favored by the younger players who didn't want to spend their money on gloves or play a game that made their hands feel as if they'd been stung by bees.

The games at Lincoln Terrace were serious. A lot of the games were heavily bet on; the quality of play was very high, and to my delight, I discovered that I could hold my own with the best players there.

I had good speed and stamina; I could hit the ball well with my right hand and was absolutely deadly with my left. I could hit a crosscourt serve that was nearly impossible to return, I had a devastating killer shot that would hit the wall at the very bottom and shoot back hugging the ground, with no chance of a return. If my opponent stayed back, I had the unsettling ability to change pace with a soft little baby shot that would dribble back from the wall, leaving the player hopelessly out of position. I had a complete game and a great arsenal of weapons. As a left-handed player, I was coming at my opponents in a way they weren't used to. I was nearly unbeatable. Nearly.

There's an old sports adage that a good big man will always beat a good small man. I was thin back then, on the edge of scrawny, but at five feet ten I wasn't small. Gebhardt, however, was definitely big. His wingspan was tremendous, and it allowed him to cover more of the court more quickly than anyone else I'd played against. That arm length gave him the opportunity to return more of my wide serves than anyone else ever could. And to my dismay, Gebhardt was good, as good as I was, and that was bad. Over the course of that first year at SIA, I played hundreds of games against Gebhardt, and I never beat him once. We'd leave the court sweating like pigs, nothing left in our tanks, too tired to gloat or regret.

Oftentimes I'd pile up points in a hurry and get out to a big lead. My momentum was surging and my confidence soaring as I approached a sure victory. But then Gebhardt would grimly claw his way back into the game. Point by point he'd doggedly gain on me, pushing his body to places I'd never thought it could reach. The game would last the entire hour of our lunchtime, and inevitably he'd overtake and defeat me. I admired him for his tenacity and hated him all the more.

The score was almost always close, the games down to the wire, and extra points often played, as the game had to be won by at least two points. But the outcome was always the same. As determined as I was to beat him, he was just as determined to not let me win, not one measly game to win some revenge for the six million.

I poured everything I had into these battles with Gebhardt. When I dragged myself off the court after each frustrating game, I had nothing left but the bitter taste of defeat and the humiliating image of Gebhardt's triumphant grin.

I could have dismissed his hatred as the misplaced feelings of a misguided soul, but what about all those misguided souls who had hunted down the six million? Why? I get the idea that everyone can use a good scapegoat now and then; the Jews have been playing that part for over two thousand years. Why us? Why are we so special?

Maybe we are. We wrote the Bible. We produced Jesus Christ, Albert Einstein, Sigmund Freud, Karl Marx, and Groucho Marx. We produced ministers, advisers, and financiers for nations around the globe. But our greatest achievement of all was we survived. Through slavery, exile, inquisition, pogroms, and the Holocaust, we survived.

I couldn't beat Gebhardt at handball, and I sure as hell couldn't beat him in a fistfight, but I could beat him at life itself, and I think that knowledge fueled his anger. I always had confidence in myself, in my destiny—a confidence that went all the way back to Union Street. Maybe it even went back six thousand years. I knew who I was, and it gave me strength. I didn't give a shit how the world turned as long as I could be myself.

Maybe that's what Gebhardt hated about me and everyone in my tribe. I knew that I was going to be somebody, that I already was somebody, and that John Gebhardt was not. It was pure arrogance on my part; I know that I had plenty of that to spare in those days. But I knew that Gebhardt was going to live out his life in the fetid swamp of his hatred, and I was going to be a king. At least, that's what I told myself. Call me a sore loser if you will, but that thought made me feel better.

8

PROM NIGHT

1960

Everything about that night was whacked, even going back to way before then. It's a complicated story.

It began the year before. Instead of a prom, SIA traditionally had a senior boat ride up the Hudson. However, the previous year's boat ride was capped by a riot, during which the celebrating senior class tossed wooden folding chairs into the river, while settling certain long-simmering grievances among the student body.

The effect of that event was the elimination of our senior boat ride. We were obviously not to be trusted as a group any place where we couldn't be tightly controlled. The new plan was to have a school dance in our tiny, falling-down, circa 1850 schoolhouse, on the ground floor where we had our daily lunchtime dance sessions.

That night I met up with my school buddies, Joey Manger and Johnny Andreolli, at the Utica Avenue station in Brooklyn. Both of my pals were good looking, muscular, and tough. I, on the other hand, was a gangly 135 pounds of smart-aleck remarks. What we shared was an irreverent sense of humor and an inclination toward bad behavior.

Getting off the subway, we headed down the same streets that we had trudged through every school day for the past three years. That night, the walk was supposed to somehow feel special. To help that special feeling along, Joey produced a pint of rye that he'd boosted from his uncle's tavern that afternoon. Along the way, we hooked up with Abe Echevarria, the fourth musketeer. Abe lived up in the Bronx, which put him just a step outside our inner circle. The biggest difference between the four of us was that I was going to college next year and they were going to work. It was a difference that I never brought up. I felt that to do so would weaken my street credibility.

We took our time ambling over to the entrance. None of us had dates that night. Dating was tough at SIA. The student body was scattered all over the five boroughs, and there weren't any girls at the school who lived close enough to me so that I could spend time in a casual way, working my way up to asking her out. Plus, I had my crippling shyness to deal with.

As we got to the door, my pals started goading me into picking a fight with Mark Famiglietti. Mark was one of the guys who always had a date. This time his date was the one and only girl I had ever taken out, the darkly beautiful and demure Sherry Mandel.

Sherry was beautiful in a quiet but devastatingly effective way. She was part of the in-crowd of sophisticated kids. She was fashion forward without being flashy, and she never seemed to run off at the mouth. Instead, she projected an aura of knowing and sensitivity; qualities that had emboldened me to get up the nerve to ask her out.

I never could relax in the presence of the opposite sex if I felt any sexual attraction to the girl. I guess my lack of knowledge and experience just scared the shit out of me. So going out on a date with one of the most desirable girls in school terrified me.

I had bought tickets to a two-man comedy show on Broadway. It starred two Englishmen, who I supposed were naturally much more intellectual and clever than anyone else. I figured that this choice would convince Sherry that I, too, was sophisticated, witty, and intelligent.

Sherry lived in Laurelton, Queens—a three-hour trip from Brownsville, involving three subways and a bus. Laurelton, back then, was a quiet, leafy, middle-class community on the far edge of Queens, with streets of neat, one- and two-story single-family homes. It may have looked like anywhere in the United States, but to me, it was Beverly Hills.

I marched up to the door in my new sport jacket and was greeted by Mr. Mandel, who shook my hand firmly while looking me up and down. For my part, I was hoping he wouldn't be able to tell just how out of place I felt. This was the first house I'd ever been in that wasn't overstuffed with too many people, too many smells, and too many arguments. Thankfully, Sherry came down the stairs less than a minute later. Elegantly dressed for the evening, her hair done up, she was truly ravishing—another reminder that I was way out of my league.

Mr. Mandel graciously drove us to the subway station, where he gave me the expected admonitions about getting his daughter back at a reasonable hour.

The subway was packed with people going into Manhattan for a Saturday night. There was only one empty seat, which I grabbed for Sherry, while I stood above her, holding on to a strap. This crowded situation made it impossible for us to talk, which was a good thing because I was tongue-tied. The very thought of revealing my inexperience with a mindless conversation had me paralyzed.

After the show let out, I suggested dinner, but Sherry told me that we had to start heading back, which brought me to the understanding that she wasn't so infatuated with me as to want to extend the evening. I realized that I had a lot of ground to make up during the trip back to Laurelton, and it would have to be accomplished with some pretty great conversation. In other words, I was sunk.

All the way back to Laurelton, I tried to drag some coherent sentences out of my mouth, but the words would rise out of my gut and get stuck somewhere in my brain, which absolutely refused to translate them into English.

We finally got to her front door, and we stood on the porch for a while. I asked if I could kiss her good night, but she said that she never kissed on a first date. I said good-bye, knowing that my first date was my last with Sherry Mandel.

It was almost four in the morning before I finally crawled into bed. On the positive side, I was way too tired to feel sorry or to be angry with myself, and I had actually gone out on a date.

So that was the basis of my claim on Sherry Mandel, and the reason, in my friends' minds, that I should pick a fight with Mark Famiglietti. By the time we entered the school, I had drunk enough of Joey's bottle of rye to actually consider it.

Once inside, however, Mark beat me to the punch, but it wasn't a punch that he beat me with. He must have been watching for me, because almost as soon as we stepped into the darkened, mood-lit space, Mark stepped out of the crowd with a couple of his friends. Armed with a huge and friendly smile, he extended his hand and said hi, and that was the end of the fight. There was nothing I could say or do to prove my point, because there wasn't any point to prove.

So instead of starting a riot, my friends and I slid along the wall, watching the dancers carry on and looking out for any mischief we could get into. It didn't take too long for us to realize that most of the people at the dance, both gay and straight, were paired up. There were the usual romantic couples from our class, and a lot of the other kids had come with their neighborhood sweethearts.

It didn't look as if an evening of fun and laughs was in store for us here. Plus, Johnny had been hitting the bottle more than the rest of us, and he announced that he had to get some fresh air. Quick.

There was a string of bars on Third Avenue that looked inviting, but they were all checking IDs at the door, and Johnny told us that he absolutely had to get home, so we decided to call it a night.

Abe was going in the opposite direction, but he came downtown with us as far as Forty-Second Street, where we were getting on the express and he would grab a train going uptown.

As we were saying our good-byes, a group of five Puerto Rican couples, about our age, arrived. I'm not sure of the reason—maybe they found Johnny's condition amusing, maybe they found the idea of a group of four young men to be funny, maybe they thought we were queer—whatever it was, they started laughing and pointing at us and jabbering away in that harsh, staccato Spanish that's typical of Puerto Ricans in New York. I couldn't understand a word they were saying, but it was obvious that they were making fun of us. Even without a translation, these were fighting words.

Abe walked over to them and had a conversation in Spanish. He came back and reported that they were going to cool it, and everything was going to be okay. Then he left on an uptown express.

Our train pulled in, and we entered the last door of one car, while the Puerto Rican kids entered the first door of the car behind. As we all walked into the train, one of the Puerto Rican guys said something to us. Whatever it was, we definitely didn't like it.

The animosity continued as the train pulled out of the station. All the seats were filled, so we were standing, as were the kids in the other car. They started pointing and laughing and taunting.

Joey became incensed. "Come on, you motherfuckers!" he yelled through two sets of doors and the roar of the train. "I'll take you on one at a time or all at once!" They couldn't hear him, but his stance and gestures said it all. They responded with mocking gestures of their own.

Through the fog of my own drunken state, I conceived of something that would scare these kids off. There was a heavy hook at the top of the connecting doors of those old subway cars. It was about two inches wide, four inches long, and an eighth of an inch thick. It was formidable, but I knew that I could bend it and pull it off the door. I had done this trick a few times already on my trips to and from school. There must have been something structurally flawed in the hook that enabled me to rip it off the door.

I stepped over to the small alcove that held the connecting doors. I reached up and slowly but forcefully pulled the hook down, then up and down again, until it snapped off. Then I threw a meaningful "don't fuck with me" look at the Puerto Ricans and casually turned back to my friends.

Before I could take a step, I was lifted into the air and slammed against the wall of the alcove. There had been a man standing there when I walked over to the door. He was a rather indistinct presence. A little shorter than I was, wearing a lightweight jacket, he had seemed like just another tired working stiff headed home at the end of a long day. But he was stockier than I, and a lot stronger, and as he pinned me against the wall with one hand, he flashed his badge with the other.

"What the fuck do you think you're doing?" he demanded.

"Nothing," I stammered, my head filled with panic and confusion.

"You planning to use that thing as a weapon?"

"No! I was only trying to scare them."

The cop motioned for Joey and Johnny to come over into the alcove, and he told the three of us that we were getting off at the next stop and were lucky that he wasn't taking us in. We readily agreed. There wasn't really any choice, and we were lucky to get out of the imminent rumble with the five Puerto Rican guys, who had us badly outnumbered, and with Johnny too far out of it to be of any use in a fight.

We got off at the next stop and started walking toward the exit. The Puerto Rican kids were at a window as train slowly pulled out.

"Why are they laughing at us?" asked Johnny. It was a rhetorical question, because he was in the process of reaching his own conclusion in his drink-clouded mind.

"Why are they laughing at us?" This time he shouted at the top of his lungs, then punched the window, smashing glass all over the Puerto Rican guys and their dates.

The train continued to leave the station, picking up speed, and we knew we had better do the same or we would soon be in more trouble than we could handle.

We climbed the steps to the street as fast as we could manage. We were on Lexington Avenue, somewhere in the thirties. There wasn't another soul in sight. It was an empty street in an empty neighborhood, a dead spot. Dark, closed-up storefronts stared out blankly at us. We started to half walk, half run down the street, figuring to get across town to the Seventh Avenue subway, which was another way back to Brooklyn. The hollow sounds of our footsteps echoed off the cement.

Johnny, stumbling along in his drunken state, slowed us down. At the end of the street, I looked back and saw the squat figure of the cop rising out of the subway. We broke into as much of a run as we could muster, turned the corner, ran down to the next street, and turned the corner again, doubling back toward Lexington. Driven by adrenaline, we raced down the street, and we were almost to the next corner when up popped the five Puerto Rican guys, all brandishing car aerials.

Joey, who was ahead of me, jumped right into it. He knocked one of the Puerto Ricans down, grabbed the aerial out of the hand of a second, and started punching a third. As I ran toward the battle, I could clearly see that Joey was good at this. But I wasn't. At all. The fact was that I couldn't stomach the idea of punching someone in the face. I don't know whether it was compassion or cowardice, but any time I got into it with another kid, I always went into pushing and wrestling, which always wound up with no one getting too hurt. I had a surly attitude and a big mouth, and that was about as far as it went.

"There's too many of them!" I yelled. "Let's get out of here."

So Joey took one last swing, knocking the third kid down, and joined me in a sprint down Lexington, with the Puerto Rican kids right behind us swinging the aerials. There was an empty taxi at the corner, waiting for a red light. Joey got there first and jumped into the back seat. The surprised driver looked up, saw me and the Puerto Ricans, and took off down the avenue, the back door still open, waiting for me.

I ran as hard as I could, the aerials whacking down on my back. Joey had one hand out the door for me and the other hand grabbing the shirt collar of the taxi driver. He alternately yelled at me to get in and at the driver to slow down.

I had just enough strength left for one last effort. I willed my legs to run faster, got a little closer to the taxi, and launched myself into the back seat, grabbing Joey's outstretched hand. We made it. There was no catching us now.

"Where's Johnny?" Joey asked.

"I don't know. I thought he was with you."

"And I thought he was with you."

We told the driver to turn a few corners and go back over the territory we had just covered. I had visions of Johnny lying in the street, bleeding to death. We started shouting out the open windows, "Johnny! Johnny!" But his name just came echoing back off the empty streets.

I looked out the back window and saw another cab speeding after us. I figured that the Puerto Rican kids had commandeered their own taxi.

"Step on it!" we told the driver. But the other car was already on us. It passed us and cut us off. The cop got out of the front passenger seat, then pulled Johnny out of the back. The game was up.

The two taxi drivers were more than happy to go their separate ways. The cop took us down into the subway station and sat us down on a bench next to a phone booth.

"Stay right there!" he commanded, then went into the booth and made a call, but not before muttering something about taking us to the station and booking us. While he was in there, I took the opportunity to take off my reversible jacket and switch it from the tough-guy black side to the goody-two-shoes side with an argyle pattern. I also slipped off the cool shades that I'd been wearing all night and put on my geeky peepers.

After his call, the cop grilled us about who we were and what we were up to. None of us had records, and we all proclaimed that we'd never been in trouble before. Johnny was surprisingly sober, Joey suddenly meek, and I kept mumbling about how this was going to screw up my college scholarship.

Then the cop asked us what we would do if he let us off the hook. Joey and I told him that we'd steer clear of trouble. Johnny said that he'd tell his father what had happened and never get into this kind of jam again.

"That's not what I want to hear!" snapped the cop. "You don't tell anybody about this, you hear? Not a word to anyone."

We all agreed to do just that. I realized what was happening. It was now close to one in the morning. The cop probably wanted to get home. We weren't dangerous criminals, so what purpose would it serve for him to waste the next hour or so filling out papers on this incident? But for him to walk away now meant that this night's flap had to disappear. If it somehow surfaced and caused any kind of ripple, it might get back to him, and that wouldn't be good.

So the cop went his way, and we went ours. The enormous weight pressing down on my head and my heart began to lift. I was alive, and I was going home, free and clear to get on with the rest of my life, at least as long as Joey didn't notice that I had failed to throw a punch the entire night.

9

THE END OF THE LINE

1960

The New Lots Avenue Subway Line, which ran thunderously past our apartment's windows, came to its final stop, appropriately enough, at New Lots Avenue, six stations down the line from where I lived. There the stairs going down to the street emptied out at a small triangle of sidewalk that was called, also appropriately, the Triangle.

This is where my buddy Joey Manger and his gang hung out. His neighborhood was even tougher than mine. It was part of a minor league feeder system for some of the Mafia families. In later years the names of some of the characters from that neighborhood came up in the newspapers, usually on one end or another of a homicide.

One early spring day, Joey and I were sitting on a bench at the Triangle, trying to figure out some mischief to get into.

"Let's go shoplifting," he said with a sly grin.

"Sounds good," I replied, although I wasn't sure it was a good idea at all. In order to hang on to my credibility, I had to hold up my end, so of course I was in for a bit of shoplifting.

The natural target for our crime was Klein's-on-the-Square, a large, low-end department store, now long gone, on Union Square and Fourteenth Street. It was the natural target because I had a part-time job there in the Layaway Department. I had this job because otherwise I wouldn't have had money to spend. No movies, no pizza, no sodas, no nothing. I'd be the only kid hanging out at the candy store who couldn't even buy a pretzel.

My parents simply didn't have any money to give me. My old man had borrowed from his sister to buy into a small business. Then his partner, a rabbi, no less, skipped town, leaving my poor father holding a bag full of debt. My mother had to find work in the office of a small textile company, something she didn't want to do, and she let my father know it big time. Finally, he got rid of his business and took a job driving a taxi.

Rather than be happy that her husband was once again bringing home money, my mother was embarrassed by his new job, and she insisted on riding in the back seat as if she were a passenger.

The idea of having to go to work three afternoons a week, rather than hanging out on the stoop of my apartment house, really pissed me off, and I directed most of that anger to Klein's and the Layaway Department. So when Joey asked me to go shoplifting with him, it had to be Klein's.

I shuddered at the thought of getting caught, it would mean getting roughed up by the cops, adding a JD card to my record, considerably lessening my chances for getting into college, losing my spending money, and getting the shit kicked out of me by my old man. But I still had to do it, or I'd be labeled a punk. Besides, even the girls back in junior high school went shoplifting, so how hard could it be?

It was spring, but it was still cool enough to warrant a coat. This job required a coat to cover up the stolen goods we would wear out of the store. Another requirement was a single-edged razor blade, to cut the tags off the clothes we were taking. Being art students, we kept single-edged razor blades as part of our tool kits.

Of course, one of the tricks was going to be to find clothes that didn't look as if they came from Klein's. There wasn't any sense in stealing clothes that looked as if they weren't worth the effort. There had to be as much pride in the loot as there was in the deed.

Joey and I took the subway to Fourteenth Street. As we climbed out of the subway, the big, gray department store loomed above us just across the street. We both wore black raincoats, and, thinking that we looked too much like two guys going shoplifting, we entered at different sides of the building and took separate elevators to the men's department.

Once there, we avoided sharing more than a passing sidelong look as we crossed each other's path searching out loot. There were lots of sweaters, but I wasn't interested in a sweater. The weather was turning warmer, and I wouldn't have any use for it. Of course, the advantage of a sweater was that it could be tucked into one of my dresser drawers, under a bunch of other stuff, and hopefully not be noticed by my mother. But I just wasn't interested; they all looked like the cheap knock-offs that they were. I moved over to the sport jackets. Here I found blazers with bright, shiny buttons that looked as if they were ready to fall apart, and lots of jackets trying to be sharp but looking like yesterday's rejects. Then I saw it, and I couldn't believe my eyes. It was beautiful and classic yet distinctive. Different from anything I'd ever seen.

This jacket managed to stand out and be quiet at the same time. Stripes of different widths and colors subtly ran up and down and across the jacket, which was a dignified shade of tan that seemed to have depth to it. The stripes were heather, gray, moss, and a very thin watery red. I reached out to touch the material. It was wool, and very soft, and it had a thickness to it without being heavy. I tried it on, and it fit as if it was made for me. I looked in a full-length mirror, and I saw a young British aristocrat looking back at me from his country estate. It was much more expensive than any of the other jackets hanging in the racks, but at the discount I was getting, price was no object.

There was a companion to this jacket in a larger size. I grabbed it and went looking for Joey. He was browsing through the suit racks at that moment, waiting for me to clear out of the sport-jacket area. We caught each other's eye. He made an appreciative face at the jacket I was wearing, and I made a show of placing the larger jacket back on the rack for him to take.

Now came the trickiest and most dangerous part of the operation: cutting off the tags. It had to be done stealthily, so that any store employee who happened to pass by wouldn't notice what I was doing.

The easiest place to accomplish this task without being seen was in the changing rooms. But that meant going in and out under the supervision of a salesperson. The job had to be done out on the floor.

I nonchalantly meandered over to the racks of raincoats, as their length seemed to give the most cover. Walking between two closely placed racks, I pretended to be perusing the coats while I surreptitiously and frantically searched out the tags. For all I knew, I was already being scrutinized through one-way mirrors placed along the walls.

Blindly fumbling around with my free hand, I managed to pull both sets of tags taut while severing their strings with the razor blade. I did this while still trying to look as if I was casually shopping for a new coat. It was only afterward that I realized how incriminating it looked for someone wearing a raincoat to be shopping for another.

Stepping out into the clear, I saw that Joey had already left the floor. I figured that he must be waiting for me outside. That was good because I was anxious to make my getaway.

I took the escalator down to the main floor, cleverly avoiding the elevator, where I could be trapped. Now all I had to do was make it past the guard, out the door, and into the street, and I'd be home with my prized new jacket.

But the guard at the door was John, a Black guy I'd become friendly with over the ten months I'd been working there. John was neither young nor old, he was a couple of inches taller than I was. I never had much to say to John other than hello, but it would be impossible to walk out without stopping to talk with him.

"Hey, I didn't know you were working Saturdays," he said.

"I don't. I was just doing some shopping, but I didn't find anything I wanted."

I tried to play it cool. I didn't want to rush things. But at the same
time, I was so nervous that I thought I would pee in my pants if the
conversation went on too long. Not only that, but the combination of
the wool sport jacket and my necessarily closed raincoat was heating
me up. I could feel floods of perspiration gathering all over my body
and the top of my head. I was praying that he wouldn't say anything
about my coat being closed on what had become a warm day.

"I guess school is ending pretty soon," he went on. I was beginning
to wonder whether he suspected that I had stolen something, and was
stalling to see what would develop. Maybe a salesperson would come
charging out of the elevator, shouting at John to grab me.

The sweat on my head was ready to come pouring down my face.
That would be a sure giveaway, so it was now or never.

"Well, I've got to get home and study for my finals," I lied.
"Otherwise I'll be going to summer school."

"You take care, young man," John said, waving me out the door.

I walked out gasping for air. Joey was down the street, waiting at the
corner. We tromped down the stairs to the subway and walked onto
the platform. Then we quickly unbuttoned our coats and flashed our
new jackets to each other with a *ta-da* flourish, and a howl of laughter.

We were waiting on the platform for about ten minutes. As I stood
there, the euphoria of our caper started to wear off, and reality began
to set in. There was just no way I could bring the jacket home with me.
My parents knew very well that I didn't have the money to pay for it,
and they certainly wouldn't believe any story I might concoct about
someone giving it to me, much less about finding it somewhere. No.
To bring home the jacket was to bring on a terrible beating and to
lose the jacket in the end anyway.

I sadly explained this to Joey, feeling like a loser for doing so. But
he totally understood my situation. He told me that he had a friend
who had a storage space and that he'd keep the jacket there for me. I
could have it any time I wanted. But I knew that would never happen.

I took off my raincoat, reluctantly slipped off the jacket, and folded it neatly before handing it to Joey. I sighed deeply and took one last longing look at the wonderful prize that had all too briefly been mine. Now it would only be a beautiful memory.

A month later I was back at the Triangle, hanging out with Joey and his pals. It was after nine, and the sun was down. Our clique and some of the older guys filled up the benches. There was a smaller group of girls who were about our age. We were drinking cans of Schaefer hidden in paper bags and smoking Lucky Strikes. Ben E. King's "Spanish Harlem" was floating out of a portable radio.

I was getting drunk and thinking that I'd better make my way home soon, while I still had the wherewithal to stand up and walk straight. I tried making conversation with one of the girls, but my IQ seemed to have been reduced to double digits, and I wound up mumbling some embarrassing drivel.

"Hey! Who the fuck are you?"

I looked up at the voice and saw that it was attached to one of the older guys. His name was Lupo, and he was one of the legendary tough guys in the neighborhood. He was big and thick, and rumor had it that he was once knocked down in a fight and grabbed the other guy's leg and bit right down to the bone. The guy went down, and Lupo got on top of him, took out his switchblade, and carved his initials in the guy's forehead. Obviously, Lupo was someone to be taken seriously.

"Who the fuck are you?" he repeated with more emphasis.

"He's with us. He's a good guy," Joey said.

"Oh yeah?" said Lupo. "What are you wearing those shades for? It's dark out."

I had my sunglasses on. I wore my sunglasses all the time in those days. Wearing my regular glasses was definitely not cool in this tough world.

"Gimme those," Lupo said as he pulled them off my face.

"Hey, I can't see without them." I tried to state my case without being too forceful.

"Yeah?" he said. "What are you going to do if I break them?"

Well, what would I do? What could I do? I could slink home without my sunglasses, or I could put up some sort of fight and get my arms and legs broken or worse.

The guys finally cajoled him into giving me back my glasses, and he tossed them onto the bench. I could see again, and I saw something way beyond the Triangle. I saw that this was a life that I wasn't remotely cut out for. I was defenseless in a world where brutality reigned and psychopaths ruled. Crime may have been a career path in that part of Brooklyn, but it was a path I could never follow. I might always be a wiseass, but I now knew that I could never be a wise guy.

10

THE JOURNEY

1960

My fashion reference for the excursion I was embarking on was two gentlemen very much in the news back in the late 1950s. They went by the monikers of "Cape Man" and "Umbrella Man," and they were the leaders of a Puerto Rican gang that had stabbed a couple of white kids to death in a turf rumble on the West Side of Manhattan.

The event I was going to called for something slick, something that told people that I was with it and had to be considered a serious person. I had bought what I called "toreador pants" for this occasion. The black pants came to a good three inches above my waist. Two rows of six buttons each ran down the front, and a skinny black belt, with a silver buckle that I cinched on the side, held the pants up. The legs tapered down sharply to the top of my ankle-high pointy-toed roach-killer shoes. I put on a clean white shirt, with a small rounded collar, then a one-inch-wide black tie, to which I added a silver collar pin and a pearl stickpin. Next came my new sport jacket: wide stripes, in what the salesman had called "wine colors" of burgundy and purple, and a single silver button. All this topped by a black raincoat and a black snap-brimmed hat, with its own pearl pin, plus my accessories of black shades and a skinny, black, tightly rolled umbrella. I knew there was a slightly hard edge to the look, but I thought it was necessary because I had to pass through enemy territory along the way.

Giving myself a good hour to get there, I walked down to the corner and caught the New Lots Avenue bus, which took me out of Brownsville and into Bedford-Stuyvesant, where I would transfer to the DeKalb Avenue bus. Once we crossed over Eastern Parkway, we were in Bed-Stuy. As I gazed out the window, it seemed to me that the action on the street was basically the same as where I lived, except that the complexions were darker. The population was mostly women, with a sprinkling of older men. Young mothers pushed carriages and strolled along with children in hand. People were gabbing on folding chairs in front of their five-story apartment buildings. Shoppers were picking at the fruit stands while the vendors shouted out, "Hands off the peaches, lady!"

I could see the cultural difference by the shops on the street. Almost every other block held a beauty parlor, a storefront church, a liquor store, and a bar. Not one delicatessen, pickle store, or nut-and-halvah shop to be seen.

My heart sank when I saw a DeKalb bus pull away from the curb as the New Lots bus approached. I figured it would be at least ten or fifteen minutes before the next one arrived. By this time, I was the only white passenger left on the New Lots bus.

I got off and crossed over to the opposite corner, trying not to turn my head as I ran my eyes up and down the street. I took up a position right next to the bus-stop sign, not wanting anyone to think that I was doing anything other than passing through. As far as I could see, everyone else on the street was what we called "the coloreds." That was, of course, when we were speaking politely.

As other people joined me at the stop, I prayed that none of the local gangbangers would happen to pass by and take offense at my being there. I knew that if any of them were caught on the wrong corner in Brownsville, there'd be blood in the street.

I'm sure that the people at the bus stop, and the people in the street, were ordinary working people and housewives, going about their daily business and wishing me no harm. But back then, I saw life through the narrow lens of the street-tough subculture that I lived in. A lens warped by sharp angles and dangerous shadows.

I think that I held my breath for the entire ten minutes it took for the next bus to come. Then I was off to what I hoped would be my new life.

I was on my way to Pratt Institute. It was the first day of freshman orientation, and I had no idea what I'd find when I got there. I felt lucky to have gotten into the school. I had scored extremely high marks on my SAT, but I had to live with my miserable grades from the ninth grade, when I was still defending my title as the worst behaved student in a junior high school filled with delinquents.

When I applied to colleges, I applied for art education programs. I didn't really want to be a teacher, but I thought that I would have a better chance of getting accepted by going that route.

My first choice had been Hunter College, but only because it was free. This was an important consideration, since my parents didn't have a nickel to spare to pay for tuition. I only made it as far as the waiting list at Hunter, but I did get accepted by Pratt, which was my real first choice. It was one of the most prestigious art schools in the country.

Fortunately, I got a State Regent's Scholarship, which together with a government loan, and what I earned at my summer job, was enough to pay my way. As far as I could see, going to college was the only way I could escape whatever life there was for me in Brownsville. I didn't know anyone who had advice about finding a way into the world beyond the neighborhood.

So there I was, my heart beating loud enough to be heard, anxious to find a path into a new life, stepping off the bus, and finding myself facing a high brick wall that ran the length of the entire street and beyond that. Looking to the nearest corner, I could see a gated entrance. I walked inside and stopped dead in my tracks. I was confronted with a vision that I had never seen in my eighteen years of life. It was a campus. With lawns, and a flagpole, and a cannon, and dorms, and big old nineteenth-century buildings. But it was the people there that had me really freaked out. I had seen blond people before, but never so many of them in one place, and never dressed like these people. Madras shorts, chinos, plaid shirts, blue oxford button-downs, tennis sneakers, and even saddle shoes, for crying out loud. And the way they were acting was even stranger: they were happy! They were throwing Frisbees, lying on the grass, laughing, and chatting away. Who were these people? Something was way out of whack in this universe, and I had the discomforting feeling that it was me.

11

WHAT I LEARNED

1963

I was at Pratt for the better part of five years. What did I learn? Not much, but they were probably the most important five years of my life.

The art classes were basically perfunctory and uninspiring. After all, we weren't studying to become artists, not even to teach people to be artists; we were merely going to teach art.

I learned that I was a better than average artist, but there was no spark to my work. I was never going to be Rembrandt or Picasso. Besides, if I did dare to put myself forward as a working artist, I had enough money saved to last until lunch.

The academic classes were a bad joke. The head of the department, Albert Christ-Janer, taught a class called the History of Art Education. He had an exalted reputation and looked as if he owned the ivory tower that he lived in. He was tall, thin, and incredibly handsome in a patrician way. His prematurely snow-white hair hung in a perfect wave over his high pale forehead. His clothes could best be described as American academia tailored by Savile Row. He could pass for an Episcopal bishop, or an English actor playing a Roman senator. He spoke in an elegant and ethe-real voice, and his words meant absolutely nothing to me. Try as I might, I couldn't make rhyme or reason out of anything he said. It was all academic gobbledygook.

The same was true for my philosophy class. I loved the idea of philosophy. I had read Plato and Socrates when I was young, and I thought that I would thoroughly enjoy a journey into the teaching of the great philosophers.

But that was not to be. Our instructor a young man in his late thirties, was another pompous dandy, although only half the age and half the size of Christ-Janer. He couldn't have been more than four feet eleven, but he compensated for that by the length of his words. No word with fewer than five syllables passed from his lips. I've always prided myself on my vocabulary, but after sitting through an hour's lecture by this little twerp, I was left feeling like a Neanderthal. There was absolutely nothing that I could comprehend. And I wasn't the only one who felt that way. At the end of the semester, everyone in the class received an F or a D, except for one person who received an A—obviously either a genius or a prostitute.

Art history was another impossible class to get through. The classes themselves were fine. They consisted of slide shows with an accompanying lecture and took us through the various periods of art through the centuries and around the world. There wasn't any analysis of what the art meant to the societies that produced it, or the relationship of one school of art to another. It was just a pleasant visual journey.

The journey, however, came to a rather unpleasant end when we were given the punishing and monumental exams at midsemester and at the end of the term. The tests were gargantuan, huge booklets of forty to fifty pages, composed of multiple-choice questions designed to trick us. For instance, "So-and-so created his masterpiece in 1623, 1625, 1632, or 1635" or "The such-and-such fountain was created by Benigni, Bellini, or Bernini."

These insipid questions covered the thousands of artists and works of art that we had studied. Preparing for these tests required spending an inhuman amount of time on rote memorization at the expense of all our other studies. And to what end? Nothing about this kind of knowledge imparted any understanding of the meaning or the societal relevance of art. The information that we were being force-fed was destined to be forgotten the day after the test, regurgitated and reviled like bad mussels. To my young, volatile mind, the only point of these exercises seemed to be a sadistic need to humiliate us.

So on the night before the final, three friends and I broke into the Art History office. We got there via a series of old and forgotten tunnels that connected the major buildings of the campus. We accessed the tunnels from the basement of the library. We were already familiar with this route, having used it earlier in the year to carry out a panty raid on the girls' dormitory.

Once in the Art History office, we picked the lock on the cabinet containing the tests and absconded with a couple of dozen of those instruments of torture, which we then distributed to our grateful friends.

The event gave me a great feeling of satisfaction. I felt like a member of an underground resistance group breaking into the armory of the occupying forces, stealing weapons that we would use on our oppressors. Two weeks later when I received my grade, a B+, I felt as if I had passed two tests: one academic and utilitarian, the other moral and more than justified.

I spent most of my time at Pratt on the lawn, pulling out handfuls of grass while watching girls walk by; in the gym, playing endless games of pickup basketball; and in the cafeteria, bullshitting with my friends.

I joined a fraternity, although I had a nagging feeling that there was something morally despicable about fraternities and that I was betraying my leftist roots. But I had to figure out some way to learn about how the world outside of Brownsville worked, and that meant that I had to get close to people who lived in that world.

It turned out to be a good move, even though the dues emptied out my already threadbare purse. It was a Jewish fraternity, which meant that all the members were either members of the tribe or guys who didn't mind hanging out with us. It also meant that the group had a decidedly urban and liberal bent. I now had a group that I could sit in the cafeteria with, glean information from, play sports with, and party with.

The guys in the group were considered winners. They were successful in class, on the athletic field, and in social situations as well. Their parties were well attended by the most attractive girls in school. This last was a huge leg up for me, as it placed me in a social situation with the opposite sex. However, I still had to overcome my shyness and social clumsiness to get to the next stage, which was actual dating, and that remained a problem, but at least it was now a problem that I could work on solving.

I was beginning to become educated. I learned the difference between a Windsor knot for my tie and a four-in-hand. I learned how to catch a Frisbee. I learned how to dribble a basketball with my right hand.

I also learned that there was food far beyond my mother's excruciatingly bland cooking. In my sophomore year, I took a share in a floor-through brownstone apartment with two older architecture students. We ate meals out at least three times a week, usually at Tony's, a small Italian restaurant just down the street under the Myrtle Avenue El. It was a typical red-sauce joint with checkered tablecloths and a red neon sign that made it look like a setting for a B movie from the 1950s. There was something special about the food at Tony's. It was called "taste," and it was something that was totally absent in what I had been eating at home. I took this lesson with me for the rest of my life.

The other taste that I honed during those years was musical. I've never been able to play an instrument, or dance gracefully, or even hum a tune on key, but I've always loved music. I feel it in my bones. My body moves to it whether I ask it to or not, even if those moves are awkward or downright clumsy.

In high school, when I wasn't playing handball during lunch, I was standing on the sidelines of the lunchtime dance crowd, too shy and too inept to ask anyone to dance, but swaying and bopping to the rock and roll and rhythm and blues that filled both the room and my head.

Now I was ready for jazz. At Pratt, the routine was to stay up late at night doing homework or studying. What better company to keep during those vampire hours than Symphony Sid and his all-night jazz show on WADO?

It was a great education and a great groove. Sid's gravel-pit voice took requests and introduced the greats of the day: Miles, Mingus, Monk, Brubeck, Coltrane, Mulligan, the Modern Jazz Quartet. They were all there blowing my mind wide open.

Better yet, I could actually see them live. This was New York, after all, the center of the jazz world. I saw Monk at the Five Spot in the East Village, wearing his trademark soft-brimmed hat and dancing by himself in a corner while his sidemen played on. I saw Miles at the Blue Note, wearing a fringed buckskin jacket, turning his back on the audience while he played. I didn't have any extra money to spend, but once every two or three months, I could eke out enough to catch someone playing somewhere.

After a couple of years, Sid changed his format and switched to Latin music. I liked salsa a lot, but I couldn't take it as a steady diet. I started tuning in to WWRL, where Montague the Magnificent played blues and soul music through the night. Montague was a great showman; between the songs, he would shout out commentary like "Send me your pillow with your tears on it, darling," after a sweet or sorrowful song, and "Burn, baby, burn," after a hot up-tempo number. Later, after Montague moved out to Los Angeles, that latter refrain became the unfortunate war cry of African American rioters who were literally burning down their city.

I fell in love with the raw, soulful sounds of blues singers like Jimmy Reed, Bobby "Blue" Bland, Lightnin' Hopkins, and Etta James. I danced at my desk while listening to Wilson Pickett, Aretha Franklin, and Marvin Gaye.

I started catching some of these acts when I could. I saw James Brown at the Apollo twice. He put moves on the stage floor that I didn't think were humanly possible. But my favorite place for music was just ten minutes away from the Pratt campus, at the corner of Bedford Avenue and Eastern Parkway, at a club called the Town Hill.

The room was dark and large yet welcoming. A large U-shaped bar, lit by colored neon strips, faced the door, manned by three friendly bartenders who were in perpetual motion. The wide, deep stage was off to the right, covered by red velvet curtains when it wasn't filled with musicians. Between the bar and the stage were thirty to forty candle-lit tables, occupied by an equal number of blacks and whites all dressed sharply for the night out, the wise guys in sharkskin suits; the brothers in suits of maroon, green, and royal blue; and the women in the latest A-line dresses and bouffant hairdos. To the left of the bar and next to the wall was another row of tables that seemed to be filled with people who didn't want to be seen.

No doubt about it, the Town Hill was important in more ways than one. Important music was played there; besides the amazing eight-piece house band, blasting out the horn-heavy *da-da-dat* rhythm and blues riffs, there were warm-up acts of up-and-coming musicians, baggy-pants comics, and tassel dancers, all topped by world-class acts like Jackie Wilson, and the Isley Brothers—acts that would cost fifty dollars in Manhattan just to get in the door, as opposed to sitting at the bar of the Town Hill and nursing a two-dollar scotch. In addition, the lounge occupied an important place in the sociology of Brooklyn. Located on the racial divide, it attracted a mixed crowd who were there to dig the music and not to fly their colors. The net effect was a peaceful universe welcome to all who dug the groove. To my young and impressionable self, it was heaven.

After three years of studying art education, I decided it was time to apply for a job as a student teacher. This was a requirement if I was going to teach in the New York public-school system. It's not that I was anxious to move ahead in that direction, but it seemed to be the logical future for me to move toward.

I visited my old grade school and stopped in to see Mr. Willen, my sixth-grade teacher. He was the only male teacher whom I had had in my seven years of grade school, and he represented, in my mind, the fact that teaching could have a masculine identity. He remembered me and was happy to see me. He offered to help me in any way he could to land a student-teaching job. But when I asked him how he was doing, he complained about not getting a promotion to assistant principal.

"They said that I was too soft, too easy on the kids," he said; it sounded like whining, which put me off a bit. It also brought home the reality that teaching could be a very political arena.

Next, I went to see Miss Kaganov, my fifth-grade teacher, who was quick to use a ruler and even her fists on me. Despite that, Miss Kaganov and I always held an affectionate respect for each other.

She too was happy to see me, but when I told her that I was going to teach, she said, "If you become a teacher, I'll kill you." She felt that teaching would be a terrible waste of my abilities. I had already felt that I might be shooting too low in going for a career in education. Now, seeing how Mr. Willen was doing, I realized that Miss Kaganov was probably right. Besides, a threat from Miss Kaganov was definitely not to be taken lightly.

And just like that, my career in education was over. But what was I going to do instead? I liked to draw, but I knew that I couldn't make it as an artist. Even if I had the talent, I didn't have any connections, and I didn't have any money. Still, I liked drawing, and I was good at it. Also, I liked hanging out with my friends and cracking wise, and I loved dreaming up ideas. So the answer to my dilemma was obvious. Advertising!

When I told my parents what I had decided to do, they freaked out. They implored me to finish the full four years of art education and to get a teaching license before switching over.

"You can always get a job as a teacher. It's a guarantee!" implored my mother.

Security was foremost in her mind, but survival was paramount in mine, and I knew that I wouldn't survive if I continued on the path I was on. I would be crushed by the cogs of a system that had no regard for singular talent or individual thought. Besides, there was still the looming threat of Miss Kaganov.

So what did Pratt do for me during the five important formative years that I spent there? Not much in terms of what I learned in my classes, but it gave me a safe perch from which I could see where I stood in the world. It was a holding pattern, a time and place for me to get my bearings and avoid being swept away by the fast-moving currents of the grown-up world. In short, it saved my life.

12

MY FIRST WIFE AND OTHER FIRSTS
PART 1

1963

I saw her across the crowded square, her knowing, enigmatic smile and her large, laughing brown eyes boring into me and connecting with mine, so that we were telling each other unspoken stories as I crossed over to the staircase where she sat. We were both with other people, who vaporized in the heat of our coming together.

It was the first night of freshman-orientation week at Pratt. It was her first and my fourth. It was a week of parties and fun and the best opportunity to check out the new girls on campus. As far as I was concerned, I didn't have to check any further. This magnetic creature was as beautiful as a fantasy, and my heart was ready to pound its way out of my chest.

Let me say something here about my history with the opposite sex up to this point in my life. Until I was eleven years old, girls were the enemy. Anyone who played with girls was a sissy, which was not the thing to be in a neighborhood where Willie Sutton, the bank robber, came in a close second to Jackie Robinson on the "whom I'd like to be like the most" list.

Then came the time when my hormones became the strongest voice in my head, and I realized that I might have been misled on this topic. In the eighth grade, I tried to remedy that situation by asking Jane Rabinowitz to the movies. I had absolutely no idea what was playing or how I was going to pay for the event. All I knew was that I had to somehow break into this foreign country called "girls." So, when I thought that no one else was looking, I walked up to Jane, a pretty and intelligent ash-blond girl with a kind, heart-shaped face and the biggest knockers in the eighth grade, and stammered out my request. She kindly but immediately told me that she was going away for the weekend with her family, although I was certain that she would have turned me down even if she had nothing else to do. I'm also pretty sure that the fact that I was staring right at her breasts the entire time I was asking her out was a turnoff for her.

That was it for myself and girls for the next four years. Unless, of course, you count the three or four times a day that I was masturbating. In my senior year in high school, I stammered my way into my first date, that pathetic outing with the beautiful Sherry Mandel—an event that emptied my bank book and whatever reservoir of self-esteem I had managed to build up.

After that it was off to college, where I struggled for a year trying to understand and bridge the differences between how almost everyone else at Pratt acted and thought, and how I approached the universe. It was a full-time job, involving a lot of watching, listening, and imitating the ways of the other students.

I felt myself drifting further and further away from life as I once knew it; but trying to expand this newly learned behavior into social intercourse with the opposite sex seemed out of reach for my freshman year.

The next year I took a share in an apartment with two older architectural students in my fraternity. I was finally breaking away! I no longer had the excuse of inconvenience keeping me from asking girls out. The only impediments I had were my inexperience and shyness, and I knew that the only way to overcome them was to get myself out there.

So I started to date, almost always going along with guys from my fraternity and their dates because I was way too unsure of myself to be out there without some support. No relationships ever developed, because I had no idea how to relate. For me, it was like trying to speak to someone in a language that I had just barely learned, without any sense of its subtleties or colloquialisms. I could say things, but I couldn't have a real conversation.

Then, the next year, my junior year, I had a girlfriend. Her name was Rosa, and I met her, of course, at a dance during freshman orientation. She was entering the Engineering School; she wanted to be a physicist. Among Pratt's major schools—Art, Architecture, and Engineering—the engineers were considered the geeks, the klutzes with slide rules hanging down their corduroy pants. Rosa stood out from that group like a flower blooming on a cactus. She was petite, dark, and beautiful, with a keen intelligence, an artistic nature, and an adventurous spirit. On our fourth date, she announced that she wanted to lose her virginity. That would make two of us, but it wouldn't happen easily, and it didn't end happily.

Without any experience under my belt, I had to guide both Rosa and myself through the uncharted waters of first-time intercourse. The best I can say of the experience is that I survived. Barely. We were totally out of sync; when I was hard, she was tight, and when she was ready, I went limp.

Things weren't made any easier by the fact that I was sharing a studio apartment with an industrial-design student who was one year ahead of me. The studio was halved by a divider, a floor-to-ceiling wall built with two-by-fours and covered with different-colored burlap squares. When Rosa and I were lying in my bed inside my tiny cubicle, my roommate was usually on the other side of the screen with his girlfriend.

Because of days filled with classes and evenings filled with homework, I only saw Rosa on the weekends. I have forgotten what we did for amusement in the early parts of those evenings, but we eventually wound up in my bed on all those nights, fighting the good but losing fight until Rosa's dormitory curfew.

Then it was the Christmas holiday, and she went home to Detroit. We got back together in January, when school was back in session. Rosa told me that she had taken care of "the problem" when she was back home. I don't know how she took care of it; I guess I didn't want to know; and I'm not sure what technical effect this news had on my already battered psyche. What I do know is that we were in sync that night, and I finally achieved what every boy and young man dreams about since the first stirrings of adolescence. But it wasn't success I was feeling; it was the accumulation of all my failures, and even worse, I wasn't feeling anything at all toward Rosa, other than that she was the vehicle and witness of those failures. I stopped seeing her. I dropped her like a sack of rotten fruit, making that lovely, trusting child-woman pay the price for my failure. Even as I write this, nearly fifty years later, I'm wretchedly ashamed of myself. Can I cry out, "Rosa! I'm sorry!" loud enough for her to hear me across the chasm of those years?

Less than two years later, I found myself walking across the campus square toward a girl who I was sure was going to be the love of my life. She told me that her name was Dorothy Crowe and that she only had an hour before she would be picked up and driven back to Plainview, Long Island. She said that she'd be moving into the city, when classes started, into her grandmother's apartment in Woodside, Queens. I figured that I could deal with that.

I took her to my fraternity house, where there was a party going on. I couldn't take my eyes off her; none of the other guys there could either. We danced a bit, and she moved like a dream, with grace and rhythm, and a mischievous gleam in her eyes which seemed to say, "I've seen this movie before, and I know how it's going to end."

Then it was time for her to leave. I walked her to where her boyfriend was waiting in a parked car, instinctively knowing that he would soon be history. We said that we'd see each other at the Freshman Dance on Friday, and said good-bye. We didn't kiss. We didn't have to; our fate was already sealed.

I was delirious with love-smitten excitement. It had already been a very different year for me, and meeting Dorothy Crowe was the capper. It was my fifth year at Pratt but the beginning of my second year studying advertising. The first year had proved to me that I was fully capable of being an advertising art director. I already considered myself the most talented designer in my class. I realized that it was my inflated ego telling me that, but on the other hand, I knew that I was good enough to have a shot at success.

The biggest news now was that I had moved back home. After years of being on a waiting list, my parents finally got a two-bedroom apartment in the building we lived in. This meant that I would have somewhere besides the kitchen table to do my work. It would also mean huge savings for me. I always had a shortfall at the end of the school year, and that was the only time I asked my parents for money. Staying at home meant I could put some money away and not have a shit-fit about the cost every time I went out.

As a reward, I bought myself a second-hand Vespa motor scooter. Never having had a bicycle, I knew driving the scooter was taking my life in my hands, but I loved the image. I had recently seen an Italian movie with the hero, a young man in his twenties, driving a Vespa and wearing a sweater wrapped over his shoulders, and I thought that could be me, riding down Eastern Parkway instead of the Appian Way. And I'd have a way to get to Dorothy Crowe at her grandmother's place in Woodside.

The Friday night after I met Dorothy, I took my kid brother Stephen along to the Freshman Dance. The four-year gap between us had always been a large one, and in the two years that I lived at school, we had drifted even further apart. But now, living at home with him, I could see that he had grown a lot, emotionally as well as physically. Next year he'd be entering college himself, so I thought it would be fun for him to go to the dance and get a preview of what it was all about, and at the same time, maybe I could become buddies of a sort with him. Maybe I also wanted him to catch a peek at Dorothy Crowe, who was supposedly waiting for me at the dance.

When we got there, it was already packed with students, dancing, prowling, and just standing along the walls. The only way to find Dorothy was to wade into the crowd. I told Stephen that I was looking for someone, that he should wander on his own, and that we'd hook up later. Then I started a slow and methodical search for Dorothy. I met lots of people I knew and stopped to chat with each one while my eyes and my heart were racing around the room.

An hour later, Stephen appeared out of nowhere with a huge smile on his face.

"I just met the most wonderful girl," he said. "She's incredible. You have to meet her."

He beckoned in the direction he had come from, and who should step out of the crowd with a cat-who-ate-the-canary grin, but Dorothy Crowe?

Not wanting to break my brother's bubble, I pretended that she and I were meeting for the first time. I asked Stephen if he minded if I had a dance with his discovery, and he agreed. It was a slow dance, and we melted into the mass of other dancers. Stephen would be disappointed, but the fates had to be served.

When the song ended, we returned to where Stephen was waiting, and I went off on my own to mingle. An hour later, Stephen tapped me on the shoulder. He was ready to go. He told me that Dorothy had already left, but he had gotten her number. That was something I had forgotten to do myself. Little did Stephen know it at the time, but that was his way of repaying me for taking him to the dance.

I woke up very early the next morning and copied down Dorothy's number from Stephen's phone book, then slipped back into bed to catch another hour's sleep. To this day, Stephen feels that I stole Dorothy away from him.

I called Dorothy at her parents' house and made a date to see her that very night. I planned to zip out to Plainview on my Vespa and go to some local place with her. I hadn't planned on Plainview being a two-hour trip by motor scooter, or on a tropical storm hitting the New York area that night.

Heavy winds and heavy rains slammed me as I made my way east on the Southern State Parkway. Gusts sometimes pushed me over into the next lane. I was way beyond being wet; I was almost under water.

Finally, after three hours of terror, I reached Plainview. I pulled into the first gas station I came to and called Dorothy from a phone booth to explain why I was late. Her father must have felt pity for me, because not only did he come to pick me up and help me get my scooter into the back of his station wagon, but he lent me the wagon to take his daughter to the city. It was probably the last time he had any kind feelings toward me.

I don't remember anything about the date itself, except that I was afraid to let anything happen to the car. With my almost total inexperience as a driver, I had the entire population of Long Island behind me on the Expressway, angrily honking their horns at my stubborn refusal to go beyond sixty-five miles an hour. I also remember that we got back to Plainview in the wee hours of the morning, and I said good-bye to Dorothy on the front lawn, telling her that I hoped to see her again.

Then, as I turned to get on the Vespa, she said to me, "Aren't you even going to kiss me good night?"

I rushed up to her, took her in my arms, and kissed her with as much love as I had in my being. This was going to be my life!

Once we were a couple, I started spending some family time with the Crowes. Needless to say, I never went there by scooter again. Neither suicide nor masochism is my thing. I took the train, and Dorothy's father picked me up. The Crowes were a picture-perfect American family. Patrick Crowe fought in Korea and came back home to marry Dorothy Cicero. He was a school custodian in the New York City education system, and he did well enough to have a nice house in the suburbs and to send three children to private Catholic schools. I could clearly see where my Dorothy got her amazing looks. Patrick was ruggedly handsome, and his wife was beautiful in a Southern

Italian, Madonna-like way. With her Irish features and Italian coloring, my Dorothy looked like a rococo doll. Her two younger brothers, Patrick Jr. and John, were handsome and mischievous towheads, taking straight after their father. Dorothy, my Dorothy, was the exotic of the family.

Some weekends I stayed overnight in Plainview. They were a religious family, and I went to Sunday services with them. It was a confusing experience for me. I did what the people around me did: when they knelt, I knelt; when they stood, I stood; when they sat, I did too. I felt foolish and phony going through those motions, and not having to go to church anymore was the best part of my later banishment from the Crowe family home.

There were also a few Sunday family dinners in Woodside at the basement apartment that belonged to Dorothy's grandmother. Tiny Ada Cicero had a modest one-bedroom place, where she hopped around on a bum leg. She struggled to make ends meet as a book-keeper at Lord and Taylor, and she made the best lasagna I've ever had. The two Patricks, the two Dorothys, John, Ada, and I would somehow fit around her dining table to gobble up huge portions of that wonderful and sustaining dish. For his part, Patrick always brought along a couple of six-packs and a caustic sense of humor. For my part, I made sure to bring along a good appetite.

During the week, a very different kind of feast was served at Ada's place, and I couldn't wait to sink my teeth into it. I'd jump on my scooter every morning, ride through the beaten-down streets of Bed-Stuy and Bushwick, past the grungy body shops and low-rise factories of the industrial areas connecting Brooklyn and Queens, past the old, worn cemeteries of Maspeth, until I finally arrived at Ada's place in Woodstock, where Dorothy would be waiting for me still dressed for bed. Lucky me.

However, my old problem reared its anxious circumcised head again. How could it do this to me when I'd met the love of my life? What was this all about? Was I gay? Impotent? Or just crippled by anxiety? I didn't think I was gay. The thought of being anally penetrated or fucking some guy up his hairy ass held no appeal for me. Impotence? Not someone who'd jerked off as many as six times a day. That left anxiety, which meant that I just had to keep plugging away, which is what I did, day in, day out, until I overcame the problem. It took me two weeks, which were then followed by another two weeks of sheer bliss, which were then followed by disaster.

Ada Cicero became ill, but that wasn't the disaster. She became ill while on the train to work. When she got to her desk at Lord and Taylor, she was feeling worse, so she turned around and went home.

Dorothy and I were locked in lust when we heard the key turn in the door. I jumped up as if shot out of a cannon, grabbed my clothes off the floor, and fled into the large storage room that was connected to the bedroom. I got into my clothes in a flash, then cowered against the wall next to the door. I figured that if Ada looked into the storage room, I'd be covered up by the opened door. I reckoned that I might have to be there all day and into the night, until Ada went to sleep.

I heard Ada talking to Dorothy in the bedroom, but couldn't make out what she was saying. Then she opened the door to the storage room. I held my breath and willed myself to be invisible, but it didn't help. She peered around the door, and there I was.

"Hello," I said, and I walked around her, through the bedroom, and out the front door. Then I got on my scooter and got the hell out of there as fast as I could.

On the way back to Brooklyn, the Vespa died. I drove it into a large puddle that was deeper than I thought. It puttered to a stop and never started up again. I wasn't too upset; I had much bigger things to worry about. Fortunately, the scooter decided to die just a few feet from a subway station. That seemed like a good omen. I left the Vespa where it was and never went back for it. I had a feeling that I was going to have to travel light for a while.

"You got me into this; now you have to get me out of here." Dorothy was back in her parents' house in Plainview, and she couldn't stand being there another minute.

What was I going to do about it? I had gotten us both into this situation, although, truthfully, we had both gotten us into it. Still, it was up to me to figure out a solution. Two of Dorothy's friends who shared an apartment in Flushing had told her that she could stay with them. All I had to do was to get her and her bed over there.

The two friends had been classmates of Dorothy's at Sacred Heart High School. They had a one-bedroom apartment but spent most nights up in the Bronx with their two boyfriends, who were also roommates. It sounded like a good arrangement to me. There was a corner of the living room that was out of the way, and it was just large enough for Dorothy's bedspring and mattress. I set it up there, returned the car I had borrowed from a friend, then went back to sleep over. Somehow, I was moving in along with Dorothy.

Now I had a lot of figuring out to do. If Dorothy and I were living together, I was going to have to feed us both, which meant I needed more money than I had. I had already come to the conclusion that I had nothing more to learn from the courses I was taking. The logical conclusion was to enter the foreign, grown-up world of work.

I went to the school's placement service, where I was friendly with the director, and she gave me a bunch of leads at some small design firms. Thus began a dispiriting, ego-crushing period. Getting work wasn't the problem; getting good work was. I worked at a series of jobs, happy to be making the money but miserable about the work I was doing. At one job, I did paste-ups for matchbook covers. They wanted to offer me a permanent position, but I couldn't get out of there soon enough. On one interview took place at a one-man shop off Times Square, then a refuge for hookers of all persuasions and dope peddlers of watered-down and sometimes deadly goods. The owner tried to convince me that the location was at the center of everything in the known universe and that he could teach me invaluable things, such as how to fold a brochure so that it could be printed more cheaply. I thanked him for the offer, then ran out of there as fast as I could. But there were jobs that I had to take because I had to have money. As it was, I made just enough money for Dorothy and me to have cheeseburgers every night at a nearby diner and go to the movies every Sunday. It was an existence, but barely.

The first semester ended, and Dorothy took a leave of absence. Her teachers were sad to see her go; she was talented and intelligent and easy to look at. Her marks had been good, but with the way things were, it would be hard to keep them up. She found a job working in an office, which was a big help in the cheeseburger and movie departments. My own marks sucked, since I was working rather than attending classes, but I didn't really care; my problem now was survival. Life was beginning to feel like a dull, throbbing pain, something to be endured as we trudged down its muddy path with no particular destination in sight or in mind.

During this period, I stayed away from home. I communicated with my parents by phone, with my mother constantly asking when I was coming home and me fending her off with a constant stream of lies like "soon" or "tomorrow." I didn't tell them anything about Dorothy, or what I was doing, or where I was staying. Maybe I was embarrassed by the insanity of seemingly throwing everything away and living in someone else's living room with an eighteen-year-old girl.

One late afternoon, however, I did go home, and it was a memorable visit. It was my parents' thirtieth anniversary, obviously an important event. My parents, my brother, and I were going out to dinner in Manhattan. Stephen was meeting my mother in the city, and I was hooking up with my dad at the apartment.

For some reason, Dorothy came with me. She wanted to see where I lived; after that she would take the subway back to Flushing. We got there in the afternoon and soon found ourselves out of our clothes and in my parents' bed. At one point, Dorothy rolled me over on my back and straddled me. I suddenly felt an uneasy presence in the room. Looking up past Dorothy's face, I saw my mother, my father, my brother, Aunt Dora, and her husband, Morris, standing around the bed, looking down on us with disapproval. I was freaked! The hallucination lasted a couple of minutes, after which I had lost all interest in taking my pleasure in the parental bed.

This turned out to be fortunate, because a few minutes later I heard my father's key turn in the lock. I leaped out of bed, threw on my clothes, and ran out of the room to greet him. We hugged, kissed, and exchanged happy greetings, and then Dorothy emerged from the bedroom. I have to say that my dad was very pleasant about the whole affair. He greeted her with a big smile and told her he was happy to meet her.

While my father got into his suit, Dorothy took her leave, returning to our corner of the living room in Flushing, where I would rejoin her after the celebration. I guess that my dad and then my mother were relieved to discover that the cause of my absence was a young lady and not some criminal endeavor. Their relief would probably be short-lived if they knew how small a corner I was painting my life into.

Then I went on an interview that changed everything. It was a larger design studio, and they did real work—book covers, record jackets, posters—work that was good enough for me to want the job badly. The creative director looked at my portfolio, then called some of the other men working there to have a look.

"How come you're not working at an advertising agency?" he asked.

I told him that I thought I was better suited to a graphic arts studio. The truth was that I was intimidated by the thought of a big corporate agency and thought it would be easier to land a job at a studio. But these guys seemed to think that my work was perfect for advertising. It was my old strategy of undershooting. The creative director said that he could offer me a job but that my talents were a much better fit for an agency.

That interview was a wake-up call for me. I went to visit a friend who was working at Doyle Dane Bernbach, at that time the premier creative agency in the world.

My friend said that my work was good, but he thought I should apply to a rival agency, Young & Rubicam, because my work would receive a better reception there. Young & Rubicam was also a highly respected creative shop, although their work tended to be more visual than cerebral.

While I was there, he showed me his own work, and something clicked inside me. I saw the difference between what he was doing as a professional and what I had done as a student. I got it. Great advertising is like a person who walks up unannounced, grabs you by the lapels, introduces him- or herself in a way that tells you everything you need to know, and does it in a way that you won't forget. It can be done with humor, fear, logic, beauty, or anything that will jolt the emotions and engage the mind.

I left the building and walked over to an art supply store, where I bought a tracing pad and some felt-tipped pens. Then I went over to Grand Central Station, sat down in the waiting room, and laid out three new advertising campaigns, each one consisting of four different ads. I was trembling with excitement and the newly realized knowledge of what worked.

I had the name of an art director at Young & Rubicam, given to me by a mutual friend. I went to meet him, and he sent me to see the manager of the Art Department, one floor up. As I waited for the elevator, my heart was in my mouth. Looking around, I was awed by the elegance of the lobby, with its Bauhaus furniture and large framed prints by legendary photographers. The people I saw were equally elegant: well dressed and gracefully at ease in their comings and goings. I questioned whether I could ever fit into this scene, but I decided I would do anything to get the chance.

The manager's secretary, Ellen, an attractive and intelligent-looking, well-groomed thirtyish woman, ushered me into his office. The manager, Andy Schmidt, was a smiling, pleasant-looking man with a crew cut. He asked a few questions about my background and education as he looked through my portfolio. Then he said that he wanted to hold on to my work for a few days and that he would call me soon. We shook hands, and I went back to Flushing, where I was prepared to hold my breath until he called.

Do you remember
the ads?

Two days later I got a call from Ellen, saying that Andy Schmidt wanted to see me that afternoon. When I hung up the phone, I was exploding with joy. I knew that I had the job! If I didn't, I would have been asked to drop by to pick up my portfolio at my convenience. But instead, I had been asked to come in for a meeting! I knew that was the protocol. Of course, I could have been wrong. Maybe the kindly Mr. Schmidt just wanted to give me a few words of advice. But the positive thoughts pushed the negative maybes out of the picture. I was swooning with the idea that I had crossed into the Promised Land. This was where my life would finally begin. Despite Brownsville, despite poverty, despite everything, I was now poised on the shores of a new world, where I was going to make my fortune.

I was so excited that, while crossing Madison Avenue on my way to the meeting, I walked right into a moving car and tore my pants. Luckily, I was early, and Ellen was kind enough to sew my pants while I waited in the men's room. Then I went in to see Andy Schmidt. He had my portfolio open on his desk, and he asked me to sit down.

"I want you to know, I wouldn't have done any of this work the way you did it," he said, sweeping his hand over the portfolio. "But I think it's interesting, and I'm going to hire you."

Whew! What a way to start a new life.

When I told my parents the good news, they were horrified. How could I possibly leave school without my diploma? What if this job didn't pan out? They even offered to pay my tuition if I stayed in school. I wasn't surprised by their reaction; they just didn't get it. Their frame of reference was still the Great Depression. This job was why I went to school in the first place. Any student in the Advertising Department would kill to be in my place.

I started working the next Monday. I was an apprentice, even lower than an assistant. I was making less than five thousand dollars a year, and sharing an office with three assistant art directors. I was in heaven.

PART 2
1965

Dorothy and I moved out of her friends' living room and into a place of our own. She was going back to school, so we had to find a place near Pratt.

We were soon setting up house in a nice one-bedroom apartment with a small balcony, on the third floor of a brownstone on leafy Washington Avenue, just three blocks from campus and around the corner from the subway. In the meantime, things progressed at work. I had fairly mastered the elementary tasks I was assigned. It was frustrating and frightening at first because, although I had studied design in both high school and college, those lessons had nothing to do with the practical applications needed on the job. On day one I feared that I was in so far over my head that I would drown, but it didn't take long to see what was needed.

I was lucky to quickly find a group of friends at the agency, and they helped me understand how to do things. It seemed that I was part of a hiring surge that put on about a dozen beginners or near beginners, all around my age. It helped that I knew Joe Toto, the staff photographer. He'd been at Pratt and had been friends with some of my friends, and Joe knew everyone in the Art Department. He introduced me to all the other new recruits.

Joe was a real character, a wheeler and dealer. He was a bit older than I was, having served in the navy before going to Pratt. He operated out of a small photo studio on the same floor that I worked on, and he did shots for presentations, layouts, and any ideas that were breaking new visual ground. He had managed to convince the agency that he required a car, rented by the year, in order to do this work. He also made sure to hire an assistant who had a driver's license and lived close enough to him so that he could get a ride to and from work every day. Luckily for me, Joe lived around the corner from Dorothy and me, so I got the chauffer treatment as well.

Aside from Joe and my group of peers, the rest of the agency seemed to be a world apart. Men with names like Butch, Chick, and Van, wearing well-fitted suits with five-pointed handkerchiefs, elegantly dangling cigarettes from their fingers, looking like the Duke of Windsor, with voices sounding like nothing I'd ever heard in Brooklyn.

I was assigned to a senior art director named Jim Tyler. He gave me his ink layouts to color, and mechanicals to paste up. After six months, he trusted me enough to give me some small-space recipe ads for Lipton Soup. This was my first opportunity to do something real, on my own. It wasn't much in the way of creativity, or, I should say, it wasn't anything in the way of creativity, but it was my own. Jim chose the photographer, but I went down to the studio to "supervise" the shoot. Which meant that I stood there, watching the photographer work, and kept my mouth shut. The work was so straightforward that there wasn't anything for an art director to contribute, even if I'd had enough experience, knowledge, or courage to make a contribution.

Jim always left at five or shortly after. I was always there way past that time, which worked out because Joe was always there late as well. One afternoon Jim told me that there was a photograph at the re-touchers, and it would be back in the office around six o'clock. He wanted me to receive it and bring it to another senior art director for approval. That man would be waiting down in Les Champs, a restaurant with an entrance in the lobby of our building.

Sure enough, at ten after six the agent from the retouching company came by with the photograph. I asked him to wait in my office while I went downstairs to have it approved. I'd never set foot in Les Champs before, and what I saw when I walked in made my eyes pop out of my head. In a setting of tiered tables and banquettes sat half the staff of Young & Rubicam, mostly coupled up, and mostly men with their younger secretaries. The place was swimming in cocktails. Lots of people were swaying in their seats, some of them to the soft music being piped in and some of them to the rhythms of their libi-dos, but many of them were just drunk.

I found the man I was looking for and interrupted his tête-à-tête just long enough for him to take a quick glance at the photograph and tell me that it was okay. Then I ran back upstairs to release the agent and think about what I had just seen. I was entering a new world, and I was certain that I hadn't even begun to fathom the depths of its strangeness. It was certainly totally different from the world I had left behind at Pratt.

As I gained more responsibilities, I started coming home later and later, arriving just as Dorothy's day was beginning. Art students traditionally do their work at night. Something about the daylight seems to distract them. Since they're working through the night, that's when they visit each other, to see what their peers are doing, to trade information, or just to smoke dope and shoot the breeze.

I'd come home and find Dorothy hanging out with some of her classmates, who always seemed to be guys. Sometimes she'd be out at somebody else's place. This was all common student behavior, but it didn't take a genius to see where it was going. Even so, what could I do about it? Every move I'd made since junior high school had been based on one thing: survival. I came from no money, and I saw how no-money people lived, and I had no intention of living that way. Would I have liked to live the life of an artist? Sure, but that wasn't in the cards for me. Only my career could take me where I wanted to go. If it seemed square to Dorothy and her fellow art students, so be it. I couldn't allow that to slow me down, no matter the consequences.

Things were going well with my career. I had my first real break-through: a subway poster for Manufacturers Hanover Bank. The idea came to me during a visit from a photographer's rep who showed me the work of two brothers who were shooting with a fish-eye lens. In 1965 the fish-eye was a brand-new development, and these brothers knew what they were doing with it. I was excited by their work and thought that if I could figure out how to use it, it would be a feather in my bonnet.

Jim was working on the Manufacturers Hanover account but wasn't doing too much with it, so that seemed to be the best possibility. Then it jumped into my head: a fish-eye photograph of a sailboat against a horizon that wrapped around 240 degrees thanks to the fish-eye, and a headline that read "Widen Your Horizons with a Manufacturers Hanover Loan." It wasn't the world's greatest idea, although no one could convince me otherwise at the time. In truth, it wasn't even a very good idea, but it was an idea nonetheless, and it worked! Not only that, but it was all mine, pictures, words, the whole shebang.

I ran into Jim's office and showed him a rough layout. He got me some money to do an experimental shoot with Joe, and within a couple of days, we were on the Long Island Sound, with a pretty secretary and a junior account executive as models.

The shots were a success. The idea was sold to the bank, and the two brothers reshot the photograph. Most importantly, I was brought to the attention of the agency's creative director.

I discovered that I was part of a movement: the so-called Creative Revolution, which was part of the rising wave of social and political awareness sweeping the world. In advertising, it was a battle between the old guard, the mostly WASP men portrayed in *Mad Men*, and the Young Turks, younger men and women who came from less privileged backgrounds but were talented and ambitious, and who as often as not came from Jewish, Italian, and Greek backgrounds.

It was also a battle between different aesthetic philosophies. Up to then, advertising had been about creating something that would capture the public's imagination and whet their appetites: a catchy jingle, a comforting family scene, a sexy portrait, or a cute character. It wasn't that the Jolly Green Giant, Speedy Alka-Seltzer, and Elsie the Cow weren't effective; in fact, they were much beloved by the general public. The problem, as seen by the Young Turks, was that those artifacts were contrary to the Bauhaus philosophies of "less is more" and "form follows function" that we had grown up with. We felt that advertising had to make sense; it had to communicate an idea, ideally a singular one, and everything in the advertisement had to support that idea. In our parlance, the advertising had to be conceptual.

The main enemy in this war seemed to be the account executives, or the suits. They were the people who sold our creative product to the clients. They were also the hand holders, drink buyers, and if necessary, pimps for the clients. In their eyes, it was their personal relationships with the clients, not the creative work, that kept the accounts in the house, and they were wary about allowing any daring or risky work to rattle their clients' cages. They'd come back from a meeting with a client and give any kind of cockeyed excuse about why the work had to be changed.

Once, an account guy gave me a reason that was so outlandish that I said to him, "What? Are you drunk?" Now, this kind of remark was common repartee in my old neighborhood, and it was considered harmless compared to something like "Your mother's a cocksucker."

Apparently, this account guy didn't see it that way. He started choking me and had to be pulled off by the other people in the room. Looking back, I can see that his problem was that he actually was drunk.

To the Young Turks, the problem was simple: the suits were in the way. The first step to change that was for the people who created the work to be in the room when the client saw the work. Otherwise, the account guy could agree to a compromise that might destroy the integrity of the work, or even not present it at all. We were not just upholding the quality of the work; we were upholding the future of our careers. If we didn't get good work produced, then our value as creative people would diminish. It was about money as much as it was about ego. We fought for the right to sit at the table so we could fight our own fight.

I had been at Y&R for a year, and was now making enough money to afford a good suit. I walked over to Brooks Brothers and ordered a made-to-measure, navy-blue, double-breasted wool suit with a chalk stripe. The axiom going around then was "Look British, think Yiddish." But no matter where the Italians and Jews got their suits tailored, we always wound up looking like thugs. So we started to develop a wrinkle on the Madison Avenue look. We pushed a gang-ster look, wearing dark shirts and light ties, sporting fedoras, looking like hoodlums in a B movie. It set us apart as creative people, and it worked because we could never be mistaken for the people in the old guard, no matter how we dressed.

It was time for Dorothy and me to get married. At least that was my mother's opinion. I'm sure she was guided by her tight-assed sense of propriety, but the reason she gave was compelling: The war in Vietnam was raging, and the draft was sweeping up every available young body. Being married, however, made me less available. Both Dorothy and I were fiercely against the war. I had the added incentive of not wanting to die. As my mother pointed out, we were living as a married couple anyway, so why not go all the way?

A few weeks later we were standing in front of Judge Seymour Liebowitz, a lodge brother and friend of my father, in some sort of neoclassical temple on a green hilltop in Staten Island. It was September, and cool enough for me to wear my new wool suit. My mother, father, brother, aunt Dora, and uncle Morris were all there, but Patrick and Dorothy Crowe were absent. Patrick, being a knight of the Catholic Church, felt that he couldn't attend our wedding if it was held outside the church. To me, it seemed that his absence was dictated by his pride and outright bigotry.

We had two wedding parties. My parents held one for our family and friends, at a wedding factory in Queens, where I sweated trying to remember the names of all my mother's cousins.

The other party was held by two friends of ours from Pratt. Charlie Brown and Bill Campeon were architecture students who shared a ground-floor brownstone apartment that had a garden in the back. Charlie was a fabulous conga player, and Bill was great on bongos. I gave them a few hundred dollars, and they threw a wonderfully wild frenzy of a party that rocked with music and rolled with rum punch and dope through the night, into the rising sun, and beyond. Half of the Art School was there, as were my friends from work, who couldn't quite believe how funky my wedding reception was, and of course tons of people whom I'd never met before or after.

Charlie and Bill, along with a few others, were up on a platform in the center of the apartment, pounding out throbbing rhythms on congas, bongos, claviers, bells, bottles, triangles, and anything they could find that would shout out a beat.

That party was the high point of my marriage. The problems started cropping up almost immediately. Dorothy went for her regular dental checkup and was told that her teeth were in terrible shape. They required surgical work costing thousands of dollars—dollars that I didn't have in my bank account. Fortunately, I worked out a time-payment schedule. Unfortunately, I didn't have the money for the first monthly payment. I was pretty sure, however, that I would be up to speed by the time the second payment was due. So, at a dinner at Dorothy's parents' house, I asked Pat if he could make the first payment. I did this with great reluctance. I was swallowing my pride, but I didn't have a choice. The dentist said that if the work was delayed, it would become more difficult to correct the problem. I was also afraid that Pat would turn me down out of his sense of self-righteousness. After all, as Dorothy's husband, I was legally responsible for her needs—not to mention the fact that I had seduced his little angel and taken her away from the church. But he agreed, and I gave him the coupon from the payment book.

I was much relieved, thinking maybe now Dorothy and I would have something like a normal relationship with her parents. But a few weeks later I started getting notices from the dentist's office that the payment hadn't been made. I figured that the check must have been in the mail, and let it go at that. But the notices kept coming and becoming more insistent. Finally, I picked up the phone and called Plainview. Dorothy the Elder picked up the phone. I replayed the entire story for her, insinuating that Pat must have forgotten to make the payment. But that wasn't the case at all. After a couple of minutes of hemming and hawing, she blurted out, "I'm sorry, Henry, but Pat's not going to pay it at all." She was apologetic and sympathetic to my plight but not helpful in any way. How could she be? She was the "good wife."

Luckily, my parents were able to help out. It seemed that my old man had finally started making enough money to sock some away. I hoped maybe that would stop my mother's ragging for a while, although I doubted it. In any event, I was happy for him and grateful for the help.

The second problem was my perception that things were getting a bit unstrung on the home front. I came home from work one evening in June. The leafy canopy over Washington Avenue was leaking golden stripes of sunlight. The street was quiet except for a curious cracking sound that randomly came in series of two. As I came up to our house, I could see Dorothy and my brother, Stephen, on our balcony, laughing and obviously having a great time. Then I saw them both fling something into the air, and watched as two dinner plates from a gift set of china came crashing down onto the sidewalk, joining the high pile of bits and pieces already there.

When I got upstairs, they took a time-out. I saw that the set they were destroying was a particularly glitzy and ugly one, given to us by one of my aunts at our wedding party. It certainly wasn't a loss of a prized possession, but there was something unsettling about the way my wife and brother chose to dispose of the gift.

Another problem, however, was clearly more serious. It had become apparent that Dorothy and I, while living in the same apartment, were not living the same lives. The most confounding thing was that we were both living the lives we should be. She, the art student, was spreading her wings and following the wildest currents of wind, and I, the ambitious young assistant art director, was working hard to make my mark. I was sure she was having an affair with one of the other students, and I was pretty sure who it was. His name was Howie; he was a lowlife posing as a hipster. He came over to our apartment a few times, so I got the chance to hang out with him. He talked shit, but he was slick. We were always getting high on weed, and he would slip things into the conversation, at a point when we were totally out of our skulls, to fuck with our minds. His art sucked as well, but he put on a good show. I really couldn't believe that Dorothy would fall for a phony like Howie, but, hey, she fell for me, so anything was possible.

Once, when Dorothy was still out at three in the morning, I went over to Howie's place, thinking that I might catch them in the act. Sure enough, she was there, but they both had their clothes on and were passing a half-finished joint between them.

They offered me a hit, and I took it; in fact I took several hits of that joint. It felt good to be in that student atmosphere again, just hanging out. But I could see that I was out of place there, and out of time as well. They were going to continue smoking, laughing, talking, and maybe even working. I was going to grab something to eat and get a good night's sleep for the workday ahead. I had no proof that Dorothy was having an affair. It didn't even matter whether or not she was having sex with Howie. It seemed inevitable to me that we were drifting apart, and I had no idea what I could do about it.

Thankfully, work was going well. It was the only thing I could look to as an answer to my problems. It was my salvation, and I poured myself into it with the dedication of an acolyte. I succeeded at every task I was given, and consequently I was gaining recognition.

I was assigned to a new art director, a man named Gordon, or Gordo, Roughouse, who specialized in television. Television was definitely the wave of the future, so I was ecstatic. My old boss, Jim, was strictly a print art director, also strictly old school. He always had a multimartini lunch with his pals Sel and Butch, and after lunch he'd just sit and stare at an ad he'd been working on for over a year, until five o'clock rolled around.

Gordo taught me wonderful things about scoring film to music, but he seemed to be more interested in working on a bottle than on a sixty-second commercial. He took me along to lunches with his pals, where three martinis were just for openers. I'd wobble back to the office after lunch, and just barely make it home.

Fortunately, I could avoid having lunch with Gordo and his pals more often than not, and I continued to concentrate on my work. Gordo, sensing my ambition and leaking his own, started to give me more and more of the work he was assigned, and I jumped all over it. What Gordo saw as chores, I saw as golden opportunities.

Soon, I was doing almost all of Gordo's work. At the same time, I noticed a very ugly turn in his attitude. He felt as if he was being bypassed by the upper echelon of the Creative Department, and became very bitter. We shared an office, sitting side by side at our drawing tables. Some afternoons Gordo would slump into his chair, mumbling curses and threats at the powers that be. He was a huge muscle of a man. He played rugby on the weekends and was a perfect bull of a specimen for that game. I became afraid that he would look up at me one day, think that I was stealing all his work, and try to kill me. I guess that I still had visions of rampaging Cossacks, because I started keeping my heavy steel T-square close by, ready to throttle him if he came for me.

Around that time, I had an illuminating experience. I was in a meeting of the creative team and the account executives on the Birds Eye account. We were discussing the strategy for frozen peas. I was mostly listening as the others talked about what the client was looking for in the advertising, but no one was talking about what they thought the advertising should be. My mind drifted out of the meeting for a while, and I dreamed up a commercial. In my vision, there were peas played by actors, and they were rowing a boatlike pod under the direction of a coxswain played by the comedian Jonathan Winters. As the meeting came back into focus, I said, to no one in particular, "What I think we should do…" I stopped in midsentence, as I realized that everyone had stopped talking in order to hear what I was about to say. It was an amazing revelation. My opinion had become important. I was now somebody!

The end of the year was coming around, and some people in the Creative Department had organized a big New Year's party to be held at a photographer's loft. I was excited. It was the first time that I felt truly accepted and integrated into the Young & Rubicam social circle. I invited a couple of my old friends from Pratt, and Dorothy asked if she could invite a couple of her friends as well. I couldn't really say no and expect to have a good time that night. Of course, the two friends were Howie and his buddy Phil. The thought of showing up at the party with my wife's lover made me want to puke, but I went along.

The night of the party, our whole group gathered at our apartment, and we smoked a couple of joints to get into the mood. I announced that I was going out to buy a pack of cigarettes and would be right back. Once in the street, I headed for the subway and went down to the station. I was beside myself, outside of myself, and inside out as well. I was on total emotional overload. I was pissed off and ashamed and didn't know what to do. So I got on the next train going out to Queens and rode it to the end of the line. Then I got on the train going back.

Somewhere halfway back to Washington Avenue, the clock struck midnight. Soon revelers were pouring onto the train, wearing party hats, blowing whistles, and rattling noisemakers. "You blew it, man!" one of them jeered at me. Little did he know how right he was.

When I got back to the apartment, everyone was still there, waiting for me. Somehow, they seemed to understand the turmoil that I was going through. I don't think that they were aware of the exact reasons for my meltdown, but they were sympathetic. Regardless of their kind understanding, it was a sad, sad moment in my life.

About a month later, another sad moment occurred. While at work, I received a call from my brother, telling me that he had just swallowed an entire bottle of aspirins and would be waiting for me at my apartment.

I dropped everything and rushed home. There I found Stephen lying in bed, holding on to his stomach. Dorothy was there as well. I asked what had happened, and she showed me a mostly empty aspirin bottle.

I half carried Stephen downstairs and sat him on the stoop while I hailed a cab, and we took him to the nearest hospital.

Once at the hospital, there was no easy way out. If someone attempts suicide, the law insists that he or she be placed under observation in a qualified institution. In this case, it meant the city hospital that I had brought him to.

Psychiatric wards in public hospitals still echo of Bedlam. They're understaffed and overcrowded. The patients are overmedicated in order to render them easy to control. These places are all painted in the dull gray light of defeat, and they reek of urine and humiliation. Stephen was there for ten days before our parents were allowed to take him home. It was only the beginning of a sad three-year journey for him.

Desperate to break the destructive pattern that Dorothy and I had fallen into, I rented an apartment for us in Brooklyn Heights. I got a great deal on the rent due to the fact that the building was owned by one of my mother's well-to-do cousins. The apartment was on the second floor of a graceful Beaux-Arts residence. It was basically a large studio with a sleeping loft, but the room was round, and the amazingly high ceiling was domed, so there was a palatial aura in that small space.

Things went along well for a while, and I began to think that Dorothy and I might have turned a corner. Then one morning as I was walking from our apartment to the subway station, I spotted a car slowly turn the corner onto our street with Howie slouched down in the passenger seat. I spun around and stormed quickly back down the street.

There, next to the entrance of the house, were Dorothy and Howie. A thick, black, angry cloud hovered over my head, and I'm sure that Dorothy sensed me before she saw me. As I arrived at the spot where they were standing, she broke into a stupid-looking grin of embarrassment. Howie turned, made tracks for the waiting car, and drove away. I don't know what I was thinking. I wasn't thinking,

I was just acting out my anger. I stepped up to Dorothy and smacked her across the face, back and forth, then turned around and walked away with the report of those smacks still echoing in the street.

Shortly after that incident, Dorothy disappeared. I didn't care. I threw myself into my work. As far as I was concerned, our marriage was over.

I heard from my brother that he had met Dorothy at the Democratic Convention in Chicago. He was there with the Students for a Democratic Society, one of the more radical antiwar groups. He was on the front lines, jeering at the police, trying to egg them into the violence that they eventually resorted to. He found Dorothy standing next to him. She threw a bag of feces at the police when they charged the crowd. Dorothy was always an enthusiast.

The next I heard from Dorothy was a phone call from her, about a month later. She was in Washington, DC, living in a commune. She said she'd be home soon. About three months after that, she did come home.

I didn't know what to make of her arrival. She seemed to be exhausted. Maybe she was just back for a rest. In any event, I decided to give all my attention to my job and none to her. I had already written my marriage off as a lost cause.

In the meantime, my career continued to rise. I was assigned to a new art director, Bob Eggers, one of the most highly regarded talents at the agency. Bob was a specialist in television, which meant that I would be doing all the print work for his many accounts. Bob handled some of the better accounts, so this was a definite move up for me.

As it happened, I got a big break on some television commercials. The Armour Foods account at our Chicago office was unhappy and ready to take its business somewhere else. So the New York office, where the best talent resided, geared up to make a presentation of new campaigns for Armour's various brands. Happily for me, there were some major problems on some other accounts that the agency considered more important. So they recruited a second tier of talent. I was assigned to the bacon business, one of the smaller accounts.

The major thrust of the agency's presentation was behind a big song and dance number for Armour Hot Dogs, their biggest piece of business. It consisted of a marching band leading a gang of kids down the main street of a small town, singing about "the dog kids love to bite." The clients loved it, and it put them in a favorable frame of mind. My commercial was much smaller in scale: an animated chicken crying her eyes out because the new, larger Armour bacon made her eggs look smaller. This too met with the clients' approval. I was in production!

It didn't take long to produce that simple commercial, and it was on the air in a couple of months. The singing hot-dog number was the big showpiece, and it got the lion's share of attention, but my crying chicken quietly won a medal at that year's Art Director's Show.

While my work life was filling up with promise and glory, the wasteland of my home life became more barren. The apartment had the stale, gray atmosphere of a dustbin. It smelled of decay. Neither Dorothy nor I wanted to be there. When an opportunity came up for me to get out of town for a few weeks, I pounced on it like a hungry cat on a canary.

I was asked to create a commercial for freeze-dried Sanka, a new product that had just been introduced by a commercial showing a close-up of an ice pick chipping away at a block of ice until the block split apart, revealing a jar of freeze-dried Sanka. It was a huge and immediate success. The client was so enamored of it that he wanted the next commercial to be based on the first, and I was assigned to come up with it. I didn't like that commercial because I had already come up with a campaign for the product and also because it wasn't my idea; however, I didn't have a vote in the matter.

At first, this depressed me to no end. Not only was I seeing my own campaign going down the drain, but I now had to create a commercial that, in my mind, had no concept other than to show the product surrounded by ice. However, there was no way I could refuse the assignment. So I determined that if I had to do the job, I was going to have a good time doing it, and I figured out a wonderful way to do just that.

Given the parameters of the commercial, it didn't need much conceptual thinking; just put the product in ice. My idea was to have a mountaineer climbing up an icy precipice and, upon reaching the summit, making a campfire and breaking out a jar of freeze-dried Sanka. The beauty of this idea was that it was spring in the United States, so we would have to shoot in a foreign locale, such as Argentina or the Swiss Alps. I had never been to either place; in fact, I had never been anywhere. So it was going to be a blast for me.

I was assigned a producer—a young guy, new to the agency, named Dennis Powers. He had hair as curly as mine, but red. He came from Los Angeles and had served in the Marines, but despite these differences, we shared something more fundamental. We had the same sense of humor, the same sense of aesthetics, and the same driving ambition. We hit it off right away.

Dennis showed me the reel of a French director-cameraman named Jacques Letalier, who we both agreed would be a perfect choice to shoot a commercial in the Alps. We didn't know of anyone of the same caliber in Argentina. So it was set; we were off to Switzerland.

The next week, I received a packet from Swissair containing my first-class ticket, slipper socks, a sleeping mask, and a menu with a choice of twenty-six entrées, plus numerous choices for the other seven courses. Whoa, baby. I started to tingle; this was the way to travel.

The meal on the flight to Geneva was, up until then, the best I'd had in my life—eight courses, and four different wines. There were three of us from the agency on the plane: Dennis, myself, and Joe Toto. Joe had decided that he needed a vacation, and asked if he could bunk with me while we were in Switzerland. Joe was a hard person to say no to under any circumstances, but considering the hundreds of times that he had given me a lift to and from work, I couldn't possibly refuse him.

Arriving in the center of Geneva, I was so excited that I immediately jumped into the Bally shop and bought my first pair of those wonderfully luxurious shoes. They were the color of butter, the shoes of a dandy.

We were shortly whisked off to the town of Zermatt, located below the Matterhorn. Zermatt was a magical dollhouse of a town. Our van had to park in a lot at the town's perimeter; no motorized vehicles were permitted inside. We rode into town in a sleigh pulled by a team of horses wearing jingle-bell collars. The constant ching chinging of those bells echoed all over the town. The buildings were all white and half-timbered. The people walking the streets were dressed in expensive clothes of quiet taste. It was Heidi's village for the wealthy.

Our production team was small and cozy. There was of course Jacques, a tall, wiry man of few words, perhaps because he spoke little English. His producer, André Moulin, spoke enough for both of them. André was smooth to the point of slick. He had the smug, well-contented good looks of a boulevardier. Carl, our local producer, spoke excellent American English. That was because he was American. He'd been living in Europe for twenty years and was equally fluent in French, German, and Italian. He was a hunky, handsome guy along the lines of Warren Beatty. He was our actor as well, and he also happened to own the Hotel Zermatt where we were staying. Another producer was a beautiful young woman named Carole. Coincidently she was also someone's girlfriend, but I never found out whose. Lastly there was Max, our mountain guide and the man responsible for our safety. Before we set out on the first day's scout, Max let us know that he required a bottle of brandy every day to keep him warm while up on the glacier. It made me wonder about our safety.

The glacier and the mountain were exuberant masterpieces of nature. Seeing the Matterhorn in person, I could well understand people's hunger for the summit. We took a cable car up to the glacier and walked around looking for shots, all the while leaping over or skirting around crevices that went all the way down to infinity.

The air was crisp, cold, and the cleanest I had ever breathed. The views were all alpine paintings. We found a great spot for our campsite location, and a few other good angles, then walked back to town. On the way down, the snow and ice gave way to the plushest green meadows I'd ever seen, making me want to roll myself downhill for miles. Of course, then I would have missed the wonderful rustic lunch we had in a rest house cabin halfway down the slope, and the sight of beautiful women in bikinis taking in the springtime après-ski sunshine and sipping aperitifs. Life was good.

The scouting and the shooting all went smoothly except for one small misstep that almost cost me my life. We were all strung together on a strong rope, walking along a narrow ledge on the glacier. Suddenly, the ice beneath my feet gave way, and I dropped straight down. Fortunately, the people on either side of me saw me go down and dug in with their cleated boots; otherwise we all would have fallen to our deaths. Max, the guide, shouted down at me to slowly dig my feet into the side of the hill and work my way back up, while he pulled me from above. I dug my foot in, but it didn't hold. The sun had warmed this side of the mountain, and the ice was soft. I tried again with the same result, then again and again, until my legs were churning like a pinwheel, all to no effect other than to raise my level of panic. Finally, Max unhooked himself and came down to get me, taking my hand and pulling me up the hill. Even when I had my footing back, I didn't want to let go of his hand.

I was safe and sound, and the shooting, which lasted over the next two days, ended well. Soon it was time to develop the film and see the rushes. Of course, there was no film lab in Zermatt, which made it absolutely necessary for us to fly to Paris.

Needless to say, we weren't staying in any old fleabag. Only the George V was good enough for us. This regal Beaux-Arts beauty was one of the Five Sisters, the grande dames of Parisian hotels. As soon as we entered the majestic lobby, I turned to Joe and told him that there'd be no room sharing here.

The man who showed us our rooms was dressed in tails. He spoke excellent English with a charming French accent. He showed us three rooms, each one grander than the last. I had never seen any rooms as elegant or as large. At the third and most impressive room, he asked who wanted which. Now, as far as I was concerned, I might never have an opportunity for an experience like this again; I was the one who had engineered this boondoggle, and I wanted it all. "I'm the boss here," I said, "I'll take this one."

The stay in Paris was short and uneventful, except for the fact that we were in the most beautiful city in the world. Everywhere I looked, everything I saw was beautiful: the fire hydrants were beautiful; even the sewer covers were beautiful. I went to the Louvre and fell to my knees in awe of the art I saw there. I felt like a Catholic in Lourdes or a Muslim in Mecca.

I also used the phone in my room to call Dorothy. I made the call at three in the afternoon, which would make it nine in the morning in New York. The phone rang and rang, until it was obvious that no one was at home. That was fine with me.

Then it was time to fly home. We were on TWA for the return flight, a step down from Swissair, as the meal was only seven courses compared to Swissair's eight, and there wasn't an advance menu to choose our entrées. We'd just have to make do.

Somewhere over the Atlantic, I finally lost it. We were the only three people in first class. There were more people waiting on us than there were of us. The entire experience of the past weeks had finally overwhelmed me in a wave of giddiness over the absurdity of it all. How could I have come out of the nowhere of my existence to be granted these rarified moments? It made no sense, except to expose the great cosmic joke of our existence, and I became unhinged by the nonsense of it all.

We had just finished the sixth course of our seven-course meal, and we were waiting for the fruit and cheese. I walked up and down the aisle of the first-class compartment and turned down all the seats into their fullest reclining position. Then, laughing insanely, I rolled myself over the seats, from the front of the compartment to the back. In the meantime, the fruit and cheese was served, the flight attendants discreetly ignoring my antics. I went back to my seat and started throwing the grapes at Dennis and Joe, who, getting caught up in my mania, threw their own fruit back at me. Then I stuffed the grapes into my ears and under my eyeglasses, screaming with laughter. Some of the passengers in the back opened the curtain separating the two compartments to see what the commotion was all about. I was laughing so hard that I could barely get the words out as I imperiously ordered the attendants to close the curtains. Once I finally quieted myself down and settled into a nap, I felt cleansed.

About a week and a half after I came back home, Dorothy disappeared again. I was relieved. Our relationship was beyond tattered. I just wanted to be able to concentrate on my work and somehow get on with my life. She showed up again about three weeks later, in the middle of the night. She was hysterical, screaming and crying and totally incoherent. I ran a cold shower and forced her into it, hoping that the shock would snap her out of it. While she was under the water, I asked her what drugs she had taken, and she rolled off a list of various items such as mescaline, methedrine, and acid. She started shouting out for Howie, which didn't increase my desire to help her. Then she showed me the scars on her wrist and told me that she had tried to kill herself. That left me with little alternative. I couldn't be responsible for any person in that condition. I got her dressed and dragged her outside, where I found a taxi to take us to the nearest hospital. There they took her to the psychiatric ward. It was a relief.

I went to visit her, and it was the same horror show as when my brother was there. She begged me to get her out, but there was nothing I could do and nothing I wanted to do. I certainly wasn't ready to take her home.

Her mother found a private sanitarium, run by Catholic nuns, on Long Island. I had her transferred out there, and agreed to pay the costs. She was there for three weeks, and I visited her every weekend.

When she was released, her mother took her home. As far as I was concerned, I was through with her. She must have felt the same way, because I didn't hear from her for a very long time. Long after she had left her parents' home.

It took me about a year to recover from Dorothy. I pretty much lived the life of a monk during that time. Going to work, coming home, going out to eat by myself, and going to bed. During the weekends I would sometimes walk over the Brooklyn Bridge, look around for a bit, then come back. I was a zombie.

Eventually I got myself out of the funk. I met Nora, a young woman whom I lived with for four years. During that time Dorothy showed up every once in a while, looking for a handout, a place to crash, or both.

Then one day she showed up needing five hundred dollars for an abortion. It was a golden opportunity. I told her that I'd gladly give her the five hundred, but she had to sign divorce papers. She didn't have much of a choice, and I knew it. Soon after that, I was on a plane to El Paso, followed by a bus to Juarez, where I got the divorce in a Mexican court. It was the best five hundred dollars I've ever spent.

I didn't see Dorothy for years after that. Then one day, after Nora and I had broken up and I had moved down to the Village, I was walking along Bleecker Street. I passed a small laundry and happened to look in. There was Dorothy, standing at a counter, folding laundry. She was working there and living somewhere in the area, although she was vague on exactly where. Our meeting was friendly, and I gave her my number, although I hoped she wouldn't use it.

But, of course, Dorothy came by my place not too long afterward. She wanted me to help her out with her living situation. She wanted to live in a loft where she could paint, and she had a place in mind and could afford the monthly rent. The problem, however, was that the landlords required more of a down payment than she could afford and also wanted someone to vouch for her. I decided to help her out. After all, I had once loved her, and I figured she could use a break.

By this time, I was a senior vice president at Young & Rubicam, making pretty good money. I had bought a two-hundred-year-old colonial house in Litchfield, Connecticut, that I went to on weekends, and a BMW 2002 to get me there. So I could easily stand to put up the down payment and vouch for Dorothy.

I went with her to a meeting with the landlords, two guys from Iran. I gave them a check and told them that I was Dorothy's boyfriend, living in Connecticut, and that I would back her financially. We shook hands; then Dorothy and I went outside, said good-bye, and went our separate ways. I never saw her again.

A few months later, I got a call from one of the Iranians. He told me that Dorothy had never paid any rent and that they wanted to evict her. He asked me if I was going to pay the rent for her. I told him that we were no longer a couple. I said I hadn't spoken to her in a month and didn't know anything about her situation. I told him that as far as I was concerned he could throw her out in the street.

Years went by, and I didn't hear from Dorothy at all. I was sure she was out of my life. I was going through big changes: a new job, a new apartment, and a new woman.

I was still at the Greenwich Avenue apartment, packing up, when the phone rang. I recognized Dorothy's voice immediately, and my heart sank into the pit of my stomach.

"I'm getting my life back together," she said.

"That's nice." I just wanted to get the conversation over with. I certainly didn't want to get Dorothy mixed into my new life.

"I just have to lose a little weight and get my skin and my hair good again."

"That sounds good."

"Then I'm going to become a call girl."

"Well, that's a plan. Good luck with it."

I ended the conversation quickly after that. I didn't give her my new phone number or even tell her I was moving. The new number was unlisted, and I was no longer working at Young & Rubicam; after eleven years, I had moved on to another agency, so there was no way for Dorothy to find me. I've never heard from her again. There were times that I got curious about what became of her, but not curious enough to chance a reconnection. That phone call was our last good-bye. I hope.

13

LIFE KICKS IN

1967

By 1967 things were beginning to fall into place, and my innate self confidence was beginning to be backed up by my accomplishments at work. Then, my Brooklyn attitude helped me to catch a huge break; although I didn't realize it at the time. I met Alex Kroll.

My first encounter with Alex was unforgettable. It was a couple of years earlier, when I was still an assistant art director scrapping for any chance I could find to prove my worth. I was sitting around the office that I shared with my boss, Bob Eggers, and gloating with Rudy Golyn, a young copywriter. I was tucked into a corner next to the door, with my drawing table and a small credenza upon which all my supplies were stuffed into a rotating plastic organizer called a taboret.

We were gloating because we had just bested our bosses. For the past nine months, they had been vainly trying to create advertising that would introduce the world to freeze-dried Sanka. When they got busy on another project, they asked Rudy and me to come up with a print campaign to serve as a stopgap until they could get back to the business.

We came up with a campaign. It wasn't great, but at least it had an idea. "The Coffee That Made the Coffee Pot Obsolete" campaign featured visuals of different kinds of coffee pots being used as flowerpots, fishbowls, archery targets, and other silly things. The clients must have been desperately waiting for something decent to come out of the agency, because they jumped up and applauded when they saw our work.

Rudy and I became heroes, and my boss was relieved that he didn't have to put any more time or energy into the project. I didn't know how Rudy's boss, Alex Kroll, would take it. I'd never met the man, but his reputation as a bully had spread all over the agency. So here were Rudy and I preening over our success, when the doorway was filled with the presence of a very large man. He stepped into the office without saying hello. I didn't need an introduction to know who he was, but a little courtesy would have been in order. The ad layouts were pinned up on one of the walls, and he stepped over to look at them closely, one by one, as if he was trying to find a fatal flaw in them. Still inspecting the layouts, he pronounced, "The logo will have to be bigger, and some other things will have to change."

Now, this man was Rudy's boss, but he had nothing to do with me. As a matter of fact, without him introducing himself, I had no clue who he was. Also, I'd had enough of bullies on Union Street to last me a lifetime. My blood was beginning to boil, but I played it cool: "Who the fuck are you to tell me anything about what should be done with my ads?"

I said it without malice, but he didn't like it anyway. He froze for a second or two, and it seemed as if time had frozen as well. Then he slowly turned to me, his jaws clenching and unclenching, the veins in his neck throbbing, his color rising as he stepped toward me. I leaned back, slickly slipped the shears out of my taboret, and held them out in front of me, just as I had seen done in countless movies about juvenile delinquents. He took another step forward, then a third, without breaking his rhythm. I quickly computed the situation, replaced the sheath, shrugged my shoulders, and said, "The logo can be bigger. No big deal."

A year later we had worked out a relationship that served us both. He recognized my talent and used it to gain power, and I recognized his power and used it to get my work sold.

That was about the time that I saved the *Life* magazine account, one of the most prestigious at the agency. The client had put us on notice, which basically meant that we had ninety days to come up with some startling new creative work or we'd be fired.

The entire creative department was put to work in the effort to save the day. I created a series of ads that were totally different from the tastefully bland work the agency had been doing up to then, boring ads that had led the client to consider changing agencies.

My ads were basically promos for the upcoming article in the weekly picture magazine, but they were arresting, edgy, and relevant. For an article about diet-pill abuse, I wrote a headline saying "How to Lose Weight. Permanently," accompanied by a large photograph of a human skull. For an article introducing the first photographs of human fetuses inside their mothers' wombs, I wrote, "Everybody's Been There. We Brought Back Pictures." My tagline for the campaign was "Life. Consider the Alternative." I have to admit that the latter was overdoing it more than a bit. On the other hand, some antiwar groups picked it up and used it as a banner in peace marches, so it was connecting to people on some level. The client loved the line. They ran two- and three-page spreads in the *New York Times* with just that line on them.

The campaign worked for a while; readership for *Life* rose to over eight million. But a year later, the magazine folded due to insufficient advertising revenue. Still, I got a lot out of the effort. I was promoted to a full-fledged art director, I got a small raise, and, most importantly, I was considered a rising star.

It was while working on that account that I met Nora. When we met I was coming off a year of living the life of a dust globule. My marriage to Dorothy was in shambles. I had no idea about her whereabouts, and hadn't for many months. I didn't really care where she was, as long as she wasn't in a position to make my life miserable anymore. One lesson I had learned for sure: don't get married to an eighteen-year-old girl with a psychotic tendency if you're only twenty-one years old yourself.

I spent my days working long hours in the office and then taking the subway back to Brooklyn Heights, a lonely table at a restaurant, and a dark empty apartment. I didn't even have a TV to keep me company; it would have gotten in the way of all the pleasure I was taking from my pain.

It was around Christmastime, and I had a last-minute print ad to do for *Life* magazine. I had to get a photograph of a family watching television, and I needed one of the agency stylists to dress them in the appropriate clothes. I'd heard about a new stylist named Nora, who was supposed to have a lot of talent, exotic beauty, and also quite a strong personality.

When I went down to the Styling Department, I ran right into her and found myself drawn like a starving man to a banquet. She was everything I'd heard about and more. I immediately commandeered her into doing the job, despite her protestations that she was about to head out of town to marry her boyfriend. I paid no attention to that last part. It just got in the way of where my mind was heading. I said that the job just had to be done and that she had to do it. There was a definite undercurrent flowing through our conversation, and a definite attraction drawing us together. I realized that I was smitten. I was also paralyzed with fear. The previous three years had weighed my soul down with old baggage filled with heavy stones, and as my soul went, so went my courage.

That day it was late and it was Friday. She invited me over to her apartment to talk about the job. I had rented a car to get me to the location for the Sunday shoot, so we walked over to Hertz together.

I had been a walking dead man for so long, I knew that if I didn't pull myself out of my self-dug grave, I'd never get out alive. My brain desperately raced around looking for something to help, and it found a song. The Beatles' "Hey Jude" flooded into my mind, and I began to use the lyrics as a mantra.

> *And anytime you feel the pain, hey Jude, refrain,*
> *Don't carry the world upon your shoulders*
> *For well you know that it's a fool who plays it cool*
> *By making his world a little colder.*

Nora lived in a four-floor walk-up on East Sixty-Second Street. It was a railroad flat; a tiny living room led into a tiny kitchen, leading into a tiny bedroom, with a tiny bathroom tacked on. But it was decorated in the most imaginative way, and at a cost of just a few hundred dollars. The living-room walls were lined with milk crates that served as storage bins, casual tables, and bases for the fifty or so plants that filled the room. It felt like I was walking into a rain forest.

> *Hey, Jude, don't make it bad*
> *Take a sad song and make it better*
> *Remember to let her into your heart*
> *Then you can start to make it better.*

Nora rolled a joint, and we started talking about a million things, even the job. Soon we were talking just to draw each other closer, and soon after that we were locked in each other's arms, devouring each other with our passion.

> *Hey, Jude, don't be afraid*
> *You were made to go out and get her*
> *The minute you let her under your skin*
> *Then you begin to make it better.*

It was like two planets colliding. Suddenly Nora wasn't getting married to her boyfriend in North Carolina, and I was moving into her apartment, or at least going back to Brooklyn to get enough clothes for the weekend.

> *Nah, nah, nah, nah, nah, nah, nah, nah, nah,*
> *Hey, Jude.*

It was three o'clock in the morning when we got in the car. I had to get to my apartment, pick up some clothes, and get back to Nora's place. I headed for the FDR Drive, which would take me to the Brooklyn Bridge. Living in Brooklyn all my life, I was unfamiliar with her neighborhood and the local entrances and exits to the drive. Finally, I found a ramp and raced onto the empty highway. Thirty seconds later I saw two sets of headlights coming straight toward me. I had gotten on the highway going the wrong way!

"You're going to kill us! You're going to kill us!" Nora screamed in a panic. I could see myself losing all the points I had gained over the past eight hours, and I couldn't let that happen.

"Cool it!" I commanded. Cool it? Where had that come from? Probably some movie. At any rate, it worked. She stopped screaming. I slammed on the brakes, threw the car into reverse, and backed down the ramp to the street as fast as I could. Backing into the street, I could see a cop car parked right next to the ramp, facing me. But the cops must have been sleeping because nothing happened except for me making a U-turn and getting out of there.

That was the beginning of Nora and me, and it was emblematic of our relationship, as we continued on with the same intensity and the same levels of tension and anxiety. We constantly raced toward each other at full speed, never knowing whether we were running into an embrace or a train wreck.

Nora was very strict in her ideals. She insisted that we live our relationship the way that Sartre and de Beauvoir lived theirs. Each day was a new beginning, not anchored by any happiness or unhappiness that had occurred the day before. To me it sounded as if I had to win her love anew every day. A person could get tired doing that, but it kept me on my toes. It certainly put an edge on our relationship.

We took a cab down to the agency every workday morning, but Nora insisted that I get out a couple of blocks before the cab got there because she didn't want to be labeled. She finally relented after ten months, when everyone in the industry, much less the agency, knew we were together.

Living with Nora, I felt truly happy for the first time in a long time, but that feeling was also a fragile one, like an egg that was cracked but still holding its shape. I felt as if I had no real right to happiness. Maybe that feeling had to do with my guilt over the failure of my life with Dorothy; or my guilt over my negative feelings toward my parents; or the feeling that, despite my recent successes, I was a fraud. Most likely the sources of that unease were all those things and a lot more, all stuffed into a huge backpack that I carry around to this day.

14

THE WINGS OF ME

1969

TAKING OFF

It was the spring of 1969. I was twenty-six years old, flying first class to spend ten weeks in London and Rome and shooting two commercials that were going to make my career. I sat in my plush leather seat, struggling to contain my excitement. I was on a journey to the stars. Little did I suspect that by the end of the trip I'd be one slip away from landing right back in Brownsville. Even if I'd known that, I wouldn't have cared because I was flying too high, straight up into the sun, living a life that was imitating art. The art was my own, and it was all about me.

Two of my colleagues were seated side by side, directly behind me: the copywriter and the agency producer. But as far as I was concerned, they were just riding my dream. This was my dream come true, and mine alone. My ego was flying as high as the airplane.

This is the dream that I had, nine months earlier while I was flush with my sense of elevation from saving the Life account and searching for the next rung on the ladder, I envisioned a young man with large white and gold wings, rising up into a deep blue sky dotted with fleecy clouds.

Of course, it was the Greek myth of Daedalus and Icarus, and of course, the young man was myself. But was I Daedalus, the genius who had created the wings that enabled him to fly? Or his son Icarus, who, failing to heed his father's warning, flew too close to the sun and fell to his death in the sea below?

But the dream was more than a self-wish; it was a vision of a commercial that would save the agency's most important account: Eastern Airlines. While not nearly the largest account, Eastern was the flagship. Young & Rubicam's creative work for Eastern had placed it in the top rank of advertising agencies, and it had been spectacularly successful in attracting new business. Lately, however, the work had become merely workmanlike, stolid, and predictable. I saw my dream as a vision of what Eastern's advertising should be. But having the vision and getting it on the screen were two very different things. There was absolutely no way that I could go to the creative director of Young & Rubicam and tell him that the advertising for Eastern sucked and that I had a much better idea. But good fortune was on my side. And three months later, the door was opened wide for me to walk through.

Floyd Hall, the chairman of the airline, was a fiercely proud man, and he did not want his company to be represented by anything less than the best. He told the agency that he was inviting other shops to pitch his account. Of course, we were invited to pitch as well.

I pounced on the opportunity like a cat on a canary. It was all hands on deck at the agency. The Creative Department of more than three hundred people became involved in a massive competition to come up with a campaign that would save the account. I never doubted I would win, because my idea was preordained.

On the day the alarm bell rang, I went to Alex Kroll my immediate superior and presented ideas for three commercials. The Daedalus commercial, of course, was first. Then I showed him a commercial about cavemen trying to touch the full moon and a commercial about a little boy freeing a songbird from its cage. The tagline for the campaign was "The Wings of Man."

He lit up like a Christmas tree. This was as big an opportunity for him as it was for me—bigger, because he was aiming for something much grander than I was. Little did I know that while I was acting out my own personal fantasy, I was taking a big role in a drama playing out on a much larger stage: Saint Stephen versus King Kroll.

Alex Kroll had been an All-American center and captain of the only undefeated football team in the history of Rutgers University. He was handpicked by the management of Young & Rubicam to be their man in a Creative Department that was beginning to assert itself over the suits. At Young & Rubicam, he was a copywriter by trade, and although he pounded out copy with the same blunt fierceness that he used to knock down opposing guards and tackles, he was a great strategic thinker and the best presenter I've ever seen. He was physically imposing and totally sure of himself. At six feet two, he may have been too small to play in the NFL, but in a group of artists and writers, he was a fearsome force of intimidation—an advantage that he used to its full extent in service of his massive ambition. With his horn-rimmed glasses, Alex looked like Clark Kent, with Superman's muscles bulging under his suit.

Alex had been hired by management with the purpose in mind of replacing Steve Frankfurt, my mentor and my hero. Steve was one of the most brilliant creative minds of his or any other era. As good as I believed my own work to be, it was, at best, an homage to the work that Steve had done for Eastern, which had put Young & Rubicam at the top of the creative mountain.

Steve's work had pushed him to the top as well. He had become the president and creative director of Young & Rubicam, advancing his creative agenda. He encouraged all of us in the Creative Department to push the envelope as far as we could. "Just make it great" was his mantra. He gave us all permission to be as good as we could.

This didn't go over too well with the rest of management – there were a chairman and vice-chairman above Steve. The suits were against pushing their clients too hard. In fact, they were pretty much against pushing their clients at all. Most of them wished that Steve would just go away, so they could put their own man in charge of the Creative Department. They had hired Alex to be that man.

So yes, Alex's face lit up when I showed him my ideas. This was the best opportunity he could hope for: the chance to take control of the very account that marked Steve's power. Alex would gain, Steve would lose, and the world of Young & Rubicam would turn over.

Of course, I wasn't aware of any of these machinations at the time. And if I had been, I wouldn't have done anything different. This was my time also, my dream, my chance for destiny. I also wanted to do it for Steve. I knew how important Eastern was to him emotionally and politically. Plus, I wanted to show Steve just how good I was, prove that I was ready and capable of carrying his standard, maybe even inheriting his mantle and becoming the heir apparent.

But having a great idea is one thing; selling it is quite another, even when there is a desperate need for it. The competition within the Creative Department was fierce. The prize was the Young & Rubicam equivalent of the Holy Grail. Having Alex on my side was both a plus and a minus. He was a great presenter, and the suits loved him, but lots of people in the Creative Department feared and detested him, and it was the heads of the Creative Department who would choose the campaign. In fact, the most heavily weighted vote in that decision would be Steve Frankfurt, the very person who had the most to lose if Alex became the Eastern go-to guy.

Eight different campaigns would be presented to a committee made up of Steve and the top creative honchos in the agency. I knew that this might be the most important presentation I would ever have to make. It had to be impressive but also surprising and entertaining. It had to be as dramatic as the commercials it was representing.

I set up in a small conference room across the hall from my office. The room was filled by a large white oval pedestal table and white pedestal chairs. Bill Waites (the copywriter), Alex, and I would be on one side, and the eight committee members on the other. The room would be crowded but intimate. It suited my plan perfectly.

The recessed overhead lights had been dimmed down to the point that the atmosphere of the room was one step into spooky. Some dim illumination bounced up from the surface of the white table, reflecting back upon Alex, Bill, and me.

The effect gave the committee members some pause when they walked in, and they took a careful look around the room and at us. What they saw must have come as a subtle surprise. I was dressed in a suit and tie for the first time in over two years. As the relaxed ethos of the late 1960s kicked in, my uniform had become black jeans and black shirts. *Viva la revolución.*

Now I was wearing a suit that I'd had custom made, tailored out of a blue serge material. It made me look like I meant business, and I did.

After everyone got seated, I began my presentation. "We see a sky filled with beautiful, puffy white clouds." The first three long haunting notes of Strauss's *Thus Spoke Zarathustra*, the same music that Stanley Kubrick used for *2001: A Space Odyssey*, accompanied my words.

Now that I was a full art director, I had my own assistant, and as I started to speak, he quietly turned on the tape recorder with the music that I had timed my presentation to. Then he went to the light switch and slowly raised the level as we had rehearsed, while I continued. "The camera pulls back, and reveals that we're looking at the reflection in a man's eye." *Ta-da!* The huge brass crescendo punctuated my first revelation. "The camera continues to pull back as we reveal a classically beautiful, bare-chested young man." *Boom, boom.* The kettle drums rolled along with me. "We see that he's standing poised on top of a high cliff, and he's wearing large white and golden wings strapped to his chest." *Ta-da!* "We pull back further as the man spreads the wings. *Boom, boom.* I stood up. "The man crouches, preparing to spring." I carefully placed a foot on one of the two black office trash cans that I had placed under the table. Then I lifted myself up on the cans to a height of seven feet, towering over the committee, who looked up at me with their mouths gaping open. "And he flies!" The final and largest crescendo continued on. "He soars up into the sky, higher and higher, sweeping through the clouds, up toward the sun, where we dissolve to an Eastern jet flying in front of the sun."

They were floored. The copywriter followed me, reading some appropriately poetic words about the eternal quest to conquer the skies. Then we went on to present the other two commercials, but the conquest on the ground had already been made.

UN SETTLING

So now Bill, the copywriter; Tom, the agency producer; and I were sitting in first class, all wondering exactly how we were going to make a man fly. We were going to work with Bob Gaffney, a cameraman and a director who had worked with Kubrick on *2001: A Space Odyssey*, and we were going to use the same front projection technology and wire-flying actors that he had used for the spacewalk shots, but we still didn't have any idea how it would all come together.

Before I left, Alex had nervously asked me if I knew how to pull this thing off, and I had blatantly lied that I had it all figured out. Then he said threateningly, "Just remember, no matter where you go, I'll find you."

We landed at Heathrow and went straight to the Young & Rubicam London office. There, we were greeted by the manager of the office, who passed us to an older woman functionary who gave us the name and address of the hotel that we'd be staying at, as well as fifty pounds each for *per diem* money. There was also a message waiting for us from Chuck Trischman, Gaffney's executive producer. He was going to pick us up at the hotel that evening and take us to dinner.

The hotel was a big disappointment. It was a dowdy Victorian hulk, located in a dull, cranky neighborhood. The rooms were dark and not overly large. It wasn't what I'd had in mind for a seven-week stay in, as it was called at the time, "Swinging London."

Chuck Trischman met us in the lobby at seven. He was American, and there was something slightly creepy about him, but I figured he was the suit of the production company, so what the hell. He apologized for Bob Gaffney's absence and promised that we would really enjoy the evening. While we drove over in a taxi, he told us that we were going to the Six-Hundred Club. It used to be called the Three-Hundred Club, when it was frequented by Princess Margaret and her crowd, but it was slightly less exclusive now, which was why we were able to get in.

The place was on a narrow street in Soho, with steps going down below street level. We were greeted by a doorman in a fancy red coat with gold brushes on the shoulders, then led to a table by an attractive hostess dressed in considerably less. After we were seated, the first things I noticed were the artists' easels spotted around a small stage. Then a waiter came dashing up to the table to take our order for drinks. Chuck generously ordered a bottle of good champagne. Then a scantily dressed young lady appeared on the stage and started to take off the few clothes she had on, while gyrating to some elegant version of the old bump and grind.

"I knew you fellows would like this place because you're artists. You can go up to the easels and sketch if you like." Chuck seemed mighty pleased with his choice of venues for this introductory dinner.

While we dined on overdone steak and overcooked vegetables, Chuck told us that Bob was busy getting a presentation ready for us. We would meet him in two days' time at Borehamwood Studios, forty-five minutes out of the city.

I went to bed that night in a funk. I didn't like the way things were going, and I intended to do something about it. This parade was too important to get rained on. We had two days before we were going to work, and I was determined to put those days to good use.

The next morning, we took a taxi to the Young & Rubicam office and marched into the manager's office. He was surprised to see us. I think he thought that he had gotten us out of his hair already.

"How do you like your accommodations?" he asked.

"Not very much," I answered. "We're going to have to make some changes. We're going to want to rent two small houses. We'll also need two rental cars, and a thousand pounds each."

I could see the man reacting even while I was still speaking. He was obviously not pleased by my colonial impertinence. I could plainly see that he thought I was a twenty-seven-year-old pisher with a fresh mouth, so I threw in, "And if you've got any questions, call the New York office."

What did these guys in the London office think was going on? That we were three accountants sent over to check the books? We were there to do something that had never been done before and to save the international advertising giant's most important account. We were going to need all our creative abilities working at full strength, and that wasn't going to happen if we were stuffed into depressing ten-by-ten rooms in some creepy hotel for seven weeks. I'd be damned if I was going to let some gray little apparatchik put us in that position so he could check us off his list. I couldn't help it if there was a marvelous convergence of what was right for the job at hand and what served my hedonistic aspirations.

Two days later, Bill and Tom were ensconced in a house in Kensington that once belonged to Ronald Colman, and I was living in a mews house two blocks north of Hyde Park. I had wanted the two houses because I didn't want to be tied to Bill and Tom for seven weeks. They were both nice enough guys who had married their college sweethearts. They ogled other women but never made a serious move. They'd never been in a peace march and had never dropped acid. They simply lived in a different world than I did.

I'm not claiming that I was a model of degenerate sophistication, but those were the waters I swam in and sometimes drank from. I was married to one woman and living with another. I got high in the office, and higher when I got home. I used to run away from the cops when I was younger, and now I sometimes dodged their clubs and their tear gas at demonstrations against the war. This was 1969, and we were going to be in Swinging London for seven weeks. There had to be two separate houses; I had to draw the line somewhere.

I loved my little house on Hyde Park Gardens Mews, and I loved the sound of that address. It was a narrow little street, around the corner from a great-looking pub called the Swan. Downstairs was a sitting room that held four small easy chairs, two end tables, and a miniscule fireplace. There was a tiny but efficient kitchen and a small water closet. Narrow stairs led up to two small bedrooms and a bathroom. The house had a little garage attached, in which I parked my little car. Everything was scaled down in these buildings, which were originally put up to house the workers who served the large homes on the main streets. It was cozy, and I found its closeness comforting. I had never lived by myself in anything larger than a one-bedroom apartment, and a house this size felt just right.

The next day, Chuck came around to pick us all up and drive us to Borehamwood Studios to meet Bob Gaffney. It took only forty-five minutes to get there, and I could see it was an easy drive. I could catch the A-5 Road just a block from my house, and then it was an easy connection to the A-1. After a couple of local roads, I'd be at the studio gates.

Chuck led us into a large office, where Bob was waiting for us with one of the happiest smiles I've ever seen. His leonine head was crowned by a mass of gray and white curls, under which sat a mischievous potato of a face, centered on twinkling blue eyes and a happy Irish drinking nose. His body was too lean for his head, save for his little potbelly, which seemed to balance things out. He was wearing an open shirt under a terrible gray suit jacket that looked as if he'd put it on for the occasion and couldn't wait to shuck it off. When he opened his mouth to greet us, the sound of the Bronx came out, and I knew I was in good hands.

Then I took a look around the office. "This is Stanley's office," said Bob. Stanley Kubrick, that is, Bob's boyhood friend from the Bronx. Stanley Kubrick, the genius who created such startling brilliances as *Paths of Glory*, *Dr. Strangelove*, and *2001: A Space Odyssey*.

A shelf ran near the top of the very high walls. It was lined with miniature figures of soldiers in every conceivable uniform from the Napoleonic Wars. Bob explained that he and Stanley were working on a film about Napoleon. Bob was producing and had just returned from a trip to Romania, where he had lined up the entire Romanian Army to be in the film. Unfortunately, Stanley soon had to abort the project. Dino De Laurentiis had already begun shooting his own version of Napoleon, with Rod Steiger starring.

"You can use the office as your own, if you want," said Bob.

If I want? Was he kidding?

Then Bob had someone bring out the wings that he had made, and I almost fainted. They were unspeakably beautiful. Made of eagle feathers, they spanned about six feet. It would take an enormously strong man to wear them while hanging from a wire above the stage. But that's what we were there for, and Bob assured us that's what we would get.

At last, the project was off the ground. Then began the series of tasks necessary to get every commercial ready for the actual shooting: casting for the actor, designing and building the mountaintop he would leap off, and finding the photographs of the sky that he would fly through.

I had a clear vision of how I wanted everything to look. I envisioned everything being hyperreal: an idealized reality more beautiful than it could ever truly be. This meant that Brian, the actor we chose, one of the wire flyers who floated in space in *2001: A Space Odyssey*, had to look like a Greek god. His steel-gray eyes were perfect for the role, but his upturned Irish nose wouldn't do for the Greek god that I had in mind. I had his nose reshaped with prosthetics and his hair restyled into golden waves. He had the fierce, heroic look of an eagle.

My vision also insisted that the mountaintop and the sky match the glory of our hero. Days and weeks went by as we reviewed new noses, hairstyles, sketches of mountains, and photographs of skyscapes.

When I was finally satisfied, we shot a test and sent it off to our, by then, anxious colleagues in New York.

In the meantime, my erstwhile social life was running into a series of closed doors, most of them shut by myself. I've always felt like an outsider. In a family where being good was expected, I was bad. In a neighborhood where toughness was prized, I was an artist. Hanging out in high school with Italian, Black, and Irish kids, I was a Jew. In a college filled with suburban kids, I was the poor kid from Brooklyn. In an industry dominated by preppy WASPs, I was out of my element. Now, on my own in London, I felt that I was all those things, and a Yank to boot.

There were pubs and restaurants everywhere, teeming with people out for a good time. I'd go and sit in a corner by myself to eat, drink and watch. John Alcott, our cinematographer, lent me his membership card to Aretusa, the chicest club in town. I'd go, stand in a corner, have a drink, and watch. I just couldn't find any way to break through. I was going through the motions of having a good time without actually having one.

During the day things were much better. I could sit back in a cushy leather chair behind Stanley Kubrick's big desk, smoke a Cuban cigar, and talk to New York over a speakerphone.

The weekends were tough, especially since the English weather was still raw, so long rambles through their beautifully manicured parks were out. The good news was that Nora, was coming over for a long visit. Hopefully, having her on my arm would give me the courage to go back into those pubs and restaurants as if I belonged there.

I met her at the airport, and she came bearing gifts other than her own precious self. She came with more than enough drugs to last us until we got back home.

Nora and I liked our drugs. There was marijuana, of course, which we smoked continuously after work, rolling one joint after another; hashish; and Thai stick, similar to grass but different.

The first thing that Nora unpacked was an ounce of grass in a baggy that she had stuffed into the bottom of a canister filled with baby powder. In those days, drug surveillance was much more lax than it is today, especially entering Europe, and the baby-powder routine was pretty much the usual way to go. She had also brought along an entire variety pack of pills: acid, mescaline, and a whole bunch of other goodies that I can't remember, probably because those particular brain cells have been irreparably destroyed.

I didn't have to worry about being an outsider anymore, because now I was a couple, a group, a world unto myself and my mate, a privileged insider of my own universe, able to partake of the delights offered by the outside world as if I were an honored visiting dignitary.

We danced the night away at Club Aretusa, dined extravagantly at Mr. Chow, toured the city's museums, enjoyed its theaters, and entertained visitors from Paris and New York. We were the toast of our own private town.

Nora was willing to come to London while I was filming there, but only on her own dime and as her own woman. This was fine with me. I was proud to stand next to a woman as strong as that. In London, we were like two songbirds inside a bamboo cage, being carried through the narrow streets of some Chinese city crowded with carnival. Then the cage was opened, and the birds flew out in different directions.

STUCK IN THE CLOUDS

At Borehamwood we were experiencing the first problem with our commercial. The clouds weren't right. The hundreds of photographs we had gone through were all very nice, but they were pretty and poetic. I needed something heroic and triumphant. We needed to take new photographs, but the skies over England were smeary and bland. We were going to have to travel somewhere to find those spectacularly glorious clouds that I had in mind.

"Somewhere" turned out to be the mountains of Bavaria, where the skies of warring clouds inspired the painters of the Northern Renaissance.

Nora, on the other hand, was going to Rome, where our friend Susan was producing a commercial for Union Carbide. Nora was already getting bored with poking around London while waiting for me to come home. She had absolutely no interest in coming to Germany, and wasn't going to hang around on her own. So it was off to sunny Rome for her. Nora could crash with Susan and also do some prep work for the Caveman commercial, which was going to be shot there.

We decided that either she'd come back to London after I returned from Germany, or we'd hook up in Rome, where I was going to supervise the Caveman shoot and Nora was going to design the costumes.

Bob, Tom, and I flew to Munich and stayed overnight. Bill, the writer, felt that since this was a purely visual exercise, his time was better spent in London, keeping his eye on the birds.

The three of us went to one of Munich's famous biergartens, where the sound of all those German voices ho-ho-ho-ing and banging their steins on the wooden tables made my flesh crawl and my hair stand up. Guys bellowing in bars, sloshing beer on the floor, and waving their testosterone around always struck me as loutish and frightening. That these particular louts were cut from the same cloth as the ones that sent people like me to the gas chambers made me sick, scared, and angry.

The next morning, we piled into a car, along with Dieter, our local connection, and headed south, toward the mountains. We were going to a region close to the Austrian border, Garmisch-Partenkirchen, and more specifically to Der Zugspitze, a peak that towered over the entire area.

The drive was only a little more than an hour. Along the way we stopped for lunch at a small rustic restaurant in the foothills. A bright sun warmed our faces as we sat at a long wooden table eating the meat dishes that the owner brought out. The meat had lots of fat on it, and I noticed that Dieter, who was sitting next to me, was mostly eating the fat, while I was mostly eating the meat. We probably could have ordered one dish between us. I realized that there must be many more cultural differences between us than met my eye.

The hotel we were staying in was a low-key, utilitarian affair at the base of Der Zugspitze. The most noteworthy thing about it was that the water stank of sulfur. It didn't matter; we were there for a purpose, and when we got what we wanted, we'd be out of there.

That night we went out to eat at a tavern in the mountains. We stepped into a smallish wood-planked room containing a bar and six tables. Fortunately, one of them was empty. Looking around, I could see that we were obviously the only strangers in the place, as all the other tables were filled with men wearing lederhosen.

The waitress came over from behind the bar. She was interested in who we were and what we were doing there, and she was flirting with all of us simultaneously. I picked up a vibe from the rest of the room. It was completely understandable. No one likes strangers walking onto their turf and grabbing the attention of the local beauties. It always leads to hard feelings and often winds up badly.

Sure enough, a tall, muscular blond beast was soon standing at our table with a tight smile forced on his face.

"American?" he asked.

"Ja, ja, American," answered Bob, sounding calm and relaxed. He seemed to have the situation in hand. Still, I was uneasy. If this situation got messy, we could all wind up beaten to bloody pulps or worse.

Despite Bob's sunny disposition, the big German kept a black cloud over his head. He started talking in German to Dieter and to the room at large. I could tell by his tone that our presence was pissing him off.

"Do you want to fight?" asked Bob, still smiling.

The guy looked over to Dieter, who gave him a quick translation.

"Ja, fight," the man answered. I could see the blood rising into his face.

"Pull up a chair. We'll fight," said Bob, placing his elbow on the table and assuming the classic arm-wrestling position.

The giant sat down, and he and Bob locked hands.

"Ready? One, two, three!" said Bob, and the German took him down in half a second flat.

"Okay. Let's do the other hand," said Bob, and he switched over to his left.

The big guy did likewise, and again, he took Bob down immediately. It was brilliant. Bob had offered no resistance at all. He put out nothing but a beaming smile. It was like an animal showing an alpha male that he was submitting to his superior force, and it worked. The man had a beer on us, then bought us a round before returning to his own table to tell his friends that the Americans were okay.

The next morning Otto, the helicopter pilot, flew in. His chopper was outfitted with a camera rig that allowed the cameraman to sit, strapped in, at the open passenger-side door with the camera suspended in front of him, hanging from a gimbal, which allowed him to move it in any direction.

Otto, Bob, and I flew up to the top of Der Zugspitze, but Bob needed more room when he was shooting, so I waited down below while Bob and Otto went up to search for the right clouds.

There I was, alone on top of a mountain, looking down over a place remembered for one of Der Führer's triumphs. This was where Adolf Hitler held his Winter Olympics for all the world to see the glory of the Third Reich.

Just then, I realized that I had to pee. Ah! An excellent opportunity for a symbolic gesture. Unzipping myself, I faced into the valley and sprayed Jewish piss all over Garmisch-Partenkirchen. What a pathetic, impotent, vainglorious gesture it was. Yet if I hadn't made that token of acknowledgment, I would have wasted the moment, not to mention a good piss.

Fifteen minutes later, Bob and Otto landed. Bob had shot nothing at all. The sky was socked in for miles around. They had wasted their time. I was glad that I hadn't wasted mine.

For the next three days, the story was the same: a dull, gray, overcast sky. It was getting boring. I managed to reach Nora by phone. We made a plan to meet in Nice, in the South of France, over the weekend. I'd fly down, and she and Susan would drive over the Alps from Italy.

It didn't matter whether I was at Der Zugspitze or not. Bob was going to go up in the chopper every day until he found and photographed the right clouds. It might happen the next day, or it might happen the next week, but sooner or later it was going to happen, whether I was there or not.

SWEPT AWAY BY THE SEA

The next day I was on a train to Munich, where I would catch a plane to Zürich, followed by another one to Nice. The train was fairly filled up when I got on, and I was lucky to get the last seat in my car. Ten minutes later we pulled into another station, and people started marching through the train, searching for empty seats.

There were a lot of elderly people in this group, and I found myself marveling at their sturdy self-sufficiency. They were well groomed and conservatively dressed, and they carried their leather suitcases and satchels, many of them obviously quite heavy, without any wavering. They seemed so much more fit, alert, and put together than the people of the same age I was used to seeing in the States.

Then some other, more cynically logical part of my brain kicked in. I began to figure how old these people would have been in the mid-1930s, when the Nazis started passing the laws that pushed the Jews out of German society; in the late 1930s, when they started to round up and throw the Jews into concentration camps; in the early 1940s, when they captured, tortured, and slaughtered millions of Jews from the Eastern countries.

There was a miserable taste in my mouth. Then I thought, what did I know about these particular individuals, happily and hardily making their way through the train? I knew nothing at all about them, and there was nothing that I wanted to find out either.

I got into Nice late in the afternoon and took a taxi to the port where Nora and Susan planned to meet me. I walked out onto the end of a long stone wall that jutted out past the port to a lighthouse. I figured that I'd be easy to spot out there. There were a couple of dozen people scattered along the wall, all looking out to the west, where the sun was getting ready to set.

I thought, "This is what the Impressionists saw, then the Fauvists after them, and Picasso, and Matisse," as the red ball melted into the turquoise waters of the Mediterranean and the sky began to take on delicate streaks of pink. It turned a darker and darker red, until it was the color of a purple fig, and finally black.

I took my eyes off the sky and looked around. The streetlamps were on, and I was the only one left on the wall. An automobile horn beeped three times as Nora and Susan pulled up and jumped out of the car.

We spent the night at a small hotel near the port, then set out in the morning for Saint-Tropez, the playground of Brigitte Bardot, where all the hip action was supposed to be happening.

Today a superhighway takes you from Nice to a point north of Saint-Tropez, and the trip still takes more than an hour. Back then it was the coast road all the way, and given that it was going to take the better part of a day, we decided we would take our time and include stops for lunch and sightseeing.

Around two, we ambled into the small and picturesque square in the center of the town of Cap d'Antibes, one of the wealthiest areas on the Côte d'Azur. We parked the car on a side street and crossed the tree-lined square as we began our exploration of this storied village.

The square was totally deserted, with the exception of one small table, where an elegant gray-haired woman in a black dress erectly sat sipping an espresso.

"Isabel?" I said incredulously, as I walked over. It was Isabel Haliburton, the casting director of Young & Rubicam and a good friend of Nora and myself.

"Oh, hello, Henry," she said, as if we were bumping into each other in the elevator. "Nora and Susan too. How nice. Let's go to the Eden-Roc for a drink."

We walked down to the water, where the grand and stately Hôtel du Cap, the most luxurious and expensive hotel on the Riviera, commanded a large point of land and continued down to the water, where the hotel bar and restaurant, the Eden-Roc, waited.

Isabel was fabulous. At almost fifty, her beautiful, fine-boned face showed no lines, only a flawless, delicate skin. She came from the theater and was good friends with notable people like Jose Quintero, Arthur Penn, and Dustin Hoffman. She swept into the Eden-Roc, asked for a table for four in her impeccable and dramatic mezzo-soprano voice, and chatted up the maître d' in her flawless French, as he led us to a corner.

What a pleasure to sit there, as if I really belonged, watching the Mediterranean gently lap the shore while I engaged in casual gossip with three attractive women who happened to be my friends.

After an hour we said good-bye, but not before I asked Isabel if she would mind extending her vacation by a few weeks and joining Nora and me in Rome to work on the Caveman commercial. It was obvious to me that Isabel, with her knowledge of maître d's and hoteliers, would be indispensable.

The rest of the trip was relatively uneventful. We found a small, not too expensive hotel with two rooms available in the town of Saint-Tropez, had a nice dinner of fresh fish, and went to a discotheque, where we danced our heads off. There we were surrounded by lots of older guys wearing tight shirts open to their belly buttons, revealing lots of gold chains, dancing with younger women who wore very little at all. We spent most of the next day baking in the sun on a small rocky beach, recovering from the night before, and smoking pot.

Then it was Monday, and we drove back to Nice, where the girls dropped me off at the airport before continuing on to Rome. I sat back gloating during the entire hour's flight to London, thinking that I had become quite the jet-setter.

OFF THE WALL

Back in London, we were ready to begin the actual shooting of our Daedalus soaring through the clouds. Bob had brought back magnificent shots of the skies over Der Zugspitze, and we were using a specially made projector to shoot them onto a screen that would reflect the image back to our motion-picture camera.

The projection wouldn't show up on the actor who was flying in front of the screen, but the wire suspending him, which was wrapped in the same material as the screen, would blend into the sky. By today's standards this is prehistoric technology. The camera couldn't move at all, and our Daedalus's movements were confined to the swing of his wire, but back then, it was cutting edge.

We started shooting Brian, our wire-flying actor, from every position and in every aspect conceivable: flying left to right, right to left, toward the camera, away from the camera, diagonally upward left to right, and on and on, in wide shots, medium shots, and close-ups. The shots were all very beautiful, bathed in cinematographer John Alcott's heavenly golden light. It was slow, mechanical work, but we would need every possible size and angle when we started the editing process.

Then, in the second week of photography, Tom, the producer, dropped a little bombshell: he was leaving us to do his required two weeks' training for the Navy Reserve.

I was totally pissed off. Tom obviously had known that he had this unbreakable commitment. How did he dare accept this assignment, which meant so much to the agency? I immediately called the head of production in New York and told him about the situation. Of course, Tom had already informed him what was happening, and the head of production was working on getting a replacement over to London.

He mentioned the names of a couple of the senior producers, neither of whom I wanted to work with because I knew they would want to put their own imprint on the commercials, and I would have to tangle with them in order to preserve my vision.

I told the head of production that I wanted to work with Dennis, who was a great producer and my friend. I told him in a way that didn't leave much room for another possibility. He told me that he'd have to rearrange Dennis's schedule, and he'd have him fly over the next week. I figured that it was the perfect moment to tell him that Isabel and Nora were available to work on the job and that I could really use the extra help, especially now that Tom was jumping ship.

I realized that I wasn't the only one with an agenda regarding this project. Of course, somewhere in my ego-consumed brain, I had been dimly aware of this, but still, when Tom made his announcement, I felt as if I had been personally betrayed. However, this unanticipated problem actually worked out to my advantage. Now I would have another friend to hang out with, as well as someone whose opinion I trusted.

The next week I was called down to Rome. Work on the Caveman commercial had to be approved. Isabel had cast some of the best stuntmen in Europe; Nora had designed costumes made from skins that were being put together; and Lear Levin, the director, had some ideas about makeup that he wanted to discuss.

I had never met Lear, whom Tom had suggested, but he had an excellent reel and wanted to shoot in Rome, which, by itself, was enough reason to make him the right choice for the job. Tom was dying to go down to Rome with me so he could hook up with his old pal, but I wasn't going to let him have his cake and eat it on my dime. If he was so anxious to go, he could go there on his own. In the end, he stayed put.

Late the following afternoon, I was in Rome for the first time in my life, and I was overwhelmed. I had been in Paris a couple of times, and of course I now knew London fairly well. But they were nothing like Rome. In its twisted labyrinth of narrow streets, the Eternal City boasted magnificent structures from every period of Western history. Traveling in from the airport along the tree-lined Via Appia and suddenly coming upon the Colosseum was an experience that defied belief. Was that really the Via Appia? Was that really the Colosseum?

Isabel, who of course knew Rome well, had booked us into the Parco dei Principi, an elegant and sophisticated hotel situated at the bottom of the famous Via Veneto. *La dolce vita*, here I come!

Nora, Isabel, and I had dinner at a little place that Isabel knew at the foot of the Spanish Steps. Needless to say, I'd never had food that tasted like that. Afterward, we went to the Piazza Navona and had a drink at an outdoor café, surrounded by the magnificent Bernini sculptures. Then we walked past the Trevi Fountain and tossed in some coins before heading back to the hotel.

The next morning Nora and I were greeted in the lobby by Raphael Piperno, the executive producer of the local company co-producing the Caveman commercial. Suave, handsome, in his early forties, and speaking broken English with an irresistible Italian accent, Raphael seemed to embody the world-weary character played by Marcello Mastroianni in Fellini's *8 ½*. He was there with his assistant, Magda, a bright and pretty young woman from Poland about the same age as Nora and myself. They drove us to Cinecittà Studios for our meeting with Lear.

I couldn't believe I was at Cinecittà, where Fellini, De Sica, Antonioni, and so many more had created their masterpieces. I was truly in heaven, and right in front of the stage we were entering was the gigantic head of a Roman emperor that Fellini had made for *Satyricon*. Life was feeling more and more like a dream.

Lear was waiting for us inside, on the stage. He was a tall, good-looking, fine-featured man with a prominent but noble nose. There was a patrician air about the way he stood and the way he spoke, not to mention in that name of his.

He was very excited about the job and was totally immersed in developing a vision of how to put it on film. As he spoke about locations and shots, I could see that he had a more fully formed vision of the commercial than I did myself.

I felt both guilty and competitive, but I told myself that this was the way it had to be. While I was in London, working on Daedalus, he was spending all his time and energy here in Rome, concentrating on Caveman. It would be good to have a director who would bring more than just technical expertise to the job.

I could also sense that he was anxious to get past this meeting and to get on with the realization of his vision. In fact, he was anxious to get past me. This, however, would only happen when I was satisfied with our direction. I had no intention of being reduced to a spectator at my own show.

But then it was time to see the show that Lear, Nora, and Isabel had produced: the actors in their costumes and their makeup.

They came onto the stage in a group: twenty-four big, strapping stuntmen from all over Europe. As they approached, Lear explained his concept to me. He had taken his idea for their look from the work of Pieter Bruegel the Elder. He wanted them to look ancient and of the earth, totally unlike the men of today.

I admired the fact that Lear had a vision inspired by high art. My own vision of how the cavemen should look was informed by something less exalted. It was a vision straight out of a *Tarzan* comic book. I saw these men as all having the same bent tribal nose, with long hair pulled back in one, two, and three ponytails. Lear's men had wild hair sticking out in all directions. They had bulbous, misshapen noses and bent faces. My first reaction was to reject this look out of hand. I wanted my vision to prevail because it was mine. But I didn't want the production of the commercial to be reduced to a competitive pissing contest, so I held my tongue while I thought things out.

I didn't have to hold my tongue for long, because there was a rational reason that the Pieter Bruegel look was wrong. These cavemen had to be inspirational characters. They represented the spirit of humanity's quest for flight—a spirit that Eastern Airlines was claiming as its own ideal. Lear's cavemen were grotesque. They looked as if they would eat children while they were still alive and squirming. If this commercial was going to succeed, that would have to change.

As I flew back to London, I was satisfied that I got my own way without being a prick about it, although I'm sure that Lear didn't quite see it that way and that Nora could clearly see that I had more than one intention in my reasoning.

I drove up to Borehamwood Studio the next morning, parked my car, and headed for the office. Along the way I passed the chief technician, a white-haired, red-faced man in a sparkling white lab coat, who seemed to belong more in a science-fiction film than on a motion-picture lot. As he passed me, he said, holding up a box with a projector bulb in it, "This is the last bulb. You've burned out all the rest. I'm going to have to close you down."

A little explosion went off in my head. It wasn't what the man had said, because the threat was laughable. This self-important, pompous prig couldn't possibly carry it out. Not only were we the largest production going on at the lot, but we were the only production. It was the way that he said it, without even breaking stride to address me. It was a pronouncement, a rubber stamp on my passport booting me out of the country. It reminded me of everyone who had ever tried to put me in my place: My embittered mother, who expected me to take her thwarted dreams of glory to places that my father never could. The block bullies who tried to keep my know-it-all mouth shut with their beatings. The Jew-haters who called me names, hoping that I would retaliate with my fists so they could beat me to a pulp. The smirks I felt behind my back, or maybe in my imagination, when I first entered the world of the ivy-clad college I attended, or the Madison Avenue offices filled with men in well-tailored suits and five-pointed handkerchiefs. I defied them all.

No, no, no to any person, movement, or event that conspired to place me in a slot that I didn't choose by myself for its shape, size, and orientation. Want me to become a doctor or a lawyer? I'll be an artist.

Want me to be good? I'll be bad. Keep my mouth shut? I'll be loud. Know my place? I'll upset the apple cart.

Perhaps coming from an argumentative and obstinate race of people, whose religious practice involves the questioning of every word in their holy texts, shaped me the way I am. Perhaps it was growing up in a household where expectations were pinned on me at birth that led me into a lifetime of refusing to allow anybody to tell me what to do.

No, this punctilious putz wasn't going to shut down my show. I'd sweep over him like a tidal wave, washing away the walls of his sand castle as if it was never there.

In truth, there was no reason to get that worked up over the man's feeble threat. But, as you can tell by my rant, he had pushed the wrong button.

Dennis was soon on board, and the shooting was approaching completion. We had already shot every conceivable angle that we needed for the bulk of the flying shots. We now needed to shoot the opening and the ending. With Bob and the camera mounted on a crane, he made a shot that started with a close-up of Daedalus's eye and slowly pulled back until it revealed him in all his glory, standing on the mountaintop. Then the shot held steady while he launched himself into the sky.

Working with the crude technology of the time meant that a move on a crane, such as Bob was making, had to be absolutely straight and even. Today this would be done with computer-driven mechanics. Then it had to be done by men with the strength, patience, and experience to keep doing it until it was right. We were at a further disadvantage, as there wasn't the video playback that exists today. We had to trust Bob's eye to judge whether or not the shot was successful. The special effects being done today are immensely more finished, seamless, and sure than they were then, but definitely not as exciting an adventure to execute.

It took Bob two days to get the shot. Then we moved on to the grand finale, where Daedalus would soar over the camera and rise up into the light of the sun. We shot this time after time, but Daedalus wasn't soaring high enough to suit us. Bob kept telling the men handling his ropes to pull him back farther and farther, in order to swing him farther up into the sun. The result was that poor Brian was pulled back so far that he was almost completely upside down, with the rope handlers backed up against the wall of the stage. This had to be the ultimate shot. The camera rolled, and the rope handlers ran forward, swinging Brian into the air. Up he went, up, and up, and up, and *whack*! Smack into the screen. Slowly sliding down to the ground like a raindrop on a window. Bob yelled at the rope handlers to give him more slack so he could slide down to the ground instead of hanging suspended against the wall like a splattered fly.

I stared at the crumpled tangle on the floor. Broken Brian, broken wings, broken dreams. A complete calamity. As the crew members rushed to Brian's aid, he took one of the hands offered, raised himself up, and pronounced himself ready to go again. Brian, sturdy Brian, the pride of County Clare, wasn't going to let a little mishap like being smashed into a screen stop him. The wings too, that product of good English craftsmanship, were almost ready for another go. It would take only about an hour's work to straighten out the wings and to let Brian catch his breath.

Then again, we all agreed we could wait until the next day to finish up. Maybe by then my heart would start beating again. In the meantime, I went back to my little mews house and started packing it up for the three-week trip to Rome.

LA DOLCE VITA

Rome, the second time, was even better than the first. There was more time, more space, and a driver to take us around. We were booked into the Borghese Gardens Hotel, a grand Beaux-Arts beauty atop one of the seven hills. Nora and I had a large suite with a huge terrace that overlooked the gardens and the city below.

We had an impressive meeting with Lear. He had a list of almost a hundred shots, many of which incorporated complicated dolly moves.

Then he took us out to an abandoned sulfur mine an hour out of the city, which he wanted to use as a location. The entire area was bone-white stone as far as I could see. There were hills and valleys and caves throughout the craggy landscape, which looked more like the moon than the earth. It was perfect!

Lear was a real student of film. He had referenced many shots in classic films by famous directors and cameramen. His knowledge made me feel as if I was flying by the seat of my pants, which I definitely was.

The casting of the commercial done, Isabel quickly stepped into another, more important role: social organizer. She showed us the restaurants of Rome with Guido, our driver, fearlessly braving his way through the fierce Roman traffic, sometimes going the wrong way down a one-way street, often parking on the sidewalk, always lamenting, "The police will kill me for this," with a big smile on his face.

Isabel organized two wonderful weekend getaways: at the hotel Le Sirenuse in Positano, where we shared a spacious two-bedroom suite with a panoramic view of the sea, and at the Grand Hotel Quisisana in Capri. Everything about Isabel was first class and elegant. She was never ostentatious, and she never made a fuss, but her presence made everyone want to please her. I loved Isabel's style and wished that I could achieve it myself, but I could never quite get there.

After the second week in Rome, Isabel couldn't pretend that there was work for her to do, so she flew back to New York. That left Nora and me with a free weekend to plan for ourselves. We booked ourselves into a resort that the Aga Khan had built in Sardinia, not the glitzy one with the marina, but the environmentally conscious one in the hills sloping down to the sea, with buildings that blended into the landscape. That was as close to being green as it got in those days.

We caught the one-hour flight to Sardinia late Friday afternoon, then rode in a taxi over rough mountain roads for another hour until we were finally snuggled up in our luxurious cabin with a delicious room-service meal, as aromatic cedar logs burned in the fireplace.

We woke up feeling so good that we decided to drop some acid. After all, we had a large unused supply of drugs at our disposal, and we were in the most beautiful place we'd been so far. You've got to open the door when opportunity knocks.

We had breakfast in our cabin and headed down to the beach and the beautiful blue sea. The resort had three beaches, one next to the other, with white sand, black sand, and pebbles, in order of distance from the restaurant and bar.

As we got close to the water, the acid started to kick in, so we wisely decided to go to the farthest and least populated beach, the one with pebbles, where there was only one other soul, reading a newspaper. We spread our mats on the ground and lay down. As the first wave of the acid washed over us, hugging the ground felt like the only safe thing to do.

I lay there watching the puffy white clouds form every animal on the planet and many that lived only in my imagination. These creatures danced, wrestled, and frolicked with each other, often changing forms, sometimes devouring their neighbors, constantly accompanied by a symphony played by the surf lapping up against the shore, then rattling through the pebbles on its way back out to sea.

Suddenly, another sound pierced through this music, higher pitched, and urgent. The sound repeated itself three or four times until it came into focus: "Help! I'm drowning!" It was Nora screaming from the water.

I jumped up and saw her, out in the surf, about fifty feet out from the shore, her head arched upward to stay above the waves and her arms thrashing about wildly. I ran into the water with my lungs bursting and heart pounding with the fear of not getting to her in time. The water was up to my knees. It seemed as if there was a sharp drop just ahead. When I was just ten feet away, I leaped forward, stretching my body out toward her. I landed on my knees and face, then raised myself up on my arms. Nora was flailing around in less than three feet of water.

I burst out laughing at the ridiculousness of the situation. Nora stared at me with a frightened look still on her face. Then, realizing the truth of the situation, she started laughing as well. The man sitting on the beach barely looked up from his paper. I helped Nora to her feet and led her back to our mats, both of us laughing, crying, and screaming uncontrollably.

We lay there for a while catching our breath. Then a large ship sailed around the point of land that blocked our view to the right. It was a very large ship, a cruiser of the US Navy. Given our strong anti-government feelings toward the war in Vietnam, and given our illegal participation in the drug trade, it was only natural for us to assume that the ship had been sent there to spy on the two of us, and maybe even to apprehend us. We immediately decided to leave the beach and go to lunch at the resort's restaurant.

I can only imagine the sight we presented, through the restaurant's plate-glass wall, to the sleek and wealthy, bejeweled, gold-chained, Puccied, Guccied, Diored, and Valentinoed guests. They were perfectly tanned, coiffed, and contented, elegantly picking at their lunches, as two zonked-out characters out of an R. Crumb psychedelic commix book, projecting waves of ecstasy and paranoia from every pore and follicle, stumbled past their discreet gazes. I know that I raised a lot of eyebrows when I tried to walk through the plate-glass wall. "How did that get there?"

We finally figured out where the entrance was, and the maître d' quickly rushed us to a table in a back corner, as far away from the other guests as he could manage without putting us in the kitchen. I guess I had some catching up to do, if I was ever going to match Isabel's style and finesse.

Meanwhile, between weekend adventures, there was work going on, and a competition was continuing to develop between Lear and me. Our first day of shooting was on the stage at Cinecittà, where Lear had a small landscape of rocks built. We only had one scene sched-uled for that day, but it was complicated and potentially difficult, and it was the closing dramatic sequence of the commercial. One of the cavemen was supposed to run onto a pinnacle of rocks and leap up-ward in a last attempt to touch the moon. The camera then moved up from his outstretched hand into a black sky filled with stars, finally arriving at the full moon just as an Eastern Airlines plane entered the picture and crossed in front.

We needed a lot of shots because I was going to build a montage of overlapping images that would extend the caveman's leap, so that it seemed to go on and up for an extraordinary time and distance.

We chose one of our best cavemen for the assignment and started shooting him in wide shots, as he left the rest of his comrades behind and ran up the pinnacle and into the air. Then we gradually shot the same action tighter and tighter, until only two shots remained: a close-up that moved up his torso, passed through his straining face, and continued up his outstretched arm, and an extreme close-up that traveled up his arm, past his reaching hand, and into blackness.

In order to extend our caveman's hang time, Lear contrived to have him grasp a rope that was wrapped around his hand and wrist, then looped over an overhead bar and back to the ground, where three sturdy crew members would pull him up higher than the high-est point of his leap.

I had serious doubts about this approach, particularly regarding the possibility of wrenching the man's arm out of its socket, and I presented my objections to Lear. But Lear insisted that it would work and that he'd get the shot in just a couple of takes, so that the strain on the man's arm would be minimal. He was adamant about having his way. He may have been pissed off at the way in which I had vetoed his idea about the look of the cavemen, and anxious to begin putting his signature on the film, or it just may have been a clash of egos. In any event, I gave in to him.

Isabel had said that Lear was a Jewish prince. I had never heard that term before. In my old neighborhood of Brownsville, Brooklyn, there were gorillas, brains, chiselers, guys with connections, and a lot of poor schmegeggies left in the middle. There were a lot of Jews, but no princes.

Very few shots in a commercial get done in just a few takes. Particularly when it's the final shot and involves the expression on a man's face. Everything has to be perfect: the action, the timing, and the man's face.

After close to thirty takes, I had to step in. It was looking more like a lynching than a filming. We were going to do serious damage to the poor guy, despite his protests that he was all right and could continue. But continuing the torture was not on the table as far as I was concerned. Besides, given the man's depleted condition, he wasn't going to do any better than he had already done. He was cooked.

As much as he wanted to continue, Lear knew that I was right. The poor actor was untied and helped back to the dressing room, after being assured that he had done a good job, and he had. He had given it everything he had to give. Of course, now we were without our final shot. The next day we were scheduled to begin three days of shooting in the sulfur mine, so picking these shots up then was out of the question. Lear told us not to worry; he would do whatever it took to get the two missing shots after we left town. He knew what the shots had to be, and he guaranteed that he would take care of it.

Indeed, he did. A few weeks after we were back in New York, the missing shots arrived, with Lear himself playing the caveman, sporting a long wig tied into a double ponytail. He looked perfect. He didn't even have to change his nose in order to leave his signature indelibly on the commercial.

The evening after the shoot, when Dennis, Nora, and I showed up at the sulfur mine, Lear and his cinematographer had already been at work for hours, setting up tracks for the camera dolly and the huge banks of lights that would approximate the full moon. For the next three nights, Lear did a masterful job, creating exciting and beautiful shots of the cavemen spilling out of their caves, running, and leaping over the rocky surfaces. His choreography and composition were masterful. His energy carried over to the crew, and we were getting all our shots at an amazing pace.

Finally, we were at the end of the third and final night, and we were setting up for our final shot. The camera was inside a cave, facing out. A campfire burned at the mouth of the cave. The cavemen all waited behind the camera, and, on cue, they would all race past the camera and the fire, out into the night.

The sun was beginning to come up, but luckily it was rising behind the cave, so we were still looking out into black, but we had to hurry. We had to wait while the cinematographer tweaked his lighting. Time was getting tight. I felt something whiz past my head. With the sun coming up, the bats were beginning to return home, flying in from three different openings. Lear called for the camera to roll. An assistant put the slate in front of the lens to mark the shot. Lear called, "Action!" Nothing happened. No one moved. Only the bats kept swarming in. I was standing next to the camera, and I turned around to see what was holding up the actors. I saw thirty of the toughest stunt men in Europe squeezed into a tight huddle, hiding behind my back in fear of the incoming bats.

"Action!" I screamed, and pointed toward the mouth of the cave. "Action! Move! Get out there and act!" I did everything but kick them in their asses, until they seemed to wake up from their collective nightmare and became stuntmen again. Off they went into the night, not a moment too soon. We were done.

A HARD LANDING

So that was it. The only thing left was a victory lap—a weekend in Paris to visit some friends and an overnight in London to see Bob's director's cut of "Daedalus," then pack up the film and head home. Except there was also time for one more little incident that could undo everything I had accomplished over the past three months.

Nora and I had seven bags between us—six more than we needed for one night in London, where we would be picking up five large boxes of exposed film and negatives. So after landing at Heathrow and clearing customs, I secured a large locker and stashed all our bags save one, in which we both put everything we would need to stay overnight.

Bob had booked us into the Hilton, which was a bit of a disappointment, but as a surprise treat, he had booked the Presidential Suite for us. The suite was so large that a grand piano sitting in a corner of the salon hardly put a dent in the cavernous space. Two walls were filled with large windows that overlooked Hyde Park and Buckingham Palace. We had a sumptuous dinner from room service, along with a nice bottle of wine. We placed our breakfast order for the next morning, then got into bed and finished off the last of the pot.

In the taxi on the way to the airport, Nora suddenly got an alarmed look on her face. She turned to me and asked, "Do you have the pills?"

"I've got them in one of the suitcases at the airport."

"We've got to get rid of them before we get on the plane."

"No problem."

But there was a problem. I had cleverly packed the remaining pills into a small matchbox. They fit perfectly in one layer, allowing me to cover them with two layers of matches. Then I put the matchbox into a pocket of one of the suitcases. The day before, when I rearranged things to put our overnight stuff into one small bag, I couldn't find the matchbox. I figured that it would show up with a more rigorous search when we took the bags out of the locker.

"Those customs agents in New York are real fuckers."

Nora's reminder encouraged my armpits to sweat. We got to the airport in plenty of time and lugged the six boxes of film over to the lockers. We had seven bags in all, including the one we had taken into town. I sat down on the floor and went through every bag, and every container in every bag, and every pocket and every article of clothing in every bag. There were clothes for three seasons, silverware, bedding, and a portable radio, but no matchbox anywhere.

Nora went ballistic. "How can you do that? How can you fuck up like that? You're going to get us locked up. Is that what you want?"

"Come on, I didn't do it on purpose. It was an accident."

"There's no such thing as an accident. Everything is done on purpose, whether you realize it or not."

This little piece of psychology stopped me cold. Could it be that I had a secret desire to get us, or myself, arrested, in some sort of career-death wish?

"Listen, man," she continued, with a hard look in her eyes that I knew all too well, "when we get to New York, I'm not with you."

"Okay. I'll say that all the bags are mine. No problem."

We hardly said a word to each other on the long flight to New York. I was hoping that the flight would never end, because I was scared shitless of what was waiting for me when we got there.

As all good things must come to an end, our flight landed. I was just praying that the life I had been building and getting used to wasn't about to come to an end as well. We deplaned, went through immigration, and got our luggage—that is, I got the luggage, except for one bag that Nora had carried on.

The customs agent that I had to pass through was a young guy, and I thought that maybe he would go easy on me, but I was wrong. The first thing he wanted to know about was the boxes of film, which he sent off to a customs film center, where they would check the contents to make sure I wasn't bringing pornography into the country. Then he went through the six bags I was bringing in. He went through every compartment of every bag—through every box and tube that was in every bag. He emptied small containers and sniffed bottles, while my heart was beating loud enough to be heard in Manhattan. But he didn't find the box of matches. Then he was down to the last bag, which had two large compartments and three pockets. He went through the compartments first, taking everything out and opening everything up. Then he went through the pockets, finally getting to the last, the one that the portable radio was stuffed into. He had to jiggle the radio to get it out, and when he did, the box of matches that was wedged in behind the radio popped out and flew into the air, turning end over end in extreme and excruciating slow motion as it floated up, then down. I reached out my hand as casually as I could and caught it before it could hit the table.

"What's that?" he asked.

"Matches," I said, as coolly as I could manage, and slid the box open to show him the matches, neatly lined up. He nodded his okay, and I closed up all my bags and dragged them past the barrier, where Nora was waiting.

We didn't say a word. We got on the taxi line, then into a cab, and headed into the city. After a while, I looked over at Nora, and she looked back. Her eyes had softened, and a little smile formed on her mouth. As we sat there in silence, the thought came into my head that maybe I really could fly after all.

15

FOUR TRIPS TO JAMAICA

1970

THE FIRST TRIP

Top of the world, Ma! King of the hill! I was the twenty-seven-year-old conqueror of Madison Avenue. I was living the dream. What more could I possibly want? But of course, there was more. It was time to collect the spoils.

Now that I was creatively in charge of the account, I had power, and I intended to use it...on a vacation, or as I labeled it, a research trip. I asked some of the people who had previously worked on the account for their favorite destination of all the places on the Eastern Airlines map. The answer was unanimous. The place to go was an exclusive resort called Frenchman's Cove, in a quiet corner of Jamaica called Port Antonio.

Reservations for four nights at Frenchman's Cove and two first-class tickets for Nora and me showed up on my desk within days. All the suits agreed that it was important that I familiarize myself with Eastern's destinations, and since Nora was going to be working with me, it was critical for her to take this little tour as well.

This unusual acquiescence on the part of the suits was due to the fact that they couldn't figure me out. All they knew was that the account had been saved, they were still on the gravy train, and I was the chef making the gravy.

The drive from Kingston Airport to Port Antonio took three hours, all filled with terror, along a narrow, twisting road hugging steep cliffs that drop down straight to the sea. The fact that our driver knew the road didn't give us any solace, as he seemed just as suicidal as the drivers hurtling toward us from the opposite direction, everyone claiming the center of a road only wide enough for one and a half cars. Nightfall offered a little help for our nerves, as we could no longer see how close we were driving to the edges of the cliffs blurring by.

The farther we drove from Kingston, the more traffic thinned out, until we were alone in the darkness. The narrow beams of the headlights illuminated only the road directly before us, the undulating rumble of the sea lulled us into a drowsy state, and our fear of running off the road barely kept us awake. Not a word came from our driver during the seemingly endless drive.

Then, as if out of nowhere, a towering stone wall rose out of the forest on the seaward side. The wall's evenly level top seemed to be about sixteen feet up, and it went on for about a quarter of a mile, until the words "Frenchmen's Cove," wrought in large metal letters set into the wall, appeared, telling us we had arrived.

We drove through a wide iron gate into beautifully manicured grounds that rolled on into the night toward the music of lapping waves. The car eased up to a large open pavilion, and the perfume of jasmine and hibiscus filled the air as we stepped outside. Towering royal palms, giant ferns, and huge wide-leafed succulents were illuminated by just enough in-ground lights to make the darkness comfortable.

Two large and friendly Jamaican men dressed in uniform khaki shirts and shorts welcomed us as we climbed the three wide steps. They didn't seem the least put off by my appearance. Back then, thick and wiry hair haloed my head in a large Jewfro that was matched by a full, thick beard. It gave me the appearance of an Old Testament prophet with mischief on his mind.

The pavilion was open in front, with louvered walls on the two sides. There was a large, handsome desk in the center of the room, surrounded by comfortable leather club chairs. Two overhead fans kept the breezes moving, and shaded lamps gave the space a shimmering glow that was both rich and inviting.

A large leather-bound guest book was waiting on the desk to be signed, and I wrote my name just a few lines below that of Juan Trippe III, the man who just happened to own Pan American Airways. I felt as if I had just entered hallowed ground, and I wondered just what business I had being there.

Moments later we were in a golf cart, being driven to our villa by one of the Jamaican men. Our bags were right behind us, in a golf cart driven by the other Jamaican. We drove along a meandering path through a landscape as lush as that at the entrance. There were just enough lights along the path for us to see where we were going without infringing upon the perfect moonlit atmosphere.

From the outside, our villa was a long, simple, low-slung building with a thatched roof. Inside, it was the lap of luxury. Louvered walls enclosed a great room, twice as large as my entire one-bedroom apartment, that held three separate seating areas filled with exquisite furniture carved out of mahogany and covered with gorgeous tropical prints. Large vases, filled with vibrantly colored bird-of-paradise, sat atop side tables. The room stepped up to a dining area featuring a table that could seat twelve, then stepped up again to a kitchen wall of sleek and expensive appliances, and wall cabinets holding fine china and glassware. The ceiling was lined with four large overhead fans. Beautiful oriental rugs dotted the marble floor. Large table lamps were arranged in such a way so that the lighting was both soft and dramatic.

We hadn't seen another building on the way from the pavilion, and there wasn't another building in sight from our villa. The kinds of guests who came here liked their privacy.

The two Jamaican gentlemen carried our luggage into the bedroom, which was situated on the far side of the great room. This room was as sumptuous as the larger space, and much more romantic. The centerpiece was a large four-poster bed, draped in white mosquito netting.

The men wished us a pleasant stay, They told us that our cooks and maids would arrive in the morning and that our butler would be by shortly to see if we needed anything.

They took off in one of the golf carts, leaving the other for Nora and myself. My eyes slowly swept over the room, taking in the fruits of my success. Nora stood over by one of the open louvered walls, staring out into the lush tropical night. I was sky-high, floating a mile up in the air on a cloud of self-congratulations.

Nora quickly slammed me back to earth. "This is bullshit, man! You've got to get us out of here, right now."

When it came to her politics, morals, ethics, or principles, Nora took no prisoners. I realized that for her this was all about the money. Everything beautiful about this place, all the primping and pampering of nature, was accomplished by lots of money. Everything that was good about this place was bad in Nora's eyes.

"Yeah, but, Nora," I stammered, "it's ten o'clock at night, we're three hours out of Kingston, and I don't have a clue what's around here."

"Well, then first thing in the morning, I want to get out of here."

Just then, who should appear outside the window, walking along the large manicured lawn, but our butler, wearing a fresh white shirt and a black bow tie, carrying a silver tray loaded with freshly cut fruit.

"I don't want him in here!" Nora was now fully wound up. I walked outside and intercepted the man, who obviously didn't have a clue about the storm that was brewing inside the villa. His name was Robert; he was about thirty years old. His voice and his face were sweet and gentle, and he was more than a little confused when I took the tray from him. He seemed disappointed that he wouldn't be serving us in some helpful way, so I made a special request for the morning, hoping it would relieve the pressure that Nora was putting on our dream vacation.

The river flowed to a reggae beat, and the fortunes of our vacation rolled along with it. This was the second part of my plan to set our vacation back on course. The first part occurred in the morning when Robert appeared along with a maid, a cook, and an envelope containing enough choice marijuana for a couple of joints.

Being as hungry as I was, Nora allowed the cook to prepare breakfast. The maid had finished tidying up by the time we were done eating. Then, having the place all to ourselves, I put on some Antônio Carlos Jobim and lit up a joint.

Would a joint make Nora change her mind? Not necessarily, but it was a start.

The second part of the plan was to get Nora out on a raft on the Rio Grande, which ran not far from Frenchman's Cove. I wasn't sure about this part. I had heard that it was a beautiful experience, but that was hearsay. In truth, I didn't know whether it would be a great ride or a bummer, but it was all I had to work with.

Robert had arranged for a car to take us to where the rafts and their captains were stationed. The rafts were long, narrow affairs, made of bamboo logs that were lashed together. A small seat for two, also fashioned out of bamboo, was set about two thirds of the way back on the raft. The captain stood balanced on the logs, either fore or aft, depending on the current, and used a long pole to push and guide the raft down the river.

Our captain was Albert. He was about our age, which is to say somewhere between twenty-four and twenty-eight, and we took an immediate liking to him. After we rounded the first bend in the river, losing sight of the launching dock, we asked him if he knew where we could score some grass. Albert whistled into the bush and immediately received an answering whistle.

So there we were a few minutes later, drifting down the winding river under a perfect canopy of palms, walled in by the lush and infinite forest, toking on some delicious Jamaican herb. There were a few rapids here and there, nothing vicious, just enough for a playful change of pace. I tried my hand at poling the raft for a while and was happy not to wind up in the river. Large herons gracefully swept across our path. Every now and then we'd see a solitary angler, or someone walking along the banks, or, once, three children playing in the shallows. Each had a smile and a wave for us. Otherwise, we were in our own magical universe.

Albert offered some tourist information from time to time. "There's blue herons and there's white herons, and they all get along." We nodded in unison to the reggae beat in our heads, marveling at the profundity of his words.

After three hours, our breaths were taken away as the river opened up to the sea. Albert tucked into a landing, where a car and driver were waiting for us. Nora was beaming. It was a great trip. We had found something wonderful, a beauty made of light and shade, color and form, and an unquantifiable mood. We wanted to devour it, wear it, sing it, rub it into our pores; we wanted to live in it.

We got our chance to do just that, two days later. We were packed and braced for another harrowing three-hour drive. We had been down the river one more time, again with Albert. We had spent another day swimming in the actual Frenchman's Cove, a small and perfect tropical beach. We had consumed delicious meals of fresh fish, prepared by our cook in the villa. We had made love under the mosquito netting, then lain awake in the dark, listening to the whir of the overhead fans. We had done everything we had hoped to do on this four-day jaunt, and we still weren't ready to leave, but leave we must.

Robert showed up and wanted to talk to me. I had left a nice big tip in an envelope for him. He was the savior of this vacation. It could have come to an untimely end without him. Since I hadn't given him the envelope yet, I thought he wanted to talk to me about money.

But that was the furthest thing from Robert's mind. He told me that he was part of a religious community up in the mountains and that he had spoken to them about me. He said that he believed I was the reincarnation of King Solomon, the wise king of the Hebrews. He made no mention of the famous "cut the baby in two" line. Robert and his community wanted me to live with them, as their leader.

Hearing this offer was like an out-of-body experience. Picturing it in my mind was like seeing myself in a science-fiction movie. Just a mere half hour ago, Nora and I had consumed every last bit of the grass we had bought on the river. Now I was in an extremely malleable and receptive state of mind. However, as crazy as I was, I still wasn't that crazy. Ten minutes before, I had been trying to figure out how to spend as much time as possible in this magical paradise. Now that a way had presented itself, I couldn't wait to get the hell out of there.

THE SECOND TRIP

I was determined to recreate the rhythm and mood of that river in a commercial—the psychedelic colors that gathered in the shadows as the sun went down, the music created by the changing currents, the mystery, and the smile. I had to tell the story of how that river won my heart.

I wanted to accomplish a lot, but once again, it was a dream that gave me the narrative. It would be the story of an old Jamaican man, walking in the lush landscape with a melancholy air. He step walk through the forest and the fields, and along the river, passing young lovers and children at play. It would seem as if everyone had a place in this paradise except the man. He would come upon a young woman and her daughter at the river's edge, and look at them longingly. Then the child would look up and see him. She would shout, "Grandpa," then leave her beaming mother and run into his open arms. It was a good dream.

And so, less than a year after I left, I was back in Port Antonio, at Frenchman's Cove, with Nora and a full-blown film crew led by Dick Miller, a talented cameraman-director and a friend of mine.

It was the high season for tourism, and Frenchman's Cove was busy, so we were lucky to get two villas, each with two bedrooms— one for Dick and his producer, another for Nora and myself—and two trunks of clothing the color of Jamaican sunsets. Along with the voluptuous landscapes and golden light, that clothing would give this commercial its look.

The second bedroom of our villa was for John Scott, the agency producer. John was a dainty and fastidious man with a sly and gentle sense of humor. His job was to make sure that the production company delivered my vision and also that I didn't suddenly go crazy and come up with new ideas that would break the bank.

The rest of the crew and the two actors that we had brought down from New York to play the old man and the young mother stayed at a nearby resort—a nice enough place, but not in the league of Frenchman's Cove.

There weren't many places in that league. The people who stayed there considered costs to be secondary to pleasures, and they had the connections to know about these places and to get into them. I, on the other hand, had neither money nor connections, but I had the good fortune to be working for Eastern Airlines.

I didn't see many of the guests. They tended to stay at their villas. The few I happened to see had a particular look about them, one that I hadn't actually seen before but could recognize. I'd encountered lots of confident, egotistical, and arrogant people in my life. The advertising business was full of them, as was the Upper East Side of Manhattan, where Nora and I lived. But the guests here were much more than that. They oozed an aura of ownership as if the world belonged to them, and in truth, a goodly part of it did.

One evening, while driving a golf cart back to my villa, I passed another going in the opposite direction. The driver was a huge man with shocking white hair and a big crimson face that looked as if it had been hit with an axe. He wore tennis whites and had draped a navy-blue sweater over his beefy shoulders. Next to him was a tall, shapely brunette who was at least fifteen years younger than the man, and one of the most beautiful female creatures I had ever seen. The man glanced at me very briefly, with a look of immense disdain, as if I were an inconvenient horsefly who had slipped into his screened veranda.

We were on a ten-day schedule: two days to cast the young lovers, the children, and the granddaughter; three days to scout for locations; a day for any last-minute production adjustments; and four shoot days. It was a good schedule for a locale with no production help, but there wasn't any fat in it either. The days were all going to be long, starting before the sun rose and ending way after dark.

After the second day of scouting in the baking heat of the Jamaican sun, we staggered into the dining room of Frenchman's Cove. We were beat, only able to pick at our meals, although that didn't stop us from draining a bottle of wine. After dinner, I found that my golf cart was gone. This was a fairly common experience, and a problem that was easily solved by taking someone else's cart, which is what I did. I guess I was just too tired to notice the navy-blue sweater draped across the back seat of the cart.

We said quick good-nights. John went to his room, Nora and I to ours, where I threw off my clothes and collapsed on the bed while Nora jumped into the shower. After thinking about the day for about two minutes, I fell into a deep sleep, and was soon dreaming. In my dream, I was caught in an earthquake. The ground rumbled and the earth shook. The rumble became a roar, and the shaking grew more and more violent. Then the roar became distinct. I heard the words "You stole my golf cart," shouted over and over again. I forced my eyes open to find my field of vision completely filled with the angry florid face of the big man with white hair. His hands were around my throat, choking the life out of me.

Nora came racing out of the bathroom, a towel wrapped around her, screaming at the guy. He jumped back, and I leaped out of the bed, ready to do battle. I immediately realized, "Aagh! I'm naked!" Just then, John came bursting into the room, fully dressed and hair perfectly coiffed. He had obviously made himself presentable for company. In a short-lived and totally absurd turn of events, John and the red-faced giant had a brief conversation as if it were a gentlemen's disagreement about tee time at the country club.

"Who are you?" boomed the big man.

"John Scott, and who are you, and what are you doing here?" demanded John.

"I'm Cliff Van Dusen," the man replied. Now that he was confronting a civilized person rather than some long-haired hippie, he began to act accordingly.

"He stole my golf cart," he offered as explanation for his attempt at murder.

I slyly slipped into my underpants, then jumped right into this new turn of events, quickly asking, "Do you know Bert Van Dusen?" He was one of my clients at Eastern.

This Van Dusen stopped to think, then shook his head.

We took advantage of his hesitation to start to back him out of the bedroom, shouting at him to get out. He kept backing up into the large living area, where I spotted a small metal-framed end table that was just the right size for a weapon. I reached down and swung it up over my head. To my shock and surprise, it weighed next to nothing. The metal tubes of the legs were obviously hollow. The table was more of a liability than a weapon. I put it down faster than I had picked it up. Luckily, Van Dusen was looking the other way at that moment, trying to get his bearings. Nora grabbed the telephone and announced that she was calling the cops. Van Dusen backed toward the door. Sensing the momentum, John and I gave him a bum's rush out the open sliding glass door and locked it as soon as he was outside.

I was perplexed about what to do about this assault. The guy had obviously been drunk. Still, he had broken into my villa and attacked me. However, I was way too exhausted to do any serious thinking, so I crashed for the night.

The next morning, I tried to see the manager of Frenchman's Cove. I was told that he was in town for some errands but would be back later. I left a message saying that I'd like to talk to him when I returned at the end of the day.

That evening, I asked for the manager again. This time I was told that he had been called away on business and wouldn't be back until the next week. This answer didn't sit too well with me. I suspected that the manager was trying to avoid an altercation involving one of his rich customers. I couldn't stand the position that it left me in; I felt like roadkill. I told the assistant manager that I wanted to see the police that night and that there would be trouble if I didn't.

When I returned that night, two plainclothes cops were there, waiting in my villa. One was sitting down, the barrel of his pistol sticking out of his pants pocket like a pair of pliers that he was intending to use on a quick repair. I don't know if it was intended as some sort of code, like "this isn't really serious" or "everything is going to be backward," because he started questioning me as if I was the one at fault. It was obvious that he had already gotten Van Dusen's version of things, and it also became obvious to me that Van Dusen was a much more valued visitor to Jamaica than I was. Whatever the deal was, one thing was sure: I wasn't going to get any satisfaction from Jamaica's finest.

We had originally planned to shoot only two scenes a day, in the early morning and the late afternoon, when the sun was low in the sky, casting thick, syrupy dollops of golden light onto the deliciously dark shadows. Magic hour, the cinematographer's dream, that brief period after the sun goes down when the sky is still lit, would be a bonus.

We discovered, however, scenes that could be shot midday and still allow us to achieve an equally dramatic feel. Scenes such as one in which the old man walked across a field of towering palm trees, through columns of sunlight shafting through the fronds, passing large, gray, hump-backed Brahma cows peacefully grazing as they watched him go by.

Or a scene of a gaggle of young uniformed school children, seven and eight years old, running through the forest along a narrow tree-canopied dirt path, kicking up clouds of dust pierced by strands of sunlight. The children would laugh with joy as they raced past the old man.

Or a similarly fortunate location on the bank of the river. The old man would walk along a shaded path, on a rise above the gently flowing water. Just below him, five or six boys, around ten and eleven years old, would sit on large rocks at the water's edge, one or two slipping into the shallow stream. The sunlight wouldn't hit any of them directly, but would bounce up from the river and reflect up into the scene in a mysterious shimmer.

For that scene, I wanted the camera to be placed in the river, looking toward the bank, looking at the boys, who were looking out toward the water. I also wanted the camera to glide past the boys, as it followed the old man walking behind and above them.

Accomplishing this was technically simple but physically difficult. The camera was mounted on a raft. We arranged the shot so that the old man walked in the same direction that the current was flowing. Since the current was moving at a gentle pace, this made the job of tracking the old man easy. He just had to walk fast enough to enter the scene, overtake the camera, and exit. The raft would move along with him at a slower pace. The boys slipping into the water did so at a signal from the raft. The hard part was setting up for another take. There were lots of variations in the speed of the old man's walk, his attitude, the direction of his gaze, the boys who would slip into the water, and the timing.

For each take, the raft had to be pulled back against the current to its original mark. This involved all our local crew getting into the water and hauling the raft by a thick rope. To my surprise, they were joined in the water by Lou Stroller, our assistant director, a bear of a man with a ready smile. Lou had the ability to make a good, workable schedule and to organize and energize a local crew. He was a key member of the team, and he didn't hesitate to do whatever it took to get the shot done.

The midday shots enabled us to finish our schedule a day ahead of time. We were all delighted. We knew that we had gotten fantastic shots and wonderful performances. We were bringing the job in under budget, and we now had a day off coming to us.

That night Frenchman's Cove threw a beach party. The timing, coinciding with the successful conclusion of our shoot, seemed apt. Those of our group who were staying at the resort sat at one of the long tables set out on the small beach. Food and drink were plentiful, and a joyous mood lit up the night. Suddenly, I became aware of some sort of heavy presence just behind my back, a powerful aura that was generating a strong gravitational pull. I looked back over my shoulder and quickly turned away. The profile of the man sitting directly behind me was unmistakable, even though I could only see a quarter of it. I took another quick look. That nose, those cheekbones, the Tahitian woman by his side. It was Marlon Brando sitting less than three feet away from me.

To say that I was in awe of the man would be an understatement. Being shy by nature, I would never intrude upon his privacy. Even if I were more outgoing, I wouldn't have dreamed of breaking into anyone's quietude at this ultra private hideaway. I was even reluctant to bring his presence to the attention of the others at my table for fear of creating a ruckus.

Then he did a very Brando thing. He stood up and walked into a small empty space of beach, looking down at the sand, just as hundreds of just-born turtles magically began to claw their way to the surface, as if they had expected his arrival. He stood there for a few minutes as the hundreds became thousands. Then he bent down and picked one of the tiny creatures up, holding it close to his face so he could study it, tilting his head in that Brando way. I'd seen the expression on his face so many times on a giant movie screen, that expression of apparent interest or concern that obviously masked a thousand opaque thoughts. While he stood there, the planet stopped spinning on its axis; the wheel of the universe ground to a halt. No one else stepped into the invisible circle that he had somehow drawn around himself. The chatter of the beach party gave way to a hush. Then he carefully put the tiny creature back on the ground and disappeared into the group at his table.

The party went on as if he wasn't there, but thoughts started to bang away inside my head. I began to think about the commercial we had just shot and ways to make it better. Maybe being in the presence of greatness made me press harder to make my own project as great as I could.

Back at my villa, I edited the commercial in my head, putting all the pieces together in every possible combination. It looked good. The scenes all played out well, and the ending had a real emotional punch. But there was one thing missing: a beginning, a shot in which the old man begins his journey. It would place him in the spotlight from the get-go, tell the viewers that this was his story. I called Dick and told him to get everything ready for one more shoot day. "We only need one shot," I said, so we wouldn't have to leave before sunrise. We could go out after breakfast, raft down the river, and find the right spot. Then we could wait for the light to be right, grab the shot, and be done.

The next day Dick and I led a flotilla of seven rafts down the river. The rafts contained the crew, the equipment, and lots of beer. As soon as we left the landing, the spliffs came out, and everyone lit up. A portable radio boomed out reggae tunes. This was definitely going to be the best workday of the week.

After an hour or two, the local guys went fishing and caught lunch. We stopped at a little island in the widest part of the river and roasted fresh fish over an open fire. The beer washed down the fish, and the ganja made us laugh. Fortunately, I had the self-discipline to remember that it was time to move on.

Floating down the river again, I saw a spot on the riverbank that I thought would be perfect for the shot. By then everyone was totally zonked, but we managed to pull ashore and get all our equipment unloaded. Dick estimated that we had about an hour until the sun would reach the best position. Nora got the actor in his wardrobe, while the crew built a platform for the camera at the river's edge, where the actor would walk along the elevated bank.

Finally, the shot was set up and rehearsed, the actor was in position, and the light was right. The camera rolled, and Dick called, "Action." The old man stood resting on his walking stick. He took a breath and started to walk along the riverbank. Dick panned along with him for a few beats, let him walk out of frame, then turned off the camera. It was perfect.

Dick called out to the old man, "Okay, George, you can stop." The actor kept on walking.

Dick called out again. "Stop, George!" The old man didn't stop. "George! Stop!" Dick started shouting, "Stop! Stop! George, stop!" to no effect, except that everyone in the crew, including myself, doubled over in laughter. Dick, who had a famous temper, became red in the face. He took off his hat and threw it on the ground. "George! God damn it, stop!"

Holding my sides and trying to control myself, I walked up to Dick and whispered in his ear, "His name is Walter." Dick's eyes almost popped out of his head; then he too fell down laughing. Walter kept on walking.

THE THIRD TRIP

About nine months later I was sitting in my office with Nora, surrounded by almost fifty photographers' portfolios. It was close to eight o'clock in the evening, and we were bleary eyed from looking through all that work.

I was preparing a campaign to promote winter family vacations in the Caribbean. I had already sold the concepts to Eastern; one commercial was going to be about a father and son rafting down the Rio Grande. A second commercial was going to consist of a child's drawings that recalled her vacation in Jamaica. We also needed a big print campaign to back up the television, and that was what we were now struggling with.

I wanted photographs of a family exploring the Jamaican countryside. This wasn't going to be about fancy hotels or restaurants, but about the simple pleasures that created a bonding experience. I wanted the photographs to reflect a feeling of warmth and even spirituality. They had to have a soft, gentle feeling, while still being recognizable as hip and au courant. Back then "hip" and "au courant" were much softer edged than today.

The photographer who had immediately jumped into my mind was Sarah Moon, a Parisian photographer whose work I had admired for years. But she was busy shooting for French *Vogue*. There were two Americans who were also right for the job: Arthur Elgort and Maureen Lambray. But they were also busy on other assignments. So I had the agency's art buyers call in the books of every photographer they could think of who might be right for the job.

However, after hours of poring over lots and lots of very good photography, Nora and I still hadn't found anyone who had the right feeling. We were stymied, and I was afraid that I would have to consider going in another photographic direction, because, after all, there was a deadline to meet.

"You know who would be great?" I said. "If Ira Mazer would shoot again, he'd be perfect. I'd get Sam Cooperstein and his family to be the models. They're friends of Ira, so he'd be comfortable. But that's not going to happen."

Ira was a creative and sensitive photographer who had quit the business and gone to live on a Greek island. He had just had enough of the pressure and walked away from a successful career. Now, two years later, he was back in the United States, but he wasn't shooting. Sam Cooperstein was an art director I knew. Neither he, his wife, nor his two children were models, but they all had angelic faces crowned by halos of honey-colored curls. It was a great idea, but only that.

I heard some people talking out in the hall. I had thought that Nora and I were the only ones in the office, so I went out to see who it was. I couldn't believe my eyes. There was Ira Mazer with an attractive young woman, walking down the hall toward the art buyers' offices.

I was taking a lot of drugs in those days, and coincidences of the sort seemed to happen all the time. Still, this was special. I corralled Ira and the young woman and pulled them into my office, where I laid out my scenario. To my great satisfaction, Ira was up for it. He loved the idea of using the Cooperstein family as models, and I immediately called their house. Sam was in, and he liked the idea, but he wasn't sure that he could sell it to his family or that they would be able to stand the rigors of being in front of the camera for hours on end. I sweetened the deal by offering to send them all down to Jamaica five days in advance of the shoot, so they could have some real vacation time. I rationalized that this would give their fair skins time to tan and also give them time to settle down.

It didn't take more than a few minutes before the Cooperstein family was on board. Ira was happy. He said that he wanted to do the job with very little crew and very little equipment. For crew, he would take his girlfriend, Karen, the young woman accompanying him, and his friend Aaron.

Aaron Rose was a noted photographer in his own right. In fact, he was infamous for going on location for *Vogue* and sending them only one picture of the hundreds that he had taken. This was unfathomable to the editors at *Vogue*; they wanted to have choices. It was inconceivable that they wouldn't have them. Still, Aaron sent only the one shot. He told them to take it or leave it.

The week after I met Ira, we all flew down to Kingston. Because of the delay in finding a photographer, there hadn't been time to apply for the necessary working papers from the Jamaican government. However, since Ira was taking very little equipment, we figured that we wouldn't have any trouble entering the country as tourists, and once we were in Port Antonio, we figured that we would be far enough out of the way that no one would be the wiser. We figured wrong.

Ira was basically broke, his money all spent on legal fees involving the dissolution of his studio. So the agency was going to have to front all the money. Consequently, Nora was carrying $10,000 in expense money.

Going through customs at Kingston Airport, we were asked how much cash we were carrying. Nora didn't want to be caught in a lie—the idea of spending even a minute in a Jamaican jail was unthinkable—so she told them the truth. Back then, ten grand was an awful lot of money.

The customs officer had all of us wait on the side while the rest of the passengers disembarked and passed through his desk.

It was a full plane, and it took the better part of an hour. Finally, the officer beckoned us to line up in front of his desk. He asked us all to present our passports. Aaron was last in line. When the officer said, "Show me your passport," Aaron gave him the "I don't give a shit who you are" look and tossed his passport on the desk.

"Pick it up!" commanded the officer, and Aaron casually retrieved his passport.

Alarm bells went off in my head. Aaron obviously had a problem with authority, and this particular authority now obviously had a problem with Aaron. The customs officer confiscated all our passports and told us that we would have to go to the customs office in Kingston to collect them. But that couldn't happen until the next day. In the meantime, we could stay in Kingston.

Kingston then, and still today, had the reputation of being one of the most dangerous cities in the world. This was not going to be fun. We got a few rooms at the Hilton. The only good thing about Kingston's murderous reputation was that the hotels weren't booked up.

The next day I took a taxi to the customs office. I went by myself. I certainly didn't want Aaron showing his face around there, and I thought that Ira's constitution might not be able to handle the stress; I needed him to be in good shape for the shoot. Also, I wasn't too sure how safe the women would be in those surroundings. Just to be on the safe side, I went alone.

It wasn't until the third morning that I was able to leave with our passports and proper working papers in hand. Even at that, it had taken calls from Eastern Airlines executives to their connections in the Jamaican government to make it happen.

Eventually we arrived at Frenchman's Cove, my would-be home away from home. The Coopersteins had already been there a week. They were ready to go home. So now I was behind schedule, with a television shoot coming up in two weeks. The models were anxious to leave the country, and, to my dismay, Ira turned out to be much more emotionally fragile than I had thought.

To begin with, he didn't want me around when he was shooting or even looking for locations. It put too much pressure on him to contend with another opinion. I wasn't happy with this condition, but I didn't have much choice in the matter, and I trusted Ira's taste. I would stay behind and get reports of the day's shooting, at least whatever reports I could glean from a mostly silent Ira.

Then Sam's kids, who were five and eight, decided that they didn't want to wear the clothes that Nora had picked out for them. Karen had come up with some alternatives from the kids' own wardrobe, but Nora was adamantly against those choices. I didn't back her up because I could foresee that if the kids were unhappy, it would show up in the photographs. Nora blew a gasket and ordered a taxi to take her to Kingston Airport. I caught her just as she was getting into the taxi and pleaded with her not to abandon me to what was threatening to become a lunatic asylum. She took pity on me and stayed. I guess that living with her gave me some leverage, although I knew from experience that it was limited.

The next day Ira came back without any shots at all, and the same for the day after that. This resulted in a meeting, which was more like a group therapy session, in which I had to coax Ira with encouragement and personal pleas in order to get him to go out the next day and shoot. The next day, however, Sam came to tell me that he and his family didn't want to shoot anymore. They wanted to go home that afternoon.

I had used up all my empathy while dealing with Ira. Now I had to use a different tactic: strong-arming. I reminded Sam that he had agreed to do this gig and that he and his family had already enjoyed an all-expenses-paid vacation at one of the swankiest resorts in the world, not to mention the fees they would be collecting for being models. I told him that if he left now, there would be consequences, although I had no idea what those consequences might be. Thankfully, Sam saw the light. He was, after all, a professional himself, and he understood how costly it would be if he bailed out on me. He also understood the price I would have to pay if the job went down the tubes, and I'm sure he knew that if I went down, he wouldn't go unscathed either.

I felt as if I were on a raft going down a series of rapids. Those manning the oars were constantly trying to jump overboard. I was the pilot of the ship, but I was navigating with a blindfold on. I wouldn't be able to see a single one of Ira's photographs until we were back in New York and they were developed. I was beginning to wonder if I would have been better off living on that mountain with Robert and his people, being worshipped as a living god, because being a mere human being was giving me a huge headache.

THE FOURTH TRIP

I was racing down the length of the huge terminal of the Miami Airport, pumping my legs as hard as I could. I was in emergency mode, pushing Nora in a wheelchair, shouting at people to clear the way, and laughing my head off.

It was two weeks after we had returned to New York. Ira's photographs were developed and were everything I had hoped for. All that anguish and anxiety had paid off. Now we were headed back to Port Antonio, but first we had to get through this.

After the trouble caused by our lack of working papers on the print shoot, Eastern had arranged for us to have a special letter from the minister of tourism, asking all governmental parties to help us in any way they could. We were meeting someone from the Jamaican Consul in Miami, who would give us the letter. Unfortunately, he was waiting for us at the opposite end of the airport from where we were changing planes, and there was only a ten-minute window for us to hook up with him, fill out the paperwork, and get back to catch our flight. By "us" I mean Nora and me. The agency wanted to have both our names on the letter, and to accomplish that we both had to present ourselves to the diplomat.

With so little time, speed was essential. Trying to push our way through throngs of anxious vacationers wasn't going to work, but racing through the terminal pushing a wheelchair and shouting "Coming through!" was like Moses parting the Red Sea.

I screeched to a halt when I spotted the distinguished-looking black man sitting on a bench, his attaché case opened next to him and a sheaf of papers in his hands. We quickly composed ourselves and walked over. After polite introductions, we presented our passports, filled out the paperwork, and said polite good-byes. Then, as the man got up and turned to leave, Nora climbed back into the wheelchair, and we went tearing off into the crowd again.

I was working with two friends, Allen Dennis and Peter Cooper, as co-directors. We had worked together before, had partied together as well, and had had fun doing both. They were both extremely talented. They liked to laugh, and they liked to get high. There was no way this wouldn't be good.

This time out we were not staying at Frenchman's Cove. Nora had found a place called Navy Island, a small private island in Port Antonio's harbor. The island contained five dwellings for guests and not much else. The dwellings were different from the villas at Frenchman's Cove, but equally luxurious. They consisted of a large round base of polished stone and a conical thatched roof that was supported by a tall, stout center post, with other posts around the circumference. The kitchen and sleeping areas were raised. Each area had its own overhead fan. All the furniture and appliances were expensive and in very good taste. The most fascinating aspect of these dwellings was that there were no walls; everything was open to the outside. Instead, wide shades of bamboo strips substituted for the walls, and they could be raised or lowered as the demands for privacy or the weather called for.

As at Frenchman's Cove, each dwelling was private, invisible from every other dwelling. A full staff of maids and cooks worked to keep our appetites satisfied and our dwellings clean. All that, plus a skiff and a boatman would provide twenty-four-hour ferry service to the mainland.

It was perfect. As soon as we organized ourselves into separate dwellings, dropped our bags, and ordered some cool drinks to be followed by dinner, we rolled up a few spliffs and congratulated ourselves on our good fortune and Nora for her excellent find.

Being on this tiny island made us feel as if we were on an adventure. Strong, wet, tropical breezes lashed our faces, made the houses shudder, and let us know that we were in a place that lived with the consequences of forces beyond our control.

The next morning, we set off to the river to scout for places to shoot. Our friend Albert, the raft captain, set us up with three rafts. He also brought along his friend Desmond, who was going to be Lou's right-hand man.

Desmond quickly became our court jester, making wisecracks, handing out nicknames, and generally having something sly and funny to say about everything and everyone. He even had a comical appearance, which may have given birth to his attitude. Short and wiry, with one squinty eye, he walked at a funny angle, and he looked sideways, as if he were slinking about on the lookout. He had an altogether mischievous presence, and we took to calling him Sportin' Life, after the character in *Porgy and Bess*.

We spent two days scouting the river, smoking lots of ganja along the way. At one point, we stopped for a while at one of the spots that we agreed would give us a great shot, and Peter, Allen, and Lou got into a complicated logistical discussion.

Totally disinterested in their conversation and totally stoned, I walked off to have a look around. I wandered onto a small island that almost filled the widest part of the river and that afforded a crossing from one side to the other. As I stood taking in the waters rushing past on both sides and the towering green walls beyond, a Rastafarian man appeared out of the forest and stepped onto the island. Despite his gray dreadlocks and beard, he seemed to be about my age. He carried a canvas satchel slung over one shoulder, and a heavy walking stick. Our paths intersected, and we stopped to say hello and remark about the beauty of the day. Then he went on his way, and I started back to rejoin my group. I got halfway back before I was struck by the realization that the Rastafarian had spoken in his native patois and that I had somehow understood everything he had said.

The next day our small cast of actors flew in. We gave them the afternoon to move into their accommodations, which were on the mainland, where the bulk of our US crew was staying. We scheduled a wardrobe fitting for the early evening.

This gave us the day off, and we decided to drive up into the mountains. The five of us piled into a car and took off, having only a vague idea of where we were going and no idea at all of what we would do when we got there.

As we climbed higher and higher, the land grew wilder and denser, and the houses became fewer and more spread out. Around one of the endless hairpin turns, we came upon two young men walking along the road. We stopped alongside them, and we greeted each other. Then we asked them the obvious question: "Where can we score some dope?" They told us to stay where we were, and they would be back shortly. Sure enough, ten minutes later, they appeared out of the bush with a very large brown paper bag, overstuffed with weed. The cost: three American dollars.

We spent a few minutes testing the product. Then, with our eyes totally bloodshot, our heads swimming, and the bag of ganja stashed in a carryall in the trunk, we headed back down the hill. We didn't get very far before we came upon one of Jamaica's finest policemen sitting on his motor scooter in the middle of the road. He was obviously expecting us.

He pulled us over and had us get out of the car. He wanted to see everything in our pockets and everything in the trunk. Even in my blissed-out, whacked-out state of mind, I knew this was bad. Being in a Jamaican jail would be a life-threatening and possibly deadly experience, not to mention the fact that we had two commercials to shoot. This was definitely not good.

We all emptied our pockets onto the hood of the car. Then we started to take everything out of the trunk. What had started as a marvelously dizzy high had now become a terror-drenched headache. One by one, our bags of cameras, bathing suits, picnic food, and drinks all came out of the trunk. Now there were only two things left in there: the carryall containing the grass-filled paper bag that would land us all in a prison filled with violent criminals with an axe to grind against white American tourists, and a leather pouch containing my own personal papers and my storyboards, scripts, and... the letter from the minister of tourism!

I frantically dug around inside the pouch, pulled out the letter, and presented it to the cop. He read it more than once, then thrust it back at me with hatred seething in his eyes. He got back on his scooter and took off up the hill. We all let out a collective sigh of relief that could be heard all the way back in New York.

The shooting began early the next morning and went on for four days. The actors were all great, although they didn't have that much to do. The two actors playing father and son had to sit in a raft, talk to each other, and point at the various sights.

The actors playing the young daughter and her parents had to run down the stone stairs to the beach and smile while doing it. The difficult parts were getting the camera into positions in the middle of the river, hauling it onto a slippery bank, and dragging the raft back into position for another take. It was hard work for both the local crew and the New York guys, but they were up to it, and Lou did a great job organizing the operation.

We got a lot of wonderful shots of the rafting trip from every conceivable angle. The most memorable shot was one with the camera set up in the middle of the river, pointed upstream. The raft came around a bend in the river and headed straight for the camera. Just as the father was pointing at something, I saw an egret swooping toward the river. I thought to myself how great it would be if it got low enough to cross through our picture, and sure enough it did. It was a perfect moment, a magical accident.

After four long days, we were done, totally exhausted, and totally exhilarated. The five of us who were staying at Navy Island went back there for a nice dinner, then plopped ourselves down on a patch of open grass by the water to watch the stars. Someone passed around some pills of psilocybin, and after a while I felt as if I were much closer to the stars than I was to the earth.

Somewhere in my consciousness, I heard a motorboat, but I paid it no mind until a heavy Brooklyn accent boomed out, "So, that's how you guys spend your time out here." It was the real-life father of the nine-year-old actor. He and his son had come over for a friendly visit, but we were in no condition to be gracious hosts.

Nora, Lou, and I were sitting farther back from the water than Peter and Allen, both of whom somehow got up on their feet to greet our guests. While they engaged in what seemed to me incomprehensible conversation, the three of us slipped back into the shadows and made our way to the dock, where the skiff and captain were waiting to ferry us across to the town.

As we approached the mainland, I saw the silhouette of a man standing on the pier. I recognized the shape and called out, "Albert? Is that you?"

"Yeah, mon," was the response.

"What are you doing here?"

"Waiting for you, mon."

I couldn't even begin to figure that one out and didn't bother trying. We all piled out of the boat and followed Albert into town. He led us to a huge tent, where what seemed like the entire population of Port Antonio, including all the guys we had worked with, were partying their heads off. A band was playing reggae, and everyone was dancing. Soon we were all dancing as well, first with each other, then with everyone else. Desmond was there too, slinking around the dance floor, making sly remarks and insinuating glances, calling me out for "going for the big-legged woman" as I danced with a large Jamaican lady. Lots of ganja and rum were going around, although we certainly weren't in need of any assistance in the getting-high department.

The sun was getting ready to break the horizon when Nora, Lou, Albert, and I finally staggered out of the tent. As we made our way back to the dock, I invited Albert to come over to the island with us and catch some sleep before heading home.

"No, mon," he said. "We've worked together. We've had fun together. Now it's enough."

16

THE ROAD TO ADVENTURE GOES NOWHERE

1972

"Wouldn't you know we're riding on the Marrakesh Express…" Nora and I played that song by Crosby, Stills, and Nash over and over on our cassette player on the train ride west through the arid, brush -filled stretch from Casablanca to Marrakesh. This was going to be our great adventure.

We had decided it was time to go someplace totally outside of our world, somewhere mysterious, spiritual, and maybe even a little dangerous. Somewhere where they had excellent drugs. India was our first choice, but monsoon season coincided with the month we had available for our vacation. Next on our list was Morocco, the land of Casbahs, spices, desert, and hashish. It would be a blast: three weeks in Morocco, starting in Casablanca and ending up in Tangier, before heading off to Spain for a week.

We only spent an hour or so in Casablanca, between getting out of the airport and getting to the train station. We had just enough time for a coffee at a café in the Art Deco French section of the city, but we were more than happy to move on. This frenchified version of Morocco was not what we had come for. It was time for the adventure to begin.

We arrived in Marrakesh after four hours and detrained with our bags into the jarring chaos of the teeming station. From what I could see, we were the only non-Moroccans on the train or in the station. The men were mostly wearing long djellabas, leather slippers, and turbans. The women were mostly in black, their heads covered in shawls and their faces by veils. Through the crowd I spotted Moroccans in shabby Western garb: old suits, tired-looking shirts, and ties, but almost always with the ubiquitous yellow leather Moroccan slippers with their backs crushed down.

People were running around, getting on, getting off, greeting people, and hustling people. Hawkers were plying their wares to everyone and one another. The din was incredibly loud and stimulating, in that we didn't understand a word that was spoken, and we allowed our imaginations to run wild.

We pushed our way out of the station through the crowd and grabbed one of the few waiting taxis. I gave the driver the address we wanted, but he didn't need it. Everyone in Marrakesh knew where the Hotel La Mamounia was.

Winston Churchill famously stayed at La Mamounia during his many visits to Marrakesh, as did anyone who was anyone while in the city. La Mamounia was one of the world's greatest hotels and was, in my mind, a great way to kick off our great adventure.

Our taxi pulled through the massive gates and drove down a long row of towering royal palms, up to the entrance of the pink palace, where two tall majordomos stood, dressed all in flowing white coats over white belted tunics, flowing white pants tapering down to white stockings, and white leather slippers, all topped with white turbans.

One of them took our bags and escorted us inside, silently ushering us down a seemingly endless columned corridor, beneath richly elaborate chandeliers, and around fountains, pools, and statuary. The corridor occasionally opened up on the sides to various dimly lit salons and nooks that seemed sumptuous, elegant, and mysterious.

At the end of the corridor were a large mahogany desk and two Moroccan men in tuxedos. It only took a moment to be welcomed and to register, before the majordomos led us to our suite.

We walked through a garden filled with fragrant flowering plants and palms. I had booked a garden suite for three nights. I figured that if we loved it here we could always book more nights, and if we wanted to adventure into other territories, then this would be a comfortable and romantic place to start out.

I had figured wrong. "This is bullshit!" proclaimed Nora, as I was gazing at the splendor of our luxurious suite. "This is bullshit. I'm not spending the night here." Ah, the sweet sound of my loved one's coos of appreciation for the tokens of affection lavished upon her.

I had heard this song before at Frenchman's Cove, another one of the "world's greatest places to stay." There I'd had the advantage of it being ten o'clock at night and in the middle of nowhere, so I had been able to beg off until morning and then ply Nora with some dynamite ganja and a raft trip down the river.

Here, I lacked those advantages. It was only four in the afternoon, it would be light for hours yet, and we were in the middle of a sizeable city. So I conjured up my best defense.

"How am I supposed to find another place to stay?"

"I don't care. You got us here; now you can get us out of here. Besides, I can't talk to anyone in this country. I don't speak their language."

This was true. Neither of us spoke a word of Arabic beyond "Salaam alaikum." The second language here was French, although not every Moroccan spoke it. I had enough French to get us a room in a hotel or a table at a restaurant. It was just enough to get by, but it would have to do, because Nora spoke no French at all.

I had the desk call for a taxi and had the driver take me around to other hotels that he knew of. This was a tall order in a place that had a small peak of absolute luxury and a huge body of squalor. I had to find Goldilocks—not too rich and not too poor, but just right. Added to that was the struggle to make myself understood, with only my high-school French, and, more importantly, to understand what it was the hoteliers were saying to me. I also had to make flash judgments as to the convenience and safety of the various neighborhoods as well as the sanitary level of the hotels. After all that, of course, I would have to sell it to Nora.

Mostly, I saw places that were too shabby, too creepy, or too ugly. Then the driver took me to a place that was just a little shabby, creepy, and ugly. It had the feeling of a place where out-of-town salespeople would stay if they were on their own dime, but at least it didn't feel as if I might wake up in the morning to find bugs, snakes, or a guy with a knife in my bed.

Our accommodations finally settled, we were ready to explore Marrakesh. The best place to start was the Jemaa el Fna. One of the world's greatest public squares, the Jemaa was filled with food stalls, storytellers, henna painters, snake charmers, fire eaters, holy men, beggars, hustlers, thieves, black nomads in blue robes from the Sahara, tourists from every corner of the globe, young hippies, and old beatniks. And everywhere we looked, there were men smoking kief, a mild herbal narcotic, through little wooden pipes with colorfully painted long stems.

As we crossed the huge square, a motorcycle with a sidecar rode in, driven by a young European man wearing a turban and motorcycle goggles, a leather jacket, and blousy pants. In the sidecar was a young woman in a flimsy flower-print dress, her hair tied up in a scarf. Nora and I stopped to watch them, then exchanged a knowing look with each other. That was what adventure looked like.

There was a relentless energy to the city. The constant beggars, peddlers, and hustlers never let up on the tourists in their sights until they got what they wanted or the tourists finally stood their ground and adamantly refused the offerings. But that wasn't easy. The Marrakeshis knew that the tourist had to fight through layers of curiosity, fascination, desire, and guilt, and they knew exactly how to work it. They knew everything about our world, through television, movies, and their relatives in the States. They knew exactly how much their wares would fetch in our stores, and they knew how little we understood about their world.

The Jemaa is right up against the great souk and its miles of covered stalls, divided into sections by the crafts they sold: leather, silver, pottery, rugs, and fabrics, going on forever in an endless maze, where strangers with a poor sense of direction would never see the light of day again without someone to guide them out. Walking through the dark, narrow aisles of the crowded, canopied souk was a bit like walking through a subway train during rush hour. We couldn't see more than inches ahead or avoid being jostled and crushed by the surging throngs of shoppers and merchants.

Besides just wanting to immerse ourselves in the excitement of the souk, we actually had a specific purpose in being there. We wanted to buy a tent, the kind that nomads live in, in the desert. We had a vague idea of buying a loft together and decorating it with a large and colorful Bedouin tent.

Aside from the entire idea being a bit whacky, just finding the tent makers was a daunting task. They were tucked away in a far corner at the very back of the souk. It took us a few days to find them, and even then, we only gained access because we used the name of a man whom we knew in New York who sold rugs and artifacts from Asia and Africa in a second-floor loft.

In the meantime, we had bought lots of stuff as we wandered through the souk. Rugs, kettles, robes, and a pair of camel-riding boots made from old rugs. We didn't buy any of the multicolored cylindrical beads that came from the far south of Morocco. My secretary, Jane, had requested those. But I figured that when we went to Tan-Tan, at the southern tip of the country, I would find beads that were better and cheaper than those in Marrakesh.

We had two days of discussion with the tent makers, and things were getting complicated. The tents were much larger than we had thought they were, as were the cost and the effort required to install them. The next day was a religious holiday, so the souk would be closed. The tent makers assigned two teenage boys to take us to a special place where we could partake in the occasion.

Late that afternoon we met the boys at the big bus stop in a corner of the Jemaa. Our bus filled up quickly, and the driver took us about an hour out of town, to a stop at the base of a mountain, where everyone got out.

It was dark by the time we started up the mountain; more than dark, it was pitch black. There was a narrow path winding up the mountain, and we very carefully made our way up in single file, practically hugging the mountainside on our left, out of fear of falling off the sheer drop-off on our right. We would occasionally feel the edge of the cliff when the path narrowed, and we would have to stop in our tracks in order to regain our courage to continue. We used little Bic lighters for whatever illumination they could shed, which wasn't nearly enough to allay our terror.

I have no idea how long it took us to get to the top of that mountain. Time had lost all meaning, as we felt that we were facing an imminent drop into eternity.

At the top, we found magic: a scene straight out of *One Thousand and One Arabian Nights*. The top of the mountain was a wide rim, surrounding a deep bowl. Below the pitch-black, star-dotted sky, the bowl was filled with hundreds of tents, lit by torches and cooking fires. There were tents with musicians, tents with belly dancers, tents with wrestlers, and many, many tents filled with food. The entire wide-screen scene was colored orange by the fires, and the overwhelming and intoxicating food scent was enough to make me swoon.

We wandered from tent to tent, eating, looking, drinking tea, until the wee hours of the morning, when we couldn't stand up anymore. Our young guides organized us into a tent where they were selling lamb shish kebabs. We curled up under the counter and fell into a deep sleep, lulled into exotic dreams by the music and smells that filled the air.

We woke up early the next morning, our bodies aching from sleeping on the stone ground. We said our thanks to the men who were working in the tent and paid them some dirham for the favor of their protection. Then we set off to explore this wonderland in the daylight.

What had been a Moorish fantasy at night had become a burning cauldron in the day. The sun beat down mercilessly, and the heat reflected off the blazingly hot stone floor. The tents were all quiet now, but looking down to the floor of the bowl, we could see a small group of stone buildings separated by intersecting alleys, and people were gathering there.

We took a circuitous route, going around and down. In the daylight, the natural bowl of the mountaintop looked something like an arena, with people heading for the exits. More and more people passed us as they hurried down to the buildings at the bottom. We thought that they were going there to get out of the heat, but upon asking, we discovered that there was a mosque down below, and they were all going to pray.

The closer we got to the mosque, the thicker and more frenzied the crowd became. When we entered the area where the buildings and alleys began, we stopped and let the throngs surge past us. It was beginning to look like a stampede.

Down at the very bottom, we could hear people screaming and shouting as they struggled to maintain their footing and gain access to the mosque. Then a squad of soldiers appeared. They dived into the crowd, swinging their rifle butts and smashing heads, as they tried to maintain some sort of order. The people in the crowd seemed unable to control themselves. They had worked themselves into a religious frenzy, and they seemed oblivious to the blows raining down upon them. This seemed like a good time for Nora and me to step away.

But stepping away came with its own price, meted out by the sun. We could not escape the fierce, dry, desert heat. We could actually feel ourselves drying up. Then we spotted some people going in and out of a small building up by the rim of the bowl. When we got there, we saw that it was a teahouse.

We quickly went inside and found ourselves a table. No sooner had we sat down than the burly owner came over to take our order, immediately followed by a waiter with two glasses containing mint leaves, and a kettle of boiling water.

We sat there, happy to have a roof over our heads, slowly sipping our tea and watching the goings-on in the teahouse. The hulking owner constantly patrolled the tables to make sure that no one was taking up space without buying something to eat or drink. At one point, he forcibly pushed some poor soul out into blazing daylight.

A moment after we had finished with our tea, the owner returned to our table. We quickly ordered two more glasses, then sipped our tea as slowly as we could. This went on for a third round, by which time we had resigned ourselves to climbing back down the mountain and hoping to find the bus back to Marrakesh.

As it happens, there were buses lined up at the base of the mountain, and we climbed aboard the next one going into the city. We were happy to have escaped the crippling heat and were overjoyed and overwhelmed by the incredible experience of the night before. As we rode along toward Marrakesh, we discussed what we would do next. We had both come to the realization that we weren't going to buy a tent; it just wasn't going to happen. The problem was that the tent makers had already shown us an incredible amount of largess. Having those two boys guide us to the previous night's celebration was no small favor. Now they surely expected us to reciprocate with a purchase. Sitting down and explaining things to them seemed to be out of the question as well. There wasn't enough shared language between us to even begin the conversation. Besides, it felt as if we had gotten ourselves in too deep to talk ourselves out. We could come up with only one solution: we had to get of town, and right away.

There was a Hertz office in Marrakesh, not too far from the square. I rented a two-door Renault with a hand shift. I had taken lessons in driving with a stick shift in New York. They had gone reasonably well, but they hadn't prepared me for the nerve-fraying task of making a U-turn in the Jemaa el Fna while surrounded by hundreds of milling Moroccans, many of whom reached into the car to ask for a *cadeau*, a gift, or just to see if they could grab something.

We got on the road and headed west toward the Atlantic coast and a city called Essaouira. Back then Essaouira was a small, quiet walled city by the ocean, a city built completely out of the local white stone. It was the perfect respite from the frantically roiled cauldron of Marrakesh.

We found a half-decent hotel just outside the walls of the city. It was a real hotel, with a lobby and a restaurant. It was a relic from the 1930s, but the rooms were of decent size, and although it was shabby, it was clean.

We set about exploring the city by car. Our first stop was a row of fish stalls on a pier just outside the city walls. Someone was grilling sardines that had just been pulled in from the ocean. A little bit of salt, a little bit of lemon, and we popped them right into our mouths. It's amazing how something so simple can taste so good.

Venturing farther into the city, we discovered Café Hippy in a large courtyard. A dozen and a half young Moroccans and young hippies were sitting around drinking mint tea and smoking hash and kief. Here was a place where we could make ourselves comfortable.

We sat down at a table and ordered some tea. Shortly after, a young Moroccan man came over and introduced himself. Somehow, between his bad French and my bad French, we were able to understand each other. His name was Youssef, and he wanted to be our friend. A week ago, the Living Theatre Troupe had passed through town, and Youssef had been their guide. He wanted to do the same for us, and he didn't expect to get paid for the service. He had loved hanging around with the Living Theatre folks, and he thought that we'd be much like them. We figured that what was good for the Living Theatre would be good enough for us.

Youssef was a great guide; one day he took us into the nearby hills, where we met up with some of his friends, drank tea with mint cut right from the hillside, and played drums all day.

Another day we toured the medina, what used to be the old Jewish section. A lot of Spanish Jews had settled in Essaouira, fleeing from the Inquisition, but almost all of them left in the 1950s, migrating to Israel.

The medina was home to many small shops that sold silver jewelry. Youssef took us into one where the work was unusually delicate and beautiful. We looked and admired but didn't buy anything. Jewelry wasn't our thing. Before we left, we made sure to tell the middle-aged couple who owned the store and made the jewelry how much we liked their work, and we thanked them for letting us see it. Once outside, Youssef said, "Nice people, yes?"

"Yes, very nice people," I responded.

"Eebaru," he said.

I had no idea what that meant, and I thought about it as we walked along the narrow streets. Then it hit me. "Hebrew." The man and woman who owned the shop were Jews. I wondered if Youssef told me that because he wanted me to see that Jews weren't oppressed in Essaouira or because he somehow knew that I was a Jew myself.

Touring around the area outside the city, we spotted quite a few campsites, some of them just one or two tents and some with as many as two dozen. Nora decided that, if we were going to have a real adventure, we should be camping, not staying in bourgeois hotel rooms. I wasn't as enthusiastic as she was about the idea, since I knew as much about camping as I did about nuclear physics. However, it seemed that I would have to give it a try.

Many of the tents we saw seemed to be plastic sheets wrapped over the tops of vans or cars and secured to the ground with enough space to allow two people to sleep. They were flimsy affairs, but they seemed like something I might be able to put together if Nora started to insist on camping.

In the meantime, we were having a grand time hanging out in Essaouira—that is, until the day we went to the beach by ourselves. The beach was extremely wide and long, and it was practically deserted. We easily found a spot from which we could see no one else: a perfect setting for romance.

We played in the surf and swam a bit, but the waves were too large, and we returned to our blanket. We had packed a picnic of bread, cheese, and grapes and had brought a bottle of water. But the one bottle wasn't enough, and after a while our thirst was getting the better of us.

Behind the beach, on the far side of the dunes, I spotted the top of a roof, and I headed over there to see if I could buy some water. It turned out to be a farmhouse, and the farmer and his dog came out to greet me. It happened that he did have some bottled water, and he could sell me a liter. We made the exchange without any bargaining, which was strange for Morocco, but I was dealing with a farmer, not a merchant, and I guess neither of us was going to haggle over something that sustained life.

I thanked the man and started walking back. Suddenly, I heard the pit-pat of little footsteps behind me. I turned around just as the dog bit me in my calf. The little fucker tore through my flimsy trousers and drew blood. The farmer angrily called his dog back, and I could hear him yelling at it as I limped back to the beach.

Rabies! The word lit up my brain like a flashing neon sign in Times Square. I cursed my bad luck. I was going to die in Morocco because I was thirsty.

We got back to town in a hurry and found the police station. The officer in charge told me that they definitely were not going to kill the dog in order to do an autopsy on his head to find out if he was rabid. Instead he gave me directions to the hospital, where they would give me anti-rabies shots.

The hospital had a regular schedule for different treatments. They gave anti-rabies shots at seven in the morning. So bright and early the next day, I left Nora sleeping and trudged over to the hospital to take my medicine like a man. There I was directed to the clinic, where a nice nurse with a three-inch-long hypodermic injected me in my stomach and told me that I had to come back every morning for the next six days.

I was shocked when I saw the size of the needle. But since the entire event seemed like a bad dream to me, I was able to disassociate myself from reality and watch the nurse pierce my stomach with this enormous thing, while I thought about how *interesting* the experience was.

The next morning the injection was less interesting and more painful; however, I considered it a small price to pay for staying alive. By the third morning, however, it was a pain in the ass as well as my stomach, and I knew that I couldn't handle coming back four more times.

"We're getting out of here," I said to Nora. "If I start acting insane or foaming at the mouth, just drive straight to the closest airport and put me on the first plane to New York."

We drove to a hotel in the Atlas Mountains. It was about halfway back to Marrakesh. It was owned by an elderly French couple, who had the place well put together in good taste and good condition. There was a nicely landscaped swimming pool behind the building, surrounded by a six-foot wall of pink stone. As soon as we unpacked, we got into our bathing suits and went out there for a swim. It seemed so tame after the wild ocean beaches of Essaouira.

Later, we sat next to the pool with a delicious lunch of seafood and a nice white wine. As we relaxed with coffee and cigarettes, we saw the top of a tour bus pull up outside the wall, and heard the muffled noise of passengers getting off and being welcomed into the hotel. I figured we had twenty minutes more of privacy left to ourselves, and sure enough, twenty minutes later two couples came out to the pool, dressed in outlandishly loud bathing suits. One of the men had a tiny blow-up tube just large enough to hold his cocktail glass with its plastic umbrella. As he floated on his back with his potbelly sticking out of the water and his drink at the ready, he started a loud conversation with the others. I was overjoyed to hear them speaking in French. It was a wonderful revelation to discover that French tourists could be every bit as boorish as Americans. *Vive la France!*

The next afternoon I wasn't showing any signs of rabies, and Nora was anxious to get back on the road. We headed south for Agadir; from there we figured to head all the way down to Tan-Tan.

Along the way we passed several campsites, and Nora started to get wound up on the subject again, and my head spun with worry that I was about to be dragged into something I couldn't handle.

Agadir turned out to be a terribly ugly city, not at all Moroccan. The city had been totally destroyed by an earthquake in 1960, and it had been rebuilt as a modern city, but not the kind of modern city anyone would want to live in. All the buildings looked alike: gray, squat, and boxy. There was no way we were going to stay there. Which put camping right at the top of our to-do list.

Before we left Agadir, I found a hardware store and bought a roll of heavy plastic sheeting, some rope, a utility knife, two sleeping bags, and some other odds and ends. I was determined to give Nora the camping experience she craved, and to prove to myself that I could do it, even if I didn't have the slightest idea what I was doing.

It was getting dark, so we stopped at the first place off the road that looked like a suitable spot for a campsite: a grove of trees that blocked the wind and guarded our privacy. I took out the plastic sheeting and the rest of the stuff, and I started to create the tent that I had imagined.

Needless to say, my plan didn't work at all. My creation never even got to the point where it could be called a tent. It was just flapping plastic sheeting, sticking out from one side of the car. I felt like a total failure, and I knew that Nora agreed with that judgment. My head felt as if a stormy sea were roaring inside it, and it wouldn't subside until I smashed my head open and let it pour out.

Night was falling quickly, we needed a place to sleep, and this place wasn't it. I bundled up the plastic sheeting and tossed it into the back seat. Then Nora and I got in the car and headed back out on the road.

"Where are we going?" she asked.

"To Essaouira."

"What for?"

"Because we can't stay here, and there's a decent hotel there."

"I thought we were camping."

"I thought so too, but if I can't make a tent, we can't camp."

"Stop the car!"

I pulled over to the side of the road. We were in the middle of nowhere. Nora reached around and pulled one of her bags out from the back.

"What are you doing?"

"I'm getting out," she said, and opened her door.

"Are you nuts?" I reached over her and pulled the door closed. "Where are you going?"

"I don't care. I just want out of here."

She opened the door again, and I pulled it closed again, and again, and again, and again. Open, closed, open, closed.

"You'll get killed out there."

"Just let me out!"

"No, damn it! It's dangerous!"

"Let me out of here!"

Nora was strong, and fueled by her rage. This was her great adventure, and it wasn't going the way she had dreamed it. The struggle went madly on with increasing violence until the door became unhinged. Somehow, this brought her to her senses.

I was able to fit it back in its hinges and secure it with rope. Then we sped off to Essaouira. Nora sat silently, her arms folded across her chest, a scowl on her face. Then she muttered, half to herself, "I knew I shouldn't have made this trip with you."

That was the crusher. It wasn't just that I had failed; it was that she had expected me to fall short. I knew that this wound would never heal; it opened up all my shortcomings. It made me into an obstacle to the life that Nora wanted to live. I was who I was, not what she wanted. Despite all my creativity and daring, I was still coming up short. I was both furious and defeated, but I held my tongue and continued on.

When we got to Essaouira, we had another disappointment; all the rooms were filled. However, the manager was able to give us one of the staff bedrooms. He called a housekeeper to clean it up, and I suppose he had two of the staff bunking together that night. The room was smelly and small, and the bed was lumpy, but the physical discomfort was nothing compared to my emotional hurt.

The next morning, I went to the small Hertz office in Essaouira and did my ugly-American act, insisting that it was the car's fault that the door became unhinged and demanding another car immediately. Sad to say, it worked.

We headed north. After the camping disaster, neither one of us wanted to test ourselves in the desert. We decided to drive up to Tangier, the northernmost city in Morocco, and from there, take the ferry to Spain. We would stop along the way wherever it seemed right.

As we drove north, the land grew greener. We passed olive orchards and orange groves, and the fertile land seemed to relax the tension between us. Coming around a particularly beautiful curve in the road, I spied a meadow through the trees and pulled over. We had fruit, cheese, bread, and water with us, all the fixings for a picnic, plus plenty of grass for an after-dinner smoke. So we laid out a blanket in a secluded corner of the meadow and kicked back.

A couple of hours later, we hit a barren stretch of road. The blacktop had given way to dirt, and there wasn't a tree on the horizon. My mind must have wandered, because I didn't see the enormous crater smack in the middle of the road until we were sliding down its front edge. If I'd had my wits about me, maybe I would have hit the accelerator and tried to speed up to reach the other side. But as it was, my body totally relaxed and went with the flow, and the car settled into the bottom of the pit.

It wasn't all that deep, maybe three feet, but there was no way to drive out of it. It looked as if I had screwed up yet again. Only this time I thought it was more serious, as this part of the country seemed deserted. But just then, help appeared on the horizon in the form of a jeep filled with American GIs. Just when we needed them, the cavalry showed up. It was surreal, almost comical, but I wasn't going to laugh in the face of my good fortune. In a continuation of the dreamlike sequence of events, the five young soldiers lifted our car out of the pit.

We sat around for a while gabbing and smoking reefer. The soldiers were from a base nearby, and luckily for us, they just happened to have decided to take a late afternoon drive. A sudden thought occurred to me, and I asked them if they sold tents at the base store. One of the young men told me that they did, and he agreed to buy one for me and to meet me here the next day so that I could buy it from him. It seemed as if I might be able to redeem myself after all.

We stayed overnight at an acceptably shabby hotel an hour farther up the road, and we woke up late in the morning. I guess that the combination of driving, doping, and almost getting stranded in the wilderness had knocked us out. I worked on our schedule over breakfast. There were three things on our to-do list—camping, Tangier, and Spain—and we only had time for two of them. For me, the decision was easy; I was here to see places I had never seen before and to have experiences that couldn't be had anywhere else. That left out camping. Nora agreed with me, although I think that her reasons also included her evaluation of my camping abilities.

The wrinkle in our decision was that I had agreed to meet that soldier later in the day and buy a tent from him. I didn't want to hang around all day just to tell the GI that I didn't want to buy a tent anymore. Besides, he might not even show up. Nora thought it was wrong to have asked him to buy a tent and then to leave him hanging. She was right, of course, but I figured that he'd always be able to sell it back to the commissary. Still, when we headed north, I felt like a heel. I added this performance to the long list of things that I didn't like about myself, and I felt the final nails being pounded into the coffin of the relationship between Nora and me.

Entering Tangier was like walking into a jackhammer. The city was relentlessly working to break down our resistance into little pieces. We had dropped the car off at the Hertz office in the port. The next leg of our journey would take place by ferry across the Strait of Gibraltar to Spain, where we would pick up another car.

Fortunately, we had the foresight to take our purchases to a shipping company before we dropped the car off. There they wrapped our treasures in old newspapers, shoved and stuffed them into cardboard boxes, tied them up with hairy twine, and assured us that they would arrive at our homes in one piece. We didn't necessarily believe them, but we had no other choice. As it turned out, they were as good as their word.

The port was like a feeding frenzy. The swarms of hawkers and hustlers were tearing at the tourists like hyenas at a carcass. I was hailed in every known Western language, including three versions of English.

Slowed down as we were by our bags, we needed every ounce of our strength to fight our way out of the port and into the main thoroughfares, which were no less crowded or less intense, but at least the target that said "new arrival" had been removed from our backs, replaced by a target that said "tourist" and marked us as only slightly less vulnerable.

As we sat at an outdoor café the next day, a Moroccan man at the table next to ours leaned over and pointed at my watch. "Rolex," he said admiringly. I nodded.

"You want to sell?" he asked.

"No, thanks."

"Wait. You'll sell."

Apparently, he had me figured for a hippie who would soon run out of money, and he was staking an early claim to my remains. It felt as if the entire city was intent on separating us from our belongings. It instilled a state of constant wariness in us. Still, the city was alive with a buzz that excited us both.

We met an artist named Abdullah at a café. He was about our age, and he spoke pretty good English. We went over to his apartment, a large, dark, loft-like space. The furniture was mostly piles of rugs and pillows. I don't remember what his paintings looked like, but his hash was first rate. I got the sense that he and Nora had eyes for each other. I don't know if it was the hash, my paranoia, or the obvious truth that was informing my feelings. Whatever it was, I didn't like it, and when he suggested that the three of us take a trip up to the nearby mountains to visit the hash factories there, I really didn't like it. I pictured myself being at the mercy of this Moroccan guy whom I didn't know from Adam but who was lusting after my old lady. Needless to say, my refusal to go along didn't make Nora happy, but she stuck with me.

The next day was the last chance I had to buy the beads that I had promised my secretary. I was going to the souk, but Nora wasn't going to join me. She was going to cruise around town, maybe visit Abdullah, as she was considering buying a painting of his.

This last put a twist in my stomach, but there wasn't much to do about it. Our relationship had always allowed for either of us to indulge our desires without guilt. We didn't see this kind of freedom as interfering with what we had together. This allowance was liberating, maybe too liberating. It may have been the reason that we didn't have a stronger, longer-lasting commitment, but I'm getting ahead of myself with that thought.

As I walked through the narrow passageways of the souk, every shopkeeper came out and tried to pull me into his store. Their aggressiveness was off-putting, and I resisted all offers. Then one merchant who was slightly less obnoxious than the others approached me, and

I realized that I had to eventually go into one of these shops if I was going to make the purchase.

The merchant sat me down and sent a young boy out to get some mint tea. I told him that I wanted to buy a kilogram of beads, and he told me that he had beauties that he had just brought back from the south. The boy came back with the tea, and the merchant told him to go back out for the beads. We sat for a while sipping tea and chatting about nothing in particular, until the boy returned with a metal box about four inches high and three inches wide, filled with beads.

I opened up the box, and the beads were, indeed, beautiful. Immediately, the merchant, seeing that I was impressed with the quality of the beads, hit me with an outrageous price. I was about to make a counteroffer, when I remembered to check the beads that were below the surface. After all, we were in a souk in Tangier, where nothing could be taken at face value.

Sure enough, just under the surface the beads were all cracked and broken. In fact, it was one of the worst collections of beads that I had seen. I was incensed that this man had figured me for a sucker, and told him so. He offered to send the boy back for better beads, but I didn't want to have anything further to do with him. I stormed out of the shop.

I didn't get very far before the boy caught up to me and tugged at my sleeve. He told me that he knew a better shop, his cousin's, where there were beads of the best quality. I didn't have any better ideas, so I followed him down through some alleys until we got to a small shop that was a step down below street level. Here, the boy introduced me to his cousin, who immediately sent him out for some tea. I was hoping my bladder would hold out for me, as I wasn't too anxious to use the local facilities.

It was the same act as the other place. After the kid came back with the tea, he was sent out for a box of beads. This time I made sure to examine the beads straight off, and again, the beads beneath the top layer were cracked and broken; not nearly as bad as the first time, but bad enough to make me unhappy. He sent the boy out again. This time he came back with a much better selection, good enough to buy. I was ready to begin the bargaining.

Naturally, the merchant opened with a price that was laughably high, and I countered with one that was just as ridiculously low. This went on for a little while, with neither of us moving too far in the other's direction. However, I was holding an ace up my sleeve. I knew the going price for the beads in the south, and I was determined to pay no more than that. Since that number was the tourist price, the merchant was still going to make a nice profit on the sale, just not the profit he had envisioned.

Following the established rules of the game, I threatened to walk out a few times and even started for the door once. Each occasion was followed by a significant drop in his asking price.

Finally, we danced down to the nitty-gritty, to a point where he wouldn't come down and I wouldn't raise. He said it was his final offer, take it or leave it. I called his bluff and stood up to leave. He started whining that if he sold it at my price, he wouldn't make a profit. "Then don't sell it to me," I said. He dropped his price again—a final-final offer—but I wouldn't budge. He started wailing that I was trying to take the food out of his children's mouths, and I could see it was his last gasp.

I walked out of the shop with the box of beads under my arm. I had bought it at the price I wanted to pay, but the process had left me feeling exhausted, soiled, and mean. I had beaten the merchant at his own game, but I had hated the game.

The boy walked out with me into a small courtyard, leading to an alley that led to the narrow street. He tugged on my sleeve and asked me for some money. "What for?" I asked. He said it was a commission for taking him to the merchant. "Get your commission from him," I responded. But the boy insisted that I owed him money. By this time, I was fed up with everything about Morocco. All the hawking and hustling and preying on every tourist in sight. I was sick of being a constant target for all of it. "Get lost!" I snapped at the kid, but he knew just how to handle me. He started screaming at the top of his lungs. Windows from the houses around the square flew open, and heads popped out. The situation was going to get very ugly in a hurry. I reached into my pocket and grabbed a fistful of coins, which I flung at the kid. "Here's your money," I shouted, and took off down the alley.

When I got back to the hotel, Nora was already there. She said that she didn't find any of Abdullah's paintings that she wanted to buy, and she was ready to say good-bye to Morocco. I couldn't have agreed with her more. Morocco is a great and magical place, but I was happy to leave it while I was still in one piece.

The next morning, after dumping the last of our dope, we were on the ferry to Generalissimo Franco's Fascist Spain. Obviously, we were interested in the country and not its government; nonetheless, we were introduced to Spain's political posture as soon as we got off the boat. Admittedly, we probably looked like hippies to the member of the Guardia Civil who greeted the boat, checking passports and pulling suspicious characters such as ourselves aside for further investigation.

We were directed to a long table, behind which stood five Guardia, dressed in starched uniforms, complete with swords, white gloves, and those funny Napoleonic-era hats. We placed down our four bags, and two of the Guardia emptied them and checked all the contents. Then the one checking my bags asked for my Moroccan walking stick. I was only carrying the stick because it wouldn't fit in the bags. The carving on the stick divided its length into a dozen sections, each one of which was painted differently, as were the spaces that separated the sections. It must have looked to the Guardia like an obvious place to hide smuggled dope.

The guy who had checked my bags took the stick and twisted and pulled at every section of it. He banged it on the table and on the ground to see if it rang hollow. But the stick didn't twist or pull apart, and it wasn't hollow. Then the Guardia next to him took the stick and went through the entire routine again, and again, he came up empty.

All five Guardia standing behind the table repeated this act. I guess that each of them thought that he was the genius who would discover what the others could not. It was a joke, but I didn't dare laugh because these comedians were deadly serious about giving us a proper welcome to their Spain.

We spent a few days exploring the coast, which was a bore. The only thing of interest was that there were hardly any people in the streets of the towns we visited, and when we did encounter people, except for one drunken man in Málaga who cursed at us, no one said a word other than those necessary to check us in and out of a hotel, to serve a meal, or to sell us the black leather pants that we bought.

We did, however, go up into the mountains, to the city of Granada, and visited the fabulous Alhambra. This Moorish palace is touted as one of the world's most beautiful buildings, and it well deserves its reputation.

First, however, we had two narrow scrapes with eternity; to this day it confounds me as to how we survived. Driving up the narrow and twisting mountain roads, we came face to face with a tour bus going down the mountain. The bus must have had the right of way, because, although the bus driver had slowed down considerably, he wasn't stopping. I guess it was just impossible for him to back up around the sharp curve behind him, which meant that I had to back up and tuck into a small space that was carved into the side of the mountain. After the bus passed us, I put the car into first, but it stalled out on the steep hill, and I quickly hit the brake as the car rolled backward. Then I tried using the hand brake as I put the car into gear, but I stalled out again, and the car rolled farther down the hill. After two more attempts, we were at the edge of the precipice. I now had only one last shot at this, but amazingly, while I was shitting a brick, I was also confident that I could do it. The wheels spun, spitting small rocks hundreds of feet down the mountainside. Then they grabbed the dirt and moved us up the road.

Incredibly, it happened again, this time with a farm truck coming the other way, and the same exact thing happened. Both times it was a case of do or die. But there was also a third option. We could have left the car where it was and flagged down some driver more experienced than I was to get us away from the edge of disaster. Why didn't I opt for that? The thought never even entered my mind. Maybe I felt that I had to prove my machismo as well as my driving ability to both Nora and myself. Whatever the reason, it was an incredible stupid thing to do, and we were lucky to be alive.

There have been three times that I have literally fallen to my knees in the presence of an artist's creations. The first time was at a gallery in New York where Paul Gauguin's large Tahitian paintings were on loan from the Hermitage in Saint Petersburg. I was floored by voluptuous colors that I had never seen before. The second time was in the Louvre, where the cumulative effect of David's huge, heroic canvases took my breath away and my legs out from under me. I was struck by awe, completely oblivious to the people looking down at me, making their way around me, somehow understanding how overwhelmed I was by this experience that spoke to me of the force that was creation. It was as if I were staring at a gate that opened up onto the source of all there was.

That is what I experienced at the Alhambra. I sat on the floor of those perfectly proportioned spaces, bathing my soul in the light and shadows orchestrated by delicately filigreed walls. I floated from room to room, passing under sensuous Moorish arches, cutting through an atmosphere that wrapped itself around me as I went. The Alhambra glowed from within, and I felt myself filled with that same light.

That glow stayed with me through the last days of our vacation, until we were sitting on the plane, somewhere over the Atlantic. I turned to Nora, and she looked like an angel sleeping next to me. But I could only think about my failures and those words: "I knew I shouldn't have gone on this trip with you." Those words were like an animal living inside my guts, gnawing at my entrails. They encapsulated all the little failures that added up to the big failure of being inadequate in the eyes of the person I loved. It was a truth I couldn't live with.

I chewed on that feeling throughout the rest of the flight and on the cab ride into the city. As much as I loved that woman, as wonderful as our tumultuous four years living together had been, I could only see tragic humiliation ahead for me if we stayed together.

The taxi stopped at her apartment house. The driver got out and opened the trunk. I helped her out with her bags, then said, "I'm going to my place. I've got to think about some things." She nodded, kissed me, and went inside. I never went back into that apartment again.

17

THE DRIFT

1971

Fierce white polka dots on a black field, large snowflakes filling the night sky, overwhelming the ground below. The highway had lost its definition to the storm. The only things identifying the edge of the road were the towering lights that lined it. It was surreal, like driving through an op-art cartoon, but this cartoon was dangerous. I had already passed several collisions, even though driving had been reduced to a crawl.

The drive had started out as a mundane event, born out of boredom and duty. It was the holiday week, between Christmas and New Year's Eve, and I was going to my parents' house for dinner. It was a trip I rarely made, and even then with only half a heart. Individually, they were sweet, caring, and well intentioned. Together, they were poison.

But I was desperately lonely. The intense four-year relationship with Nora had recently ended, and even though I was the one who had called it off, I was now leading the social existence of a potted plant. My closest male pals were all out of town or hunkered down with their honeys. I prized my independence, and I often enjoyed being alone, but now I was climbing the walls, certain that everyone in the universe was having a great time with each other, not thinking about me at all.

My life felt out of sync. The year before, I'd received a bonus that was larger than my salary. It was enough for a down payment on a weekend house in rural Connecticut, and a new BMW to get me there. I was only twenty-nine years old, my future seemed guaranteed, and I was so miserably unhappy that I was driving through a furious snowstorm to have dinner with my parents and watch them eat away at each other.

The drive started out in the cozily narrow streets of Greenwich Village, glowing in the warm light of holiday decorations. Snow was forecast, but there were only a few stray flakes floating around like solitary drunkards. I cut across Tenth Street, turned north on the wide but lonely First Avenue, and hooked around into the Queens–Midtown Tunnel.

It was a simple, straightforward trip that usually took three-quarters of an hour. But when I emerged from the tunnel onto the Expressway, I discovered that the world had been transformed into a snow globe. The snow was flying, the traffic was crawling, and everything was white.

I caught some Miles Davis on the jazz station, fired up a joint of fine Acapulco Gold, and relaxed into a comfortable daze as I geared myself down into a long, slow, careful journey.

I was in my own private world inside the raging blizzard. My head was filled with smoke, music, and dreams as I drifted past a dwarf, half-covered with snow, standing at the side of the road, trying to flag someone down. "Far out," I said to myself. Then: "*What!*" That wasn't a flashback from a Fellini film; that was a dwarf at the side of the road, trying to flag someone down!

I pulled off the road and got out of my car. Creeping along as I was, I hadn't gone far beyond the little man. He was indeed a dwarf, not a midget, which is a normally proportioned small person. This guy had a normal head and torso, which seemed too large for his short arms and legs. He was wearing a dark-gray snow parka, the hood pulled over his head, which furthered his gnome-like appearance. I asked him if he needed help.

"Flat tire!" he exclaimed in a high-pitched voice that sounded as if he had just sucked in a lungful of helium. The sound took me by surprise, and I wasn't sure what he had said. "Flat tire!" he called out again, and beckoned me to follow.

He led me around a huge snowbank to where his car was parked, snow piled halfway up the doors. Out of sight of the highway, surrounded by black sky, it looked as if it had landed on its own snow-covered planet. There was a family of dwarfs in the car, maybe four or five of them, all in hooded parkas, all peering out at me.

"Flat tire!" he cried out once more, pointing at the one that was damaged.

I asked him if he had a jack, but he didn't. It was apparent that he was counting on me to come up with one and also to change the tire. I didn't have a problem with that. The whole thing was so bizarre that I figured the more I got involved, the more interesting it would be. I trudged back to my car and took my jack out of the trunk. As I was doing that, I realized that cars were passing by at an uncomfortably close distance. I became afraid that someone, not expecting my car to be where it was, would accidentally drive into it. Someone was going to have to stand by, waving the other cars off. It couldn't be one of the dwarfs because they weren't tall enough to be seen.

I ran back to the dwarf's car, gave him my jack, and told him that I was going to stand guard by my car. He thanked me and set to work, while I returned to the side of the road.

Standing next to my car, waving traffic off, I started chuckling at how crazy and cinematic this whole scene was. After about ten minutes, the humor began to wear off, and the cold began to seep in. I started to flap my arms and stamp my feet to keep warm. Then, out of the whiteness, a sleek black BMW pulled up, and the driver's darkened window rolled down. It was my old friend Susan

Smitman and her girl gang, driving out to the Hamptons for the holidays. Under the bizarre circumstances, her happening upon me seemed as natural as running into her at a party thrown by a mutual friend. In her always calm, slow growl of a voice, she asked if I needed help. I told her that I was fine and that I'd explain everything to her the next time I saw her. I waved as she went off down the highway, wishing that I too was going to the Hamptons with friends.

It was taking too long. I went back to the dwarf's car to see what was happening. Nothing was happening. The dwarf was standing next to his car, my jack dangling from his hand, the flat tire still where I first saw it, on the car. "I can't do it!" he piped, frustration showing on his face. I remembered seeing a gas station on the other side of the highway from where I was parked. I told the dwarf that I would take him there.

We walked to my car. I could barely make out the faint lights of the service station that was across the highway and a little farther down the road. Sizing up the situation, I realized that I had no idea where to find the exits and entrances that would get us to the station. We were at the intersection of the Long Island Expressway and Grand Central Parkway, a confusing maze of roads and ramps.

I figured that the best way to get to the station was to hotfoot it across the road. Even though I was thoroughly stoned, this wasn't as crazy as it sounds. Traffic was intermittent, with big gaps between cars—big enough for even a guy with little legs to make it across. Still, we had to cross four eastbound lanes, climb over a divider, and cross the four westbound lanes, all in shin-high snow, knee-high for him, in a blinding blizzard.

I took the little guy's hand. "Hold on to me," I said. We waited for a large break in the traffic, then quickly made our way to the divider. We had to wait, carefully watching the headlights of the oncoming traffic. There were more cars coming in this direction than in the other. Finally, our break came. We stepped into the road. Suddenly, he whipped his hand out of mine and made a mad dash across the four lanes, wildly bounding through the deep snow with a leaping gait and diving over the low divider on the far side. He quickly got to his feet and took off toward the station, disappearing into the cascading white curtain of the storm.

I got back into my car, fired up the engine, the music, and the spliff, and continued on to my mother's waiting, and surely now dried out, pot-roast dinner. It didn't matter now, nor did the bickering that was certain to come; my evening was already complete.

18

ECLIPSED

1972

S o here I was, running at full throttle, unstoppable, at thirty years of age, the genius golden boy of Young & Rubicam Advertising. Every idea that sprang out of my head was considered exceptional and usually acted on, no matter how crazy it sounded. This story is about one misadventure that I got away with. Barely.

In 1971 I discovered that in a year's time there would be a total eclipse of the sun, best seen from the Sahara Desert. A surrealistic scene filled my mind, featuring myself dressed in Bedouin robes, dancing atop the dunes under every star in the universe. I wanted magic!

I tried to organize a concert in the desert, envisioning musicians from all over the world playing under the brightest starlit sky ever seen. I knew some people in the music business, but I couldn't get any of them interested in pursuing my dream. As it turned out, it was everyone's good fortune that it never happened.

In any event, I had an ace up my sleeve. I convinced Gulf Oil, a client of Young & Rubicam, that it would be a great idea for them to do a commercial featuring the upcoming eclipse. There was a serious oil shortage that year. The Arab states were cutting back on production as retaliation against America's support of Israel. Lines at the gas stations were backed up for blocks, and a feeling of desperation filled the air.

I wanted to tell the story of how in ancient times, when there was an eclipse of the sun, the people thought that the world was coming to an end. But, of course, the eclipse would stop, and the world would go on as before. It wasn't the greatest idea, but it was a metaphor that worked, and they bought it.

Then it was time for adventure, and I flew over the Atlantic to Dakar, Senegal, with Dennis and Bob Gaffney. Bob's producer was his wife, Sherry. Sherry was an argumentative and sometimes spiteful woman, but Bob knew that whatever went down, she would always have his back covered.

We were going to shoot in Mauritania, out in the desert, but we were mounting the production in Senegal. Mauritania was simply too wild and remote; we had to make sure that, as we gathered our equipment and personnel, we were in a secure place where the equipment could be easily replaced in case of a breakdown or unpleasant surprise. Senegal, south of Mauritania, was the logical place.

We stayed at a modern high-rise hotel on the beach, just outside the capital, Dakar. The hotel had all the necessary amenities and a fair restaurant. The beach was filled with local women in fantastically bright blouses, head scarfs, and skirts, selling trinkets and souvenirs. The pool was lined with rows of lounges filled with attractive and sophisticated Europeans wearing the latest in vacation wear.

I discovered that all those guests were from Switzerland. Three days later, a new group of guests, even more fashionably dressed, replaced them. They were, of course, French. Three days after that, the Germans came in. Not so fashionable, nor so svelte. Finally, the Americans: boxy shorts, ugly tops, stupid T-shirts, and hideous Birkenstock sandals. It would have been embarrassing if any of the Europeans had stayed to see what American taste looked like, but it was only our little crew who witnessed this spectacle, and we already knew what to expect.

Our group was augmented by three additions: Oussman, a Senegalese cameraman; François, a Frenchman who had been born and was living in Africa (François knew Mauritania and was going to connect us with local people there); and Carl, an Israeli sound engineer who would be an all-around assistant. Carl had the tight mind and body of many Israelis, and the arrogance as well. However, he knew the desert, knew the equipment, and was a positive addition to the crew.

The plan called for us to be in Senegal for ten days. It was my plan. I wanted to make sure that we had enough time to check out all our equipment and to replace anything that needed to be replaced. In truth, though, I just wanted enough time to be able to take it all in.

We spent the first few days at the hotel. Then Bob had to go into Dakar to change some money, and we all went along. Coming out of the bank, Bob spotted a saloon where they were playing live music, and in we went.

It was dark inside, but the rhythm carried us along to the bar. As my eyes became acclimated, I began to have misgivings. There might as well have been neon signs on our heads saying "White and Rich." Men sidled up to us making offers of drugs and women. Others were throwing us looks that I recognized from Brooklyn, sizing us up for a rumble. Bob had grown up in the Bronx, and I couldn't understand why he wasn't reading the same signs and getting us out of there. But when I spotted Bob through the crowded room, he was already into his second drink and laughing it up with the bartender.

In truth, I don't know whether or not I was just being paranoid, but I figured it was better to play it on the safe side, and I've always felt unsafe in a bar filled with drunken bravados. I sidled up to Bob and said, "I'm not sure about this place." He took a good look around and, to my relief, agreed with me. As we made our way out of there, the entreaties for us to stay became more and more adamant, until we literally had to pry people's hands off us.

After that misadventure, we kept ourselves mostly to the hotel and the pool. We tended to stay away from the beach, where the ladies selling cheap trinkets swooped down on us like a swarm of mosquitos.

The only safe excursion seemed to be to a small market, next to the hotel, where there were stalls selling local crafts such as sculptures, baskets, rugs, and the like. I saw two beautifully carved drums, about the size of congas, that I liked. It was clear from the ridiculously high asking price that this was to be a bargaining session. I had learned the ritual when I was in Morocco, where it was impossible to buy even a small box of matches without bargaining. The Senegalese were nowhere near the hard-driving level of the Moroccans. This was a much easier game to play. I would make an embarrassingly low counteroffer, which would eventually get me to the middle price that I wanted.

A few days after buying the drums, I went with Dennis back to the market. I didn't want to buy anything else, but it was a break from the monotony of the hotel. Meandering through the stalls, I came upon a group of young women in stewardess uniforms—very attractive young women. One honey-blond beauty in particular caught my eye. As they picked through the tables of one of the stalls, I hovered nearby, trying to overhear what language they were speaking. To my delight, it was English. From a safe distance, I took a longer look at the blonde. She was delectable. Nothing will cure boredom so well as a romantic possibility; however, I couldn't figure out how to break the object of my interest away from her group.

Then opportunity struck. She was interested in buying a particular statuette, and I could see and overhear that the price was way too high for her. The vendor offered to hear a counteroffer, but she was so dismayed by the asking price that she didn't want to take it any further.

As she walked away, I approached her and said that I couldn't help but overhear the exchange, and I offered to get the statuette for her at the price she wanted to pay. She seemed doubtful but told me her price anyway. Five minutes later, the statuette was hers, and I was a hero. I offered to take her to dinner, but she already had plans to be with her crew, and she was leaving the next evening. That gave me precious little time to claim my reward.

We met on the beach the next day. The hotel had packed lunch and a bottle of wine for us. Lying on the sand and taking in her lovely figure, I regaled her with my many creative and corporate accomplishments and my international adventures. I piled the bullshit on as high as I could, while trying not to be trying. But I was trying hard.

After lunch and a swim, we walked back to the hotel. I asked her if she wanted to see my drums; it was the only line I could think of. My heroic gloss must have still been on me, because she agreed to come to my room.

I knew that the timing was way off. This was all happening much too fast. If I'd had one more day, it would have been a beautiful interlude, but the way it was unfolding just wasn't cool. However, what choice did I have? It was now or never.

Arriving at my room, I put some bossa nova on my cassette player. I took out my drums and softly played along with the music. Then I took her in my arms and kissed her. She kissed me back. Our tongues glided into each other's mouths. My heart was beating loudly and pumping blood into the veins of my stiffening penis.

Then she said, "No." Too late, she had to pack. Too sandy, too messy, too stupid. She gave me her number, said good-bye, and left. I felt like an idiot, but that was okay. It would have to do.

My libido aroused, I started to check out the waitresses in the hotel restaurant. One day, as I was finishing my lunch, romance came calling again. A young native waitress with whom I had been half flirting came up to my table and told me in French that she liked my T-shirt. It was a black, with a picture of an American flag made up of red, white, and blue matches, with one lit match at the corner. My high-school French allowed me to understand what she was saying, but her eyes were saying much more. Aside from the message of welcome, and the beauty of the messenger, there was an intelligence in those eyes that I found exciting.

That afternoon I sent the T-shirt out for cleaning and pressing, and the next day I presented it to her as a gift. Her smile washed over me like sunshine. I asked her if I could take her to lunch the next day, and she accepted. She told me to wait for her, after lunch was served at the hotel, on the road outside.

Of course, I realized that I had no idea what I was getting myself into. What did I mean by asking her out to lunch? I didn't know. Where was I going to take her? Into Dakar, where I was scared shitless? I was letting myself be swept along by a current of my own making. But I was okay with that. After all, this trip was supposed to be an adventure, so I might as well let it rip and see what happened.

The next day, I borrowed the car that Bob had been renting, and waited outside the hotel. I turned on the radio to keep me company, and hopefully to create a mood for when she showed up, but all I could find was static. Soon she appeared and walked over to the car. Now what was I going to do? I had absolutely no plan.

"Where shall we go?" I asked her after she got into the car. She directed me down the road, then, after a while, off onto a dirt side road. She had me park next to a mosque, which was next to a large stockaded village.

Inside the gate were smaller enclosed areas that I guess were family compounds. We walked into one that contained a large group of small wooden shacks with thatched roofs. She led me over to one of the shacks, and we climbed up the three rickety steps. Inside, a wizened old lady was reclining in a cloth hammock. It must have been her mother or an aunt. They spoke for a while in a language I couldn't understand. I shook the old lady's hand and said *bonjour,* although I have no idea if she spoke any French. Then we walked over to another small shack, which I guess was hers. There seemed to be two rooms. The first was furnished with a simple table and four chairs. A door led to a back room that must have been the bedroom.

Before I had finished taking the entire room in, a young man, about eighteen years old, came in: her cousin.

He brought a small transistor radio with him, and he tuned in a station that played American soul music. We chatted in broken French for a while, mostly about the music.

"James Brun, c'est bon!"

"Oui, James Brun est bon."

"Otis Redding, c'est bon aussi."

"Otis Redding est mort."

"C'est mort?"

"Oui, il est mort."

"Quel dommage."

In the meantime, I was feeling as if I were sinking deeper and deeper into quicksand, and I had no idea how I was going to get myself out. What had been in my mind when I asked this beautiful young woman to lunch? It certainly hadn't been a lucid thought. Inside my pants, my penis had been doing all the thinking, without any consideration of the new territory it was operating in.

They asked me if I was hungry and wanted something to eat. Not wanting to take food off their meager table, I refused. They asked me if I wanted to go to the beach. I refused this as well. I think that by this time I was so confused and even frightened by my total lack of a social, emotional, or logical compass that I became fearful about being on a "native" beach. Probably some form of racial paranoia.

The third time that they asked me about eating, it dawned on me that they might be hungry and that I was keeping them from their dinner. This time I said *oui*, and off we went, walking across the compound to another shack.

This shack was larger than the others, and packed inside were what seemed to be all the women in the village. There were *bonjours* and smiles all around as I was ushered to the center of the room, where a large pot sat atop a low fire, bubbling with some kind of stew. In front of the pot was a stool. As far as I could see, this was the only piece of furniture in the room, and it was reserved for Prince Henry.

I thanked them all and sat down. They handed me a fork and invited me to eat.

Now, two facts jumped to the front of my brain in bright-red letters: One, there had been seven years of an ongoing drought in this area. Two, if I ate this food, I would die. But what could I do? I absolutely couldn't use the fork. It had certainly been washed in water that would make me deathly ill. That was easy to refuse, since the others were going to be using their hands. In fact, it was downright egalitarian of me.

I scooped up a small handful of whatever was in that soupy pot. There was some kind of grain and a bunch of other stuff that I couldn't make out. I made a ball of the stuff in my hand and started nibbling at its edges, while declaring how delicious it was. In the meantime, what was left of my brain raced around at a million miles an hour, trying to figure a way out.

Then I had it. I didn't know anything at all about these people; their customs, their habits, their way of life were all a blank to me. So it was reasonable to assume that they knew very little about me and my way of life. I spoke to the cousin, who had the best grasp of French. I told him that in my country we only ate two meals a day, one in the morning and one at night, and I wasn't used to eating in the middle of the day. Then I said that I had to get back to work, thanked everyone profusely, got up, walked out of the hut and the village, got into my car, and got out of there as fast as I could, my tail between my legs and "asshole" branded across my forehead in big capital letters.

Fortunately, the next day was our last at the hotel. It was time to get the expedition on the road. Unable to face the young waitress, I ordered a room-service breakfast and slipped out of the place as quietly as I could.

We drove north toward the border in two Land Rovers and a Volkswagen bus. The Rovers were the kind that had made that company's reputation: olive green and clunky. They looked like distant relatives of a rhinoceros, with truck-sized engines and four-wheel drive that could go almost anywhere.

The three vehicles were packed to the roof with equipment, provisions, and, most importantly, water. Given the draught, we hid the water away, beneath everything else. It was the thing we could least afford to lose. If we lost the camera, it would be very bad. Returning home without the commercial would be a career-damaging horror show. But dying of thirst in the desert would be much worse.

It was too long a drive to make it in one day, so after many hours of driving through the bush along the dusty, one-lane highway, we stopped in the town of Saint-Louis, once the colonial capital. We turned off onto a long, straight road that went on for miles before ending at the entrance to the town.

The town was picturesque, quaint, and seriously decrepit. We stayed at a colonial-era hotel, and we may have been the only guests that evening. The lobby was filled with potted palms, rattan furniture, and large wooden ceiling fans. It was pretty but very worn out. Dinner was kind of French and decent. The wine was better than the food.

We were all tired from the long drive, and after hanging around for a short while, we all went to our rooms. My room was too hot. The barely working air conditioner made more noise than anything else. The mattress was on the lumpy side, probably as old as the hotel. I had an uneasy feeling, which wasn't helped by the sight of a cockroach as large as my fist working its way across the wall by my bed. Fortunately, the roach wasn't as large as the boot that I squashed it with.

Late next morning we arrived at the Senegal River, the border with Mauritania. We pulled up to the end of a line that stretched half a mile to the ferry station.

As vehicles continued to line up behind us, and with no forward motion, it became obvious that this was going to take a while. We all piled out of our hot vehicles to get some air and stretch our legs. I was in the lead Land Rover. Right in front of us was a battered stake truck with a tarp thrown over the cargo. The driver was a tall, muscular black man wearing greasy old trousers and a sleeveless undershirt. I noticed that he had started to sweat profusely. It wasn't heat sweat either. It was the perspiration of fear that was pouring down his forehead. He was staring down toward the head of the line with a look of sheer terror in his eyes.

I followed his gaze and spotted the cause of his fright. Marching down the line was a short, wiry man in a tan uniform. He was only about five feet three, but he was ramrod straight, and he slammed his heels into the dirt with every step he took. His short beard was the blackest of blacks, but it was more than matched by the two blazing coals that were his eyes. He was a Mauritanian customs officer. He carried a small automatic pistol in a holster around his waist, but he didn't need any weapon to assert his authority. I had read about how the Arabs of the North had come down to Senegal and enslaved the people there. Now I could see how it had been done. These desert people, made of steel cable, had a fire inside them that couldn't be matched by the easygoing people of the forests. They had conquered the southerners just by the force of their wills. Guns had probably had something to do with it as well.

After an hour, we finally made it to the head of the line. Even with all our equipment, we weren't worried about customs. We had a letter of introduction signed by the Mauritanian minister of tourism, who also happened to be the princess of that monarchy.

The ferry turned out to be a huge raft made of large logs. It could hold four vehicles and lots of people and animals. The river was as wide as a city block, and the current was running fast. Our three vehicles carefully rolled onto the raft. I kept looking into the water for crocodiles or hippos, while thinking to myself, "We're really in Africa now."

Across the river was a road and nothing else. While Senegal had been forest and bush, across the river, Mauritania was nothing but desert sand, right to the horizon, which itself was invisible under a thick layer of sand-filled atmosphere. A straight blacktop road cut the desert in half, and as we drove down this line for hours, the infinite desert took on the aspect of visual white noise.

Sand swirled onto the road, sometimes building up into eddies that we had to plow through in low gear. Once, the Volkswagen got stuck in one of them and had to be towed out by one of the Rovers. It was humbling, if not humiliating, that I, the great leader of this expedition, was driving the Volkswagen at that time.

After several hours, there was a vision in the distance that, at first, we thought was a mirage. It seemed as if there was an immense field of diamonds on one side of the road. As we came closer, we could make out areas of green, sparkling next to those of white. Coming up on it, we saw that it was miles and miles of broken glass, laid out on the desert floor as if it were a gigantic recycling area, which it probably was.

Not too long after that, we started to pass tents pitched in the desert. The tents became more and more numerous, until they formed a tent city, which then became the actual city of Nouakchott, the capital of Mauritania.

In reality, the city contained more tents than buildings. There were only about fifty substantial buildings in Nouakchott. Our hotel, Hotel Oasis, was one of them.

The hotel was like something out of an old Hollywood movie. A graceful white four-story Art Deco structure, facing a small square, surrounded by one-story cubed buildings built out of mud or concrete. Inside, behind the reception desk, centered in a small circular lobby, was a beautiful Asian woman with ivory-colored skin, wearing a white suit. The guests seemed to be business types, older Europeans, Arabs, and North Africans. One North African man had skin the color of green olives, something I'd never seen before or since. Off the lobby, there was a bar, where we went to wet our whistles while our rooms were being readied. I half expected to find Sydney Greenstreet there, dressed in a white suit and a fez.

Everything seemed to be going according to plan, until a truck pulled up to the hotel, containing a two-man committee from the local Teamsters Union. They insisted that we accompany them back to their headquarters in the Government Building.

They wore the long, hooded djellabas favored by most North African men, the skullcaps worn by all devout Muslim men, and the traditional leather slippers. They also had that universal grim scowl traditionally worn by thugs of all nations.

Bob, François, and I somehow squeezed into the back of their truck's cabin, and we headed off. As soon as we left the hotel, the two Mauritanians started hitting on a hash pipe, which they put away when we got to the Government Building. I took the fact that they didn't offer us any smoke as a sign that we were in for some difficult negotiations.

The Government Building was the tallest in town, all seven floors of it. We walked up three flights of stairs and down a long hallway to the Teamster Office. Their deal was pretty straightforward: we had to use local Teamsters and their trucks while we were in Mauritania.

In their eyes, this was an offer that we couldn't refuse. In our eyes, it was an offer we couldn't accept. Once our equipment was on their trucks, it was as good as gone. But maneuvering our way out of this situation would be next to impossible.

Then, a wonderful sound filtered into the office from the hallway outside—the melodious tones of an English woman. The three of us stood up as one and stepped outside to meet Princess Ellen of Mauritania.

The princess was an English woman who had met the prince when he was at Oxford. She moved here with him and took on the Ministry of Tourism, an especially important job at the time, with many visitors coming to see the eclipse. Sadly, the prince had recently passed away. Happily for us, the princess decided to stay on at her post. It took her less than five minutes to sort out the Teamster Committee and get us a ride back to the hotel.

We left after breakfast the next morning. I had decided that it was time to don my desert attire, and I appeared outside the hotel dressed in a long navy-blue djellaba, a matching turban, and camel-driver boots made of carpets, all of which I had purchased on my trip to Morocco. Sunglasses and protective goggles completed the look. I felt like the Jewish Lawrence of Arabia.

We drove hundreds of miles north through the endless desert, eating lunch on the move, stopping only when one or another of the vehicles got stuck in the sand. There wasn't one sign of life out there, nor was there a sign of anything that could sustain life. It seemed as if this was a place where the earth had died.

We drove until nightfall and stayed the night in Akjoujt, a mining center, where we slept in the dormitory along with about a thousand astronomers who had come for the eclipse.

The next morning, we were back on the desert road. A few hours into our drive, the road began to rise, and we climbed hills that were nothing but rock; we saw no vegetation of any kind. It was as completely barren as the sand down below; I couldn't even make out where the road was. Fortunately, François knew the territory and guided us through the hills.

At what seemed to be the highest point, François had us change direction with a sharp left turn. After about a mile, he brought us to a halt, and we all got out of our vehicles. Now I could make out the bare trace of a road. In front of us, where the lead Rover had stopped, a line of small brush stretched across the road. François said something in a native dialect, and two small children suddenly appeared from behind the brush. He spoke to them for a few minutes, and they removed a strand of barbed wire that had been hidden within the brush. I guess it was there to rip the tires of any vehicle that didn't stop at this almost invisible barrier.

We drove on, descending into a ravine. Down and down; the farther we went, more vegetation appeared. First grasses, then ferns, larger and larger. The humidity increased palpably as well. It was like entering a different world. Finally, we arrived at the bottom, where there were palm trees and reeds.

We parked, got out of our vehicles, and walked forward, following a path into the depths of the ravine. We entered a clearing and found a small village of reed huts, totally unlike the adobe-like buildings elsewhere in the country. People were sitting in the doorways of some of the huts. I felt as if I were walking into some kind of Tarzan adventure.

We exchanged astonished looks as we wordlessly walked on through the village. The path continued on behind the village through dense tropical foliage. By that point the humidity had become thick, and I could hear the cascading water. We came to the back end of the ravine, where sheer walls lined three sides. To our right there was a waterfall, with a small group of people sitting at the top. I asked François who those people were, and he told me that they were praying. One of them climbed down and approached me. He was a young North African man of about twenty-one years old who spoke French. He asked me what we were doing, and I told him that we were shooting a short film about the eclipse. He asked me if we needed any actors. I was floored. This was all too surreal to be true. I answered that we had all the actors we needed. Then he told me that he wanted to go to the United States, and I became wary. I told him, truthfully, that things weren't great in the American job market, as there was a recession going on. He said that he didn't want to work; he wanted to go to school in Arizona, where he wanted to study the American Indians. This was all getting to be too trippy to be true. I gave him an orange that I had in my pocket. He sold me some arrowheads that he'd found in the area. Then we left, in a state of awed bewilderment.

We drove out of the ravine, off the hills, and back onto the desert floor before finally arriving at our evening's bivouac, an abandoned air force base at Atar—a real find, since there weren't any other accommodations for hundreds of miles around.

The base consisted of two long, low-lying buildings, one dormitory and one administration building, right next to an airstrip in the middle of absolutely nowhere. Whose airstrip? I never found out. The dormitory was a series of small, bare rooms, one next to the other. There was a communal bathroom at the end of the hall, which was poorly lit by widely spaced bare bulbs of low wattage. We unpacked the sleeping bags we had brought, and each took a room.

We had our dinner out of cans, then bullshitted for a little while. Mostly we talked about the incredible oasis in the ravine and the strange encounter with the young Mauritanian. Oussman admired the arrowheads I had bought, and I happily gave them to him. Then we retired to our little quarters and tried to get some sleep.

At one o'clock in the morning, we were all rousted out of our dreams by banging and screaming in the hallway. I scrambled out of my sleeping bag and threw open the door, but it was pitch black out there. Then someone turned on the hall lights, and there was Oussman writhing on the floor. He seemed to recover just as Bob and Carl got to him. We were all afraid that he was having an epileptic seizure, but he was only having a nightmare. He slowly got to his feet and told us that he was "fighting with ghosts" who had attacked him because of the arrowheads he was holding.

After his explanation, Oussman lost no time in tossing the of-fending arrowheads out into the desert, and we all went back to sleep.

The next morning three men on camels came calling. They were dark-skinned nomads, possibly Tuareg, one of the most feared of the desert tribes. They handed us a bill for our stay at the base. It includ-ed water, electricity, and rent for the rooms. It was for $90,000. This was almost the cost of our entire production; remember, these were 1972 dollars.

Bob told the men to come back in an hour and said we would have their money. As soon as they were out of sight, we packed up the vehicles and got out of there. We had expected to be overcharged for most things, but we could not accept grand larceny.

Why did those three men trust us? They must have thought that it would be too dishonorable for us not to be good for our word. It's fascinating how many different ways a word like "honor" can be interpreted.

Our next stop was two hours away: a collection of two-story mud buildings that housed an extended family. These were people

François knew. This was where we were going to pick up our actors and extra crew.

We were adding three men and a camel to our party: a young man, who would be our actor, his grizzled father, and a family slave. I was flabbergasted to discover that slavery still existed there. Although this man seemed to be treated as an equal, he was not equal. I found it repugnant, but there was nothing I could do about it. At the same time, I could understand the dynamics that cause the existence of that institution to this very day. There is simply no way to survive in that cruel and meager place without the support of a clan. To be alone in Mauritania is to die.

With the three Mauritanians packed into our vehicles, and the camel tied up to the back, we continued on for another hour or two into the desert, before arriving at a spot that Bob determined would perfectly suit our purpose.

We unloaded the vehicles, set about pitching two-man tents, and checked out the equipment and supplies. As we prepared to settle down for a dinner of various canned foods, four men on horseback rode up. They made no pretense about their purpose. This was their territory, and they wanted money for the right to camp here. One look at these rough characters, as their greedy eyes hungrily devoured our carefully laid out equipment, told their story.

This was no time to be in a giving mood. Carl, François, and the Mauritanians made a show of their firearms as we spoke to the four intruders. I'd had no idea that any of us were packing weapons, but I was happy to see them. With the older Mauritanian interpreting, Bob told the four men to get lost, saying that we were in constant radio contact with the Mauritanian Army, which was patrolling the area. Although a blatant lie, this last had the desired effect, and the men wheeled their horses around and rode off.

That night we slept with our weapons next to our sleeping bags. My own weapon was a clasp knife that I'm sure would have done no good at all, but at least it made me feel that I was doing whatever I possibly could for the cause.

The sun rose after a thankfully uneventful, if uneasy, night's sleep. This was *the Day*. We had only one chance to do this thing right. There would be no second take.

But the day had a troubled beginning. I reached over for my boots and fortunately remembered enough movies about the desert to peer inside. Sure enough, down at the bottom of my left boot was a scorpion.

"Aaaaaaagh!" I screamed, jumping so high that I must have hit the top of the tent.

"What's wrong!" shouted Dennis, catching the mood of my panic.

After racing around the tent in a frenzy, I finally got up the nerve to dump the poisonous thing out of my boot, and Dennis smashed it with a heavy camera case. It took me another five minutes to come close to regaining my equilibrium.

We drove out until our camp was no longer visible. This took a while, given the flatness of the terrain. Then we set up a Bedouin tent and tied the camel up in front of it. This was our set, where the younger Mauritanian would experience the terror of the eclipse. We then took one of our two cameras and set it up to capture a shot of the entire scene, wide enough to include the sun. This camera was attached to an intervalometer, a device that would control the speed of the film running through it. It was set to shoot one frame every twelve seconds. In this way, the one roll of film in the camera would photograph the entire duration of the eclipse. We secured the camera with sandbags and rope and went on with our work.

The next job was to photograph the "dramatic acting" part of the commercial. We shot a close-up of the Mauritanian looking up at the sky, becoming frightened, then looking relieved. Bob talked him through these steps, with François interpreting. Next, we shot a close-up of the camel. Being a finicky animal by nature, it easily got upset, which was the attitude we wanted. Then we shot a wider shot of all the action, including the Mauritanian grabbing the camel's reins, trying to control it and calm it down.

This took time, but it all went well. The only thing left was to wait for the right time to turn on the other camera and photograph the shadow of the moon covering the sun, revealing the heavens in all their glory, until the sun reappeared, making the day whole again. The camera was set facing the back of the tent, in a position where it wouldn't see the Mauritanian or the camel.

The time came, and the camera was turned on. Every twelve seconds we could hear a satisfying click as the film advanced one frame. Everything seemed to be falling into place, until the laws of physics took center stage in our little production.

When a solar eclipse occurs, the air temperature can fall forty degrees in about thirty seconds. This sudden drop can cause winds of hurricane force to rise. At sea, this often results in huge tidal waves. In the desert, it means a devastating sandstorm.

As the wind and sand kicked up, we moved our vehicles into positions that would hopefully block the camera from the worst of the storm. But as things continued to worsen, we realized that our own position was getting perilous. Soon the sand would be blasting hard enough to tear the skin off our faces. Forget about dancing under the stars; this was now about running for our lives. We crammed ourselves into one of the Land Rovers and raced back to camp.

We got there not a minute too soon. Some of the tent stakes were already coming loose. We jumped out of the Rover and furiously set to fastening everything down. Then we raced into our tents and zipped them up tight.

Dennis and I sat on the floor of our tent, just staring at each other, afraid to voice our thoughts as the wind outside thundered as loud as cannon fire, and the continuous wall of flying sand blasted the tent.

It seemed to go on interminably. We were exhausted and hungry. Fortunately, we had tins of beef jerky, a variety, in fact, that we happily wolfed down.

After a long time, it sounded as if the wind had abated a bit. The brain-splitting howl of the wind had reduced to a very loud scream.

I cautiously unzipped the tent enough to look outside. I could see that the wind was still blowing hard, but not with the same fury as before. The other tents seemed to have held up, with everyone still inside. The camel was hunkered down behind one of the tents. It was covered with sand, but its nose was sticking out.

Then I spotted some movement through the blowing curtain of sand. I stared at it until I could make out the form of a man walking toward the camp. I called Dennis outside to see this impossible thing or to tell me that I was hallucinating.

But it was real. A Mauritanian man, his turban covering all his face, save for his squinted eyes, aided by a walking stick, was walking determinedly and briskly through the vicious sandstorm. He walked right through the center of our camp. I held a bottle of water out for him as he passed, but he didn't even look at me. He just continued on in a straight path, one sandaled foot ahead of the other, unfalteringly moving ahead, until he disappeared into the swirling sands.

After a while, the storm finally stopped, and we all emerged into the open. We swept most of the sand from the Land Rover and headed back to the shooting location, desperately hoping that the camera was still in place and intact.

Approaching the location, all we could see were mounds of sand where our vehicles had been parked. It seemed as if everything had been buried. We got out of the Rover and walked around to the other side of the mounds. The first thing we saw was the tent. While the sand had covered most of it, the top was still exposed.

The sandbags guarding the camera were covered with sand, but they had done their job well. The camera lens was uncovered and clean, and the camera was still clicking away one frame every twelve seconds.

Two days later we were driving back into Nouakchott. The vehicles and we all looked as if we had been through desert warfare, but the smiles on our faces spoke of victory. I felt particularly heroic. I had

had a dream about an eclipse in the desert, and I had overcome the odds to make that dream come true.

We pulled up to the Hotel Oasis. It felt like home. While the others busied themselves unloading the equipment, I got my room key at the desk, then swaggered into the hotel bar, my desert finery still encrusted with sand. There were two young European women at the bar—attractive, young European women. They were dressed in expedition outfits. I supposed they were there for some sort of adventure. Well, here I was, Mr. Adventure himself, bronzed by the desert sun, hardened by the elements, filled with tales of derring-do. What a way to end the trip. I asked the bartender for a bottle of water. I wanted to quench my very deep thirst while I figured out how best to approach the situation. He handed me a liter bottle of Evian. God, did that clean, cool water taste great. I couldn't take the bottle away from my lips. It went down in one greedy gulp. I ordered a second bottle and did the same.

Now I was ready to make my move. I rakishly wiped my mouth with my sleeve as I took a step back from the bar with an air of bravado, and I turned toward the women. That's when the water flushed right down to the bottom of my intestines, like a depth charge on the verge of exploding. I froze and felt my face take on the mask of panic. I spun around and walked as quickly as I could, then ran up the stairs to my room.

After thirty sweat-soaked minutes on the toilet, followed by a hurried shower and a quick change of clothes, I raced back down to the bar, but the girls had already left. Glory is such a fleeting thing.

19

VIVA LA CAUSA!

1973

Maurice and I hit the first roadblock somewhere between Mexico City and Cuernavaca. They were a rag-tag dozen, unevenly uniformed, in their late teens and early twenties. Some of them had yet to shave for the first time.

We climbed out of the cab with our friendliest smiles and invited them to search the camper, opening cabinets and drawers to make it easier for them. I didn't know if they were looking for drugs or guns, or if it was just an old-fashioned shakedown. I did know that their automatic rifles were loaded and that the nervous looks on some of their sweaty faces were making me very uncomfortable.

Maurice, on the other hand, seemed to be chatting some of these fellows up, despite the fact that he didn't have a word of Spanish, and they, I'm sure, spoke none of the languages he was fluent in. It didn't really surprise me; Maurice was always able to chat up and charm absolute strangers. That's what made him the most successful pickup artist I'd ever seen in action.

Now he was working his magic with these young soldiers, easing their fingers off their triggers. They might not have known what he was talking about, but it was clear that they saw him as a friendly figure. For sure, he wasn't a gringo; there was nothing remotely

Anglo-Saxon about him. Although I'm certain they had no idea what he was, unless they were familiar with Moroccan Jews and an accent that was threaded with Arabic, French, Hebrew, and American English. However, they did know that he was someone closer to their world than to the vanilla behemoth north of the border, and the tension between us all relaxed.

At the time, Maurice was my best friend. He was an odd bird, with a first-world education in Israel but a third-world upbringing in Morocco. He had a macabre, even demonic look, with deeply set coal-black eyes, sunken cheeks, pocked sallow skin, and a wire-thin body. Most men immediately became suspicious of him, but many women found him attractive. For my part, I found him to be intelligent, funny, and quirky, a good companion.

So when I decided to use my four weeks of vacation all in one shot, I had asked Maurice to come along. The idea had been to fly to Mexico City, rent a camper, and drive south along the Pacific, down past Acapulco, then swing east to the Caribbean, winding up in Oaxaca. I had heard that all the best artisans and craftspeople were in that city. Pottery, silverwork, weaving, all the fabulous stuff made by Mexican craftspeople was even more fabulous there, and I was very curious to see what made the place so special.

Carlos, the creative director of Young & Rubicam's office in Mexico City, set me up with a reputable company that rented out campers. The one we got was small, barely accommodating two people, but we weren't looking for luxury in that department. Shortly after leaving Mexico City, the side-view mirror fell off. When it happened, I didn't see it as an omen, but as I was standing at the side of the deserted road, while nervous young Mexican soldiers went through the camper, I began to wonder whether I had let my curiosity about Oaxaca get the better of me.

Five minutes later we were on the road again. Fortunately, we hadn't scored any drugs in Mexico City. Not that we would have turned down the opportunity, but none was offered. So we were once more on the road, heading for Acapulco. We hit another roadblock between Cuernavaca and Acapulco, but this time we knew what to expect and relaxed, sitting by the side of the road, in the shade of the camper, while the soldier boys did their duty.

Late that afternoon we rolled into Acapulco on the main road that ran along the ocean, lined with majestic royal palm trees. The last time I was there, I had stayed at Las Brisas, a resort in the hills overlooking the ocean, where the ultrarich sunned themselves in opulent private villas, each with its own pool. Of course, that was on the company dime. Now Maurice and I were staying in a camper parked in a public lot. At least it was by the sea.

The social standings of our accommodations came more into play that evening when we went to a swank club for dinner and disco. The club was called Romeo. It was set at the edge of the beach in a circular building meant to resemble an ancient Greek temple. It was open all around, so the sound of the waves crashing onto the shore could be heard whenever the ear-splitting music abated. Maurice and I sat there, eating, drinking, and checking out the ladies on the dance floor to see who was attractive and available.

I had never been one for picking up women at discotheques. Back in New York, I was very much a bachelor in demand. I had gained a large and wide reputation in the advertising industry as a brilliant rising star and a fun-loving, pot-smoking, all-around wild and crazy guy, and women kept coming around my office and my apartment to see what the fuss was all about. This kind of attention tended to make me lazy in the picking-up-ladies department. The fact that I was still intensely shy and unsure of myself was another major factor.

However, to paraphrase an ancient adage, "when in Acapulco, go for the gold." Maurice was already out there. He had picked out his target and dashed out to corral her on the dance floor. He did some kind of half-disco, half-Arabic dance, waving his hands in the air and staring intensely into the woman's eyes. She was pretty, blond, and dressed expensively in an out-on-the-town-for-a-good-time kind of way. She was laughing out loud at the things that Maurice was speaking into her ear as they danced. It looked as if he was already set for the night.

I made my way onto the floor and danced with a few different women before settling on a pretty brunette who smiled at me in a way that seemed to be genuine. We talked as we danced, introducing ourselves to each other. I was getting into a nice groove, and I started to wonder whether this was going to go anywhere. Then I remembered that there wasn't any place for it to go, at least not on my end. I certainly couldn't take her from this glitzy club back to the little camper in a parking lot. So this was going nowhere except where it was, which was okay with me.

I took a look over at Maurice, and he was still getting on with the blonde. I wondered what would happen if he took her back to the camper. Maurice could get away with a move like that, whereas most guys, like myself for instance, wouldn't even try. But what would happen if he did? Would I have to wait outside until they were done? Would I have to wait outside until morning? I realized that we didn't have the right equipment to deal with this town. At the end of the next song, I said my good-byes to the woman I was dancing with, then caught Maurice's eye and signaled that I was going. He, in turn, signaled that he was staying.

The sound of the ocean is as sweet a lullaby as there is, and I was soon fast asleep. I don't know what time Maurice got in, but in the morning all he would say about his night was that the lady had been "a very nice woman."

Over breakfast at a café along the water, I told Maurice that I wanted to leave Acapulco sooner rather than later, and he agreed to take off right away. But when we returned to the camper, we discovered that the battery was dead, really dead. We got a mechanic to come and give us a charge, but that wouldn't do it. We needed a new battery. Two problems in two days for the camper. I was beginning to think that it was jinxed.

We were able to take off for the South by midafternoon. I'd been to Mexico a few times before, but never south of Acapulco, and I felt a sense of adventure. I had pictures of tropical forests and lurking jaguars dancing in my head.

I did the driving, as Maurice didn't know how to work a manual transmission. I loved to drive, so it was fine with me. After several hours of running along the sea, the road turned inland and wound itself up and around a steep mountainside. At the peak, we were stopped by another roadblock of young soldiers with the usual heavy artillery. These guys took longer than the other soldiers had; they patted us down as well. I guessed that the trafficking of whatever they were looking for was heavier here in the South.

The moment we left the soldiers and started downhill, the camper began to act up. The gears refused to engage without a struggle. Soon, one by one, they stopped engaging at all, until we were bumping along the road in first. Our situation became more complicated as night fell, the twisting road now lit only by our dim headlamps.

Thankfully, we got to the bottom of the incline without mishap, and the road straightened out. Now we only had to find a safe spot to stop. After a few hours of stumbling along in first gear, we came to a house that was dark inside, but it had colorful light bulbs strung around the roofline. It seemed safe enough, and I didn't want to drive any farther in the dark, risking the one gear that we had left.

We didn't want to knock on the door. I'm not sure why. Maybe we were afraid that if the people inside weren't friendly, we'd have to drive away into the unknown. So we quietly pulled off to the side of the road and called it a night.

I slept until late in the morning, when I was awakened by Maurice, who had just come from the house bearing rolls, coffee, and the news that the house with colored lights was a bordello. He also had found out that the town of Pinotepa Nacional was just down the road, and there was an auto mechanic with a shop there.

The camper started up, which was a relief, and we chug-a-chugged into Pinotepa Nacional. The town wasn't much: a stretch of one-story cement-block buildings along the road. Here and there a dirt road led off to a sprinkling of other similar structures. We found the mechanic on the far end of the town. He had a walled courtyard in front of his house, and we pulled in there, raising dust and rousting a couple of chickens from their nap.

The mechanic came out of his house, and after I communicated with my hands and some sound effects, he kind of caught my drift. It didn't take him long to discover that the gears were all stripped, and we needed a new transmission. He told us that it would only take an hour or two to replace the transmission, but it would take four days for the part to get there from Mexico City.

Why four days? The answer was too complicated for my knowledge of Spanish, which consisted of less than a dozen words, most of them insults. The good news was that, although we were stuck in a place that seemed to be no more than a clearing in the jungle, we could stay in our camper, in the mechanic's courtyard, so at least we were safe.

I was concerned about something. All the people whom I had seen so far in Pinotepa Nacional seemed to be Mexican Indians. No Spanish Mexicans, no gringos, no tourists of any stripe. Maurice and I were the only unusual things in town, which, in my mind, made us targets. No matter how cool, hip, friendly, open-minded, generous, warm, down-to-earth, spiritual, or saintly we were, and I can't say we were any of those things, we would always be rich strangers there. We had it, they didn't, and some of them undoubtedly wanted it badly enough to try to take it away from us. In every group of people, no matter how peaceful, law abiding, educated, or civilized, there will be some who will try to get what they want through conning, lying, or just plain stealing. Now any those people so inclined knew where to find two likely victims.

You might think that this is a jaundiced point of view, and you might be right. But I was brought up in a neighborhood where some people would happily take advantage of the unwary and unprotected, especially if they were strangers.

The other issue before us was what to eat and drink. Mexico can be problematic in that department. Eating anything washed in unboiled water would undoubtedly make us as sick as a pig who ate a live porcupine, and I was sure that the closest doctor around had probably treated more pigs than people. Thankfully, the solution was just down the road at a small café, where we could eat fried eggs and tortillas and drink coffee three times a day. It was boring, but it would keep us alive.

The coming days of doing nothing in the mechanic's courtyard threatened to bore us to death. Besides the mechanic's place and the café, there was a sparsely supplied grocery and a similarly stocked hardware store. As it turned out, we were the only entertainment in town.

Young people started to drop by to take a look at the two strangers. Maurice and I had to work hard to maintain friendly faces while keeping our distance at the same time. That, combined with a lack of a common language, seemed to work. Most of the visitors left after a short stay and didn't bother to visit a second time.

In between curious guests, I practiced Tai Chi. When visitors showed up while I was doing these exercises, Maurice tried to explain that I could kill people with my bare hands. We also tried to play backgammon. I say "tried" because Maurice was a whiz at the game and I was less than a novice. While the gameplay was educational for me, it did nothing to cut the boredom for Maurice.

On our second full day in Pinotepa Nacional, one of the young men who had come by the day before showed up for a second visit. He hung around for more than an hour, asking us questions about the United States in his broken English. Just before he left, he asked us if we wanted to buy some marijuana, but we turned his offer down, fearing that it might be a setup. We had heard stories of people selling tourists grass, then tipped off the cops for a reward. We were going to be here for at least two more days, and we would be sitting ducks for a scam like that.

That evening, over our dinner of eggs, tortillas, and coffee, we decided not to continue south after the camper was fixed. If we went on to Oaxaca, we'd be moving farther and farther away from any kind of help we might need, and we couldn't trust the camper not to break down more than it already had.

The next morning, the young man who had wanted to sell us weed came by again. This time he wanted to take us to see a nearby river. It seemed harmless enough, and also necessary, as we were getting cabin fever being locked up in the confines of the courtyard. We walked south along the road for about half an hour, then took a path that ran through the forest. Ten minutes later, we were on a bluff overlooking a living mural of life in the South of Mexico. From where we stood, we could see three twists in the river that made complete S-curves, and in those curves was every part of life—children playing, women washing clothes, others bathing, and a young couple making love. It felt as if God had invited me to have a look at his creation. From the height of our point of view, the images down below flattened out, accentuating the feeling of a two-dimensional painting, and our distance from the river mirrored the remove that one feels when looking at life represented by art. We feel the art without feeling the individual lives it represents. Still, this work of art took my breath away.

The replacement transmission arrived the next day, and the mechanic assured us that he would have the work completed by the evening. We'd be out of Pinotepa Nacional the next morning.

When our young friend came around again, we told him that we were headed back north and would like to buy some marijuana from him. He was happy to accommodate us, and he came back late that afternoon with about an ounce of beautiful golden buds. He asked if he could come along with us as far as Acapulco, and we agreed. We told him to meet us at nine the next morning.

That night I hid away the bag of grass. There was a recessed light fixture in the ceiling above my bunk bed, which was about four feet off the floor. I lay on my back, unscrewed the metal frame surrounding the fixture, and removed the glass. I wedged the bag of grass into the recess and taped a rectangle of heavy white paper over the opening to create a false ceiling. Then I replaced the glass and the frame.

It was a perfect job of camouflage. We could only get caught with this grass if our newfound friend betrayed us to the soldiers at the roadblock or to some cops who might "coincidently" meet us along the way.

The simple solution to that problem was to leave town at eight in the morning, an hour before he showed up at our camper door. It seemed a bit harsh and a bit paranoid, but we figured it was much better to have to live with those fleeting feelings of guilt and remorse hanging over our heads than to be in a Mexican jail.

So off we drove, guilt, remorse, and marijuana all packed away. We drove out of the town of Pinotepa Nacional, past the bordello in the woods, and up the steep incline of the mountain road before we stopped at the roadblock at the peak. There the soldiers inspected us and the camper as closely as before, but not so completely as to find our precious bag of weed hidden away in the light fixture. Another triumph of good old American ingenuity.

Miraculously, the camper didn't break down on the drive back to Acapulco, and we drove into town smoking a big doobie, a self-congratulatory celebration of our cleverness. We drove along the sea road until we saw the parking lot. Then we went to the corner and made a U-turn around the center meridian. As we turned, I spied a policeman on a motorcycle a block farther on and immediately realized that, in his greedy eyes, we were cutting him off. Sure enough, he turned on his siren and sped after us. As I pulled over, I quickly explained to Maurice what was going down.

The cop pulled up behind and waited for us to get out of the cab and walk over to him. Sweat poured off me, and fear flooded my veins as I fumbled around killing the joint, rolling up the windows, getting the rental papers and my license together, and trying not to shit in my pants. Maurice meanwhile jumped into action. His Moroccan background had taught him just what to do in a situation like this. He hopped out of the cab, offering a thousand apologies, walked right up to the scowling cop sitting atop his rumbling Harley, and by way of a further apology, placed a twenty-dollar bill into the officer's hand.

The cop grunted and nodded, Maurice got back into the cab, and we drove away. No ticket, no drug bust, no Mexican jail time.

Of all my bad-boy friends, Maurice may have been the quirkiest. He was an immigrant twice over. A Jew in Morocco, a Moroccan in Israel, and a foreign presence even in a polyglot society like New York. He must have felt alienated everywhere he went. That's why he didn't feel obligated to play by anyone's rules. His number one, two, and three priorities were survival, survival, and survival. That's why, when I knew he was bribing a cop or a client, or withholding a payment from a supplier, I always cut him some slack in the ethics department. After all, who was I to judge?

We now had two weeks to kill, and Acapulco seemed as good a place as any to kill a good part of that time. Romeo's Beach Club seemed like the right spot for our headquarters. We had lunch and dinner there and rented beach lounges by the day. At night we hung out at the discotheque there. It wasn't the adventure I had been hoping for, but it wasn't bad either.

Two days later, walking along the main road, we passed some cars that had flyers stuck behind their windshield wipers, advertising a place called La Quinta Rebecca, with a little map showing a grand house up in the hills above the city. It seemed like a good place to break up our routine of day and night at Romeo's.

That night, following the map, we found the right road and made our way up the hill. After a short while, the road went from macadam to dirt, ending in a turnaround and a small parking lot, where about a dozen pigs were scrabbling for food. Across from the lot was a high wall with an impressive wooden door, as well as a heavy rope hanging down from a bell.

We pulled the rope, and the bell sounded a deep and mellow ring. When we walked through the door, we found a large courtyard with a neatly raked earthen floor. Across the courtyard was another, higher wall with a wide stone staircase that led up to the top, where ten women appeared. They all seemed young and pretty, and each wore a different tropical-colored taffeta dress that flowed in the breeze.

They had large hibiscus flowers in their hair, and they smiled and waved to us in welcome.

As we climbed the stairs, I could hear a guitar strumming a romantic Mexican ballad, and the scent of jasmine started to waft down from above. When we arrived at the top, the ladies surrounded us, caressing us and making adoring sounds, each one looking right into our eyes with a seductive promise. Up close, I could see that the majority of these women were neither as young nor as pretty as they seemed from a distance, but they weren't all that bad either. One in particular seemed younger than the others and was actually very attractive. She was mine. Maurice chose a woman who seemed to be the wise guy of the group. He was going for the hot sauce.

Afterward, sitting on the terrace that overlooked the Pacific, smoking cigars, and drinking margaritas served by the ladies while the guitarist supplied the background, I felt as if we were in some 1940s movie about Americans living a decadent life in the tropics. Closing my eyes, I had a momentary fantasy of staying up there; then I opened my eyes and realized that the magical but delusional moment was as good as this place got.

The following day, I took advantage of another luxury that Acapulco had to offer: a phone booth. I had to call Carlos back in Mexico City to tell him about all the problems we'd been having with the camper. I wanted him to run interference for me with the rental agent. We were bringing it back with a new battery and a new transmission, and I didn't want to get any grief when I asked for a reduction on my rate. Carlos was happy to hear from me. He had unexpected news. Carl Sturgis, the manager of the Creative Department in the New York office, was looking for me.

I made a collect call to the New York office. Carl told me that they wanted me in Los Angeles in three days' time to have a meeting with Ernest Gallo, the chairman of Gallo Wines. Obviously, this was an offer I couldn't refuse; besides, I had seen as much of Acapulco as I wanted to. This also meant that half of my airfare would be covered by the agency. Maurice wasn't terribly upset when I told him the news. He was ready to get back to New York.

I caught a morning plane to Los Angeles, wearing the only clean clothes that I had: off-white linen tie-up pants and an off-white embroidered Mexican peasant shirt. I took a taxi to the Young & Rubicam office on Wilshire Boulevard, and I was ushered into the conference room, where the head of the office was nervously waiting. There was just enough time before the meeting for him to fill me in: Gallo was about to launch a new line of premium wines, a big departure for them, and Ernest Gallo himself had come down from Modesto to brief the agency, something that he'd never done before. It was clear to me that this guy was nervous at the prospect of a face-to-face with Ernest Gallo, even more so with me, my Afro, and my Mexican peasant outfit standing next to him.

A few minutes later, Ernest strode into the room, accompanied by three suits from the agency. The head of the office stood up to greet him, and Ernest shook his hand. Then I stood up to be introduced, and Ernest stopped in his tracks and stared at me.

Gallo, like all the major wine producers in California, was having serious and much-publicized labor problems with the Grape Pickers Union led by Cesar Chavez. The unions had garnered a lot of support from liberal groups who supported La Causa. Now here in front of him was a swarthy, bearded, and long-haired young man dressed like a grape picker wearing his best clothes.

I guess that my Brooklyn accent and Jewish name disarmed him, because when I offered my hand, he took it. Then we sat down to business. Ernest told us that the new line of wine would be composed of varietals, wines made from only one kind of grape. There would be Chardonnay, Cabernet, Pinot Noir, Merlot, Chablis, Syrah, Sauvignon Blanc, and Zinfandel. These would be the top of the Gallo line and, according to Ernest, comparable to any wine anywhere. This line would require a breakthrough advertising campaign to launch it, different from anything Gallo or any other winemaker had done. I told him that he'd come to the right place.

Three weeks later I was back in the conference room in the Los Angeles office, along with five other creative executives. There were two of us from New York, two from LA, and one each from San Francisco and Chicago. Each of us had brought two different campaign presentations, making twelve in all.

The head of the Los Angeles office was in charge of our show. He was assisted by the two top account executives in the business. We did a full-scale rehearsal with the account guys presenting research results and media proposals and all the creatives presenting their work. It was an impressive show. There were a couple of ideas that I would have been proud to call my own. Of course, I still favored my own work and the work of the team I had put together back in New York, but then again, I always liked my own work best.

The next morning, we were all on a commuter flight landing at the airport in Modesto, California, the Kingdom of Gallo. As the largest winemaker and distributor in the United States, perhaps the world, Gallo affected every corner of this vine-covered region. As we drove up in our rented van, the Gallo corporate headquarters loomed up on the horizon like a modern castle.

The entrance to the building was a huge glass atrium filled with tropical trees, ferns, and plants. There were streams and waterfalls, and tropical birds flew under the incredibly high glass ceiling. The walk to the elevator was the length of half a football field, past the watchful eyes of the discreetly placed security guards.

We crowded into the elevator and took it to the top floor, where we were guided to a large conference room. We seated ourselves along one side of the long conference table and busied ourselves with arranging our various presentations.

After fifteen minutes, the two top marketing guys from Gallo came into the room, sat down opposite us, mumbled hellos, and told us that Ernest would be there presently. After that, they said nothing but flipped through the presentation booklet that the agency had prepared for them. Twenty minutes later, Ernest and his son David walked into the room. Ernest took a seat at the center of the table, facing us, and David found himself an empty chair on our side of the table.

With only the briefest of introductions, we began our presentation. The account guys ran through the research results and marketing and media strategies. I could see that no one on the Gallo side was particularly interested in any of that. Clearly, the only thing they cared about was the new idea. Then we went into the presentation of the creative work. There was so much of it that it didn't matter who went first or last. The variety of the work was so great that the agency didn't have any particular recommendation, which it usually has in most client presentations. For our part, we were just hoping that the Gallo people would see something that would stick in their minds.

I presented somewhere in the middle of the group. I had two campaigns. One was a print campaign I had done myself, intended to be educational in nature, explaining the concept and taste benefits of varietals to a market that was fairly unknowledgeable about wine in general. The other was a TV campaign wrapped around a song that one of my copywriters had written. Despite my inability to carry a tune, and much to the amusement of everyone at the table, I sang the song.

While the others were presenting, I was watching the reactions of the Gallo people. Ernest was stolid and solid, staring straight at each presenter with a totally noncommittal look on his face. The two marketing guys busied themselves with checking to see that the spoken words matched those written in the presentation booklets. They obviously had no say in the decision-making process. But David was something else. He spent almost the entire presentation unfolding a paper clip and edging it closer and closer to his left eyeball. Closer and closer in tiny, incremental distances, until *bang*! It got so close to his eyeball that he dropped the clip and jumped back in his chair. Then he picked up the clip and started all over again.

From time to time, during one of the presentations, he'd shout out, "Dad! Dad! They're insulting our wine!" and he'd go on to complain that the wine wasn't being shown in a sufficiently exalted way, such as in a silver or crystal decanter, or being sipped by beautiful people in formal attire. Minor details that had no bearing on whether the advertising idea was any good or not. One time, he became so incensed that he started barking, and when Ernest told him to stop it, he crawled under the table for a while.

Finally, after hours of presentation, we were done, and it was time for them to respond. Ernest had a well-known reputation as being one of the toughest clients in the business, but I couldn't believe that he wouldn't be impressed by the length and breadth of our presentation.

The head of the LA office gave a little wrap-up speech and asked for a response. There was nothing but silence from the other side. I realized that our suits weren't going to stick their necks out until Ernest made his pronouncement. But Ernest said nothing. It was David who made the call. "It's shit, Dad! It's all shit! They're not presenting the wine with enough respect. It's demeaning!" I had the sinking feeling that I knew where this presentation was headed.

But Ernest stayed noncommittal, saying that there were some good ideas in the presentation. He asked his marketing guys what they thought. One of them immediately jumped on David's bandwagon and said that he didn't think any of the work was right. The other one wanted to seem more thoughtful. He said that he liked some of my work.

"Which one?" I asked. "The singing one?"

"No, I didn't like that one."

"The educational one," I said hopefully.

"No, I didn't like that one either."

"Then what did you like?"

"I guess I liked Henry."

I heard the toilet flushing and felt the water swirling all around me as the entire presentation went down through that little hole in the porcelain. After that, a lot of hedged statements came from both sides, with the agency trying to pry some clue as to what was wrong with our advertising and what direction we should be going in, and the Gallo folks not committing to anything at all.

Finally, Silvio Galterio, the other creative from New York, got up to say something. Silvio looked like a nobleman in the court of the

Borgias, tall, thin, and dark, with a prominent nose and piercing eyes. In a well-tailored silk jacket, fitted white shirt, and smartly patterned tie, he looked like he'd be good with a stiletto.

Silvio announced that he was aghast at the response from the Gallo people; that he thought it was the most unprofessional performance he'd ever seen; that they had made it impossible for the agency to adjust the approach because they were giving us nothing to adjust to. He was right in every respect. But he definitely wasn't smart.

After Silvio sat down, there was total silence in the room.

Then Ernest slowly got to his feet. He spoke quietly and evenly, without a hint of emotion. He used sentences like "Do you want to be responsible for your agency losing this account?" and "I'm the largest and most successful marketer of wine in the world," and "Are you saying that I don't know what I'm doing?" He spoke like a man filling up a large balloon with short, sure, and powerful breaths, his words gradually filling up the room with fear as poor Silvio grew steadily smaller, until his pants slid down off his shrunken frame, forcing him to cover himself up with apologies.

Ernest, "the most successful marketer of wine in the world," made a grand display of bullying, making mincemeat of all our marketing strategies and claims of partnering with our client, making a mockery of our creative efforts based on research and logic, pulverizing our ego-driven creative ethos, destroying our cause.

To Ernest Gallo we were the same as the Chicano grape pickers who worked for him. He bullied us the same way that he had bullied them. Only they were standing up to him. They derived their strength from their unified belief in La Causa, in their own integrity as human beings.

What was my cause? I realized just how insignificant all my so-called achievements were. Was this really the life I wanted to lead? Trying to get a bully like Ernest Gallo or his pathetic toadies to approve my work or to like me? My stomach roiled with anger and discontent. I sensed the beginning of a sea change.

20

UNCLE SOLLY

1974

U ntil recent years I've always palled around with at least one bad-boy friend. When I was a teenager, practically all my friends were bad boys, but when I found myself brushing up against some truly brutal psychopaths, I started to back off a bit. I enjoyed chaos and adventure, but mayhem, jail time, and death were definitely out of bounds for me, although I sometimes had a hard time discerning where the line marking that boundary was.

Why did I always have these bad boys around me? Surely it was part of a pattern of self-destructive behavior. Was it the desire to keep thumbing my nose at the rules of a society that I've always felt alienated from? Was it the acknowledgment that everything in life is temporary, ever changing, and random? And so, to hell with the rules of society, as long as I didn't cause anyone harm.

By the mid-1970s the massive wave of drugs and sex that we had been riding had pushed social changes way over the top. People were smoking reefer and snorting coke out in public; men and women were jumping into bed with whoever shared the itch at that particular moment. Relationships were replaced by one-night stands. Even square couples from the suburbs were having group orgies at places like Plato's Retreat.

Flower power had been a beautiful dream, but it didn't have enough juice to be a power in the real world. The Vietnam War had ended only because the little men in black pajamas had beaten back the world's most powerful army. The image of the last Americans in Saigon clambering off the roof of the American Embassy onto an army helicopter told the whole story.

Maybe the decadent turn that our love parade took was one last nasty spit in the eye of our imperialistic, money-hungry, war-mongering, self-righteous Uncle Sam. It may have been crazy, it may have been destructive and nihilistic, but it was fun.

Shortly after I had saved the account, I managed to have the entire Eastern Airlines group placed on a floor that was separate from the rest of the Creative Department.

Soon the sweet smell of ganja was wafting through those halls, mixing with the sounds of jazz and soul music coming from the station we all had our radios tuned to. Three times a week, we all gathered, usually in my office, with bongos, congas, and all sorts of percussion instruments and noisemakers. There was an ongoing Ping-Pong tournament on a table we had smuggled into our conference room. There was constant traffic from other people in the Creative Department and people from the outside, all wanting to get in on the fun. Even some of the suits would occasionally drop by for a visit and a smoke.

You might well ask, "How did management allow this to happen?" The answer is money. The most important and influential consumer group is the youth market. This group sets the tone, forecasts the future, watches the most television, and buys the most products. By the early 1970s, youth had run wild, and the captains of industry didn't understand a thing about what was going on. As Bob Dylan so aptly put it, "There's something happening and you don't know what it is, do you, Mr. Jones?" The suits, however, were smart enough to realize that they didn't get it, that they had to catch up or they would be dead in the water.

Fortunately for them, there was a young generation walking the corporate halls who were connected to what was happening. That was us. We had discarded our suits for jeans and army-navy surplus. Our hair was long, our egos were overblown, and we were creating some wonderful advertising that the suits didn't understand but for which they were happy to put on the air and collect the money.

Management needed us, or they thought they did. In any event, things were working, revenues were pouring in, the clients were happy that the youth market was being covered, and nobody wanted to upset the apple cart, which at Young & Rubicam, at that point in time, included me and my posse. In other words, things were way out of control.

So I wasn't surprised when Richie Cohen walked into my office one day with a special gift for me. Richie was a good writer with whom I had just started working.

We had hit it off right away. Not only was he a good writer, but he was fun to be with, and he was ecstatically happy to be included in the A team.

The special gift was a pretty blond woman in her late twenties. Her name was Greta, he said; she was from Germany, and she'd be very happy to blow me. I didn't know what to say. It seemed more than a little weird, and a lot more than a little creepy, but the flesh is weak and I seemed to remember an old axiom about never looking a gift blow job in the mouth, or something like that, and I graciously accepted Richie's gift.

A couple of weeks later, Richie invited me to his brownstone apartment in Cobble Hill for dinner. There I met his wife and two young daughters. Like Richie, they were all petite. They were also all beautiful and very intelligent. I couldn't quite understand why Richie would be catting around when he had a gorgeous family like this at home, but on the other hand, that's the way things were in those days. Married, unmarried, it didn't matter; when it itched, we scratched. Just as long as the moment felt good.

Then Richie's uncle Solly came into town—according to Richie, an unforgettable character I should meet. They came over to my apartment one night, and Richie was absolutely right. Solly was a genuine, old-school, New York character. Short and stout, with a cherubic face, curly gray hair, and well-trimmed mustache and beard, Solly could have been a stand-in for Edward G. Robinson. He chuckled a lot and kept calling me "Henry, my boy."

Over a joint and a bottle of good white wine, he told me that he had started out as a garmento, but he had tired of life in New York and left his wife to take off for LA. Now he was living in Vegas and was married to a tall, blond, statuesque, shiksa showgirl: the dream of every Jewish man under the height of five feet five.

But Solly had another story as well; in fact, this was the reason he was in New York. He was starting a venture with some partners that would install television screens and cameras in supermarket aisles. These would serve a dual purpose; they would help monitor shoplifting, and they would advertise products on the shelves. Solly was working with a man in store security, as well as a man whose company Eastern Airlines used for their market research, so I was immediately reassured that this was a legitimate operation.

I thought it was a good idea, and I set up a meeting for Solly and his partners with the top people working on the General Foods account. It wasn't a difficult thing for me to arrange; I was the creative director of special projects at that time, and this seemed to be one of those special projects. The meeting went well, but it never led to anything concrete, as General Foods didn't want to get involved in a deal that pushed hardware along with the distribution of its products. I think there was something else at play as well. Solly, the security guy, and the research maven, all had the rough-hewn textures of self-made, small businessmen—a very different feel and smell from the corporate suits at General Foods—and it just may have been the case that the gears didn't mesh well. However, the experience made Solly a good friend.

The following year, Solly approached me with a business proposition, and it was delightfully insane.

"Henry, my boy, we're going to start a television network, and you're going to be the creative director." He told me that it would be a network for homeopathic doctors, carrying information about the latest techniques and discoveries, discussions regarding controversial treatments, and other things.

When I replied that I didn't know the first thing about medicine, he said that it didn't matter. His good friend was the president of the American Homeopathic Medical Association, so the deal was in the bag. The annual convention was taking place in Las Vegas, where he and his friend lived, and all we had to do was to create a sales film, go to the convention, and seal the deal.

He explained that all doctors had to continue their education in order to maintain their licenses and that this network would serve that purpose. What he neglected to explain was that the "other things" in the network were going to be pornographic films that would serve as an added enticement. That, I found out later.

I was intrigued by the idea but uneasy about going into business with Solly and his doctor friend, who would be our silent partner. They were obviously both crooks.

I decided that I needed a partner I could trust, so I recruited my old pal Sandy. I first met Sandy when he was representing photographers. Now he was living in Orange County, California, with his wife, Sharon, and their two little girls, and he was working in the marketing department of a medium-sized pharmaceutical company.

I knew he was bored stiff and looking for something new to do. When Sandy was still living in New York, Nora, Sharon, he, and I had a great time together. We smoked immense amounts of weed and dropped acid together a few times. We went to the Woodstock Festival together, loaded on acid, but only got as far as the parking lot, ten miles away from the music. Our condition wouldn't allow us to navigate those ten miles with any assurance that we'd wind up somewhere on the planet Earth.

Sandy was smart and well educated. He'd graduated from Yale and gone on to Wall Street. His brother Barry was still a broker, but Sandy had lost his license in some sort of scam. He would be a big plus going into this deal with Solly.

Sandy was a great pitchman. He had a voice that was as smooth as silk. I used him as the spokesman on our sales film. The film turned out fine. If we had had something to say beyond just bullshit, it would have been much better, but you can only work with what you've got.

So off to Las Vegas we went. This was still the old Rat Pack Vegas, before it became the Disneyland with slots that it is today. The hotels were lavish, the entertainment world class, but from the time you stepped off the plane, you knew that this town was about one thing, and one thing only: taking your money away.

The convention was taking place at the Tropicana, and that's where we were staying. Solly's wife was there to greet him, and Sharon had flown in from LA to join Sandy. I was on my own, but that was okay because I had a plan.

Our large rooms oozed with the satin-slippery charm of a high-priced call girl. Of course, the centerpiece of everything was the casino. It was impossible to go from any one place to any other without crossing through that roaring monster. The sound of the casino compared only to the howling sandstorm in the Sahara Desert. The sound put my entire nervous system into overdrive. It formed a vortex that was impossible to escape, sucking me into an emotional maelstrom of unleashed primitive energy. The room was jam-packed with desperate humans flinging themselves against the furies of destiny, raging at fate, pitting themselves against the gods, more than willing to go down in flames. It was a scary place.

The convention was set up in a series of rooms and auditoriums that ran around the perimeter of the casino floor. Our booth was in one of the smaller rooms. Essentially, my job was done. I had designed a logo and a letterhead for the network, I had designed a brochure as well, and I had made a sales film of Sandy pitching the idea.

Now it was up to Sandy and Solly to make the deals. I'd stick around and stay involved in what was going on. Sort of.

I'd brought a bag of beautiful psilocybin mushrooms, each one about the size of a small pea. Since the idea of a "real" Las Vegas was a ridiculous oxymoron, I decided that I'd be a tourist in Hunter Thompson's world rather than Frank Sinatra's. I felt more at home there.

The next day was our big pitch day. I woke up early, showered, and got dressed in a suit, shirt, and tie. If I was going to be a network executive, I figured I had better look the part. The hallway outside my room was almost silent. I thought that everyone must still be sleeping. I took the elevator down to the main floor, where I would meet up with Solly and Sandy at our booth. The quiet of the early hour and the height of my floor made the elevator ride seem as if I were silently parachuting down to Earth.

The doors shushed open, and KABONG! I was in the deafening, hysterical energy of the casino. The gambling lions were making their first roars of the morning, and the all-nighters were making their final screams. People down to their last nickel were kissing it good-bye. Others were putting their homes on the line, their businesses, their children's educations, anything that would keep them in the game.

I squeezed through the crowded aisles and found the room where we were set up. Sandy and Solly were already there. The sales film was running on a loop on a TV monitor. The brochures were neatly stacked on a table. A banner that I had designed was tacked to the far wall. Everything was set; Sandy and Solly were ready to roll. I could grab some breakfast.

Bada bing! I was back out on the casino floor. New recruits were pouring in, ready to sacrifice their lives, or at least their houses, for some action. The wounded were limping out, wondering if they still had the carfare home. Here and there a few momentary success stories were being celebrated with champagne and showgirls. I put my head down and bulled my way through.

I took my breakfast in the hotel coffee shop, rather than the fancy main restaurant. In Vegas, you can get any meal you want at any time of day. There is no time in Vegas except for gambling time. I looked for a *New York Times* to read while I ate, and was lucky to find just one left at the newsstand. Las Vegas didn't want the gamblers distracted by something as trifling as world events.

I sat in a booth away from the slot machines lined up by the entrance, which were all being played. I had my favorite diner breakfast: orange juice, scrambled eggs with crisp bacon, hash browns well done, a toasted English muffin, and black coffee. It's not that I consider this combo particularly delicious or nutritious, but I do consider it safe to eat anywhere in the continental United States. Oh, and what breakfast of champions would be complete without a hearty helping of some magic mushrooms? I pulled a small handful of these little beauties out of a small baggie that I held under the table, and slipped them into my mouth. Now I was ready: Viva Las Vegas!

I quickly paid my bill before my brains became too scrambled to add; then I sat reading the paper, waiting for the mushrooms to kick in. When I found myself heavily engrossed in an endless article regarding the white goods industry in India, I knew I was good.

I sauntered out the door, and KAWANGA! I was back in the casino. By this time, the mob was piled up three deep on top of each other. Blackjack dealers were calling out cards like auctioneers. Showgirls were sweeping across the floor like ants at a picnic. Cowboys out for the time of their life were tossing their lariats into the crowd and proposing marriage to whomever they pulled out. Arabian sheiks were flying to the high-stakes tables on magic carpets. A quarter of the crowd seemed to be on the verge of suicide, while another quarter was ready to ring in the New Year three months early. The rest of the crowd was moving around like a bunch of marionettes, jerking around on strings controlled by an unseen puppeteer on the floor above.

I took this all in and immediately understood that I had to get to our booth quickly or risk getting sucked into the oily whirlpool.

When I got there, Sandy was deeply involved in explaining our network to a couple of doctors who didn't seem terribly interested. About a half-dozen others were idly thumbing through our brochure.

When he finished his pitch, Sandy rushed over to me and said, "You've got to do something about Solly. He's out of control."

I quickly brought myself into a condition that closely approximated focus. "What do you mean?"

"He's an animal. He grabs these guys by the throat and doesn't let go. And he's offering everyone points in the business if they come in."

"Well, maybe you have to do that for some key players to get the ball rolling."

"Yeah, but he's already given away two hundred percent of the company."

Even in my addled condition, I could recognize that giving away 200 percent was bad. I told Sandy that I'd look for Solly and have a word with him.

BAROING! I was out on the casino floor again. It was like walking into the exhaust blast of a jet engine, with frantic people with bulging eyes and sweaty brows pushing forward to the tables, desperate for a piece of the action; yahoos with ten-gallon hats and big rodeo buckles; Rotarians in polyester suits, pastel shirts, and matching white shoes and belts; Jewish garmentos and Italian wise guys in shiny sharkskin suits smoking fat Havana stogies; women swathed in minks; showgirls; bar girls; call girls; all of them climbing over each other to take the shortcut to the American dream.

Octopus tentacles were everywhere, slipping among the crowd, placing bets, picking pockets, pulling the suckers in. Gorillas and orangutans were stationed beneath the tables and in nets high over the floor, ready to pounce on and tear apart any poor sap who would dare try to break the system. Sharks and squid shot through the waters that were now filling up the casino, turning it into a gigantic aquarium. Three mermaids swam over to me, offering unspoken pleasures.

But I was on an urgent mission to find Solly, and wouldn't be deterred. Finding him in this confounding, disorienting space, with an insane melee going on all around me, was going to be difficult. I absolutely required another handful of mushrooms to level me out.

With my extra senses appropriately sharpened, I set out on my quest. I had to avoid the almost invisible quicksand pits, the palm trees behind which saber-toothed tigers were lying in wait, and especially the dark corner hiding the tyrannosaurus rex. I had to hold my breath while I passed through the area filled with poison gas. But I couldn't overcome my overwhelming need to take a piss. I spotted a men's room just in the nick of time. Luckily there was a stall available, because I could see that the men milling about the urinals were narcs on the watch for the telltale smell of psilocybin-filled urine.

Finally, I found Solly in one of the conference rooms. Sure enough, he was nose to nose with some doctor, climbing inside his suit, barking at him like a rabid dog.

I waited for him to finish his pitch, or rather for the doctor to break his hold and get away. After a little small talk, I ventured the opinion that the sales technique I had just witnessed might have been a bit on the aggressive side.

"Henry, my boy, that's the way it's got to be done." Solly said this, not like the kindly old philosopher that he'd been in the past, but with iron in his voice, sweat on his brow, and a look of desperation in his eyes. Even in my totally polluted condition, I could see that he was going to go full speed down this track, even if it led straight off a cliff.

I spent the rest of the day trying to find my way back to Sandy. Somehow, by the time I got to our booth, the day was over and my baggie of mushrooms was empty. Sandy told me that between him and Solly they had rung up a total of zero subscribers, but we did have reservations to see Lou Rawls performing in the hotel nightclub one hour later.

I went up to my room and spent nearly the entire hour under the shower. Then I put on a fresh shirt and went down to the club to join my partners and their wives.

Lou Rawls's Las Vegas act was a lot slicker than it was soulful. Still, his wonderfully oozing four-octave voice was a pleasure to get lost in. But when he broke into "Dead End Street," a bitter song about loss, I sneaked a sideways look at Solly and Sandy, wondering if they were bitter about their losses on this trip—Solly's money and Sandy's time. For me it was a free trip to Vegas, a place I'd never go on my own. I also had the advantage of having a good job to go back to.

About a year later, I got a call from Solly. He was in town, and he wanted me to meet some guys who were interested in making movies. I desperately wanted to make movies. I had begun to direct some of my own commercials, and I was hot to trot onto something bigger.

The meeting took place in an apartment on the East Side that had the look of a corporate crash pad. These guys were anything but corporate; they were serious wise guys. My brain went numb when I realized whom I was hobnobbing with.

I have no idea what they were talking about for the first half hour. But when they started pouring drinks, one of them pulled me aside to talk about "making movies." These guys were distributing porn films, and now they wanted to get in on the manufacturing end of the business. I could just imagine what the creative conferences on these films would be like. Worse, I could imagine the consequences if they didn't appreciate the finer points of my artistic vision. I told the guy that this was a big decision for me and that I'd have to give it a lot of thought. Then, when we went to join the others, I whispered my good-byes to Solly and quietly slipped out.

I didn't see or hear from Solly after that, mainly because of problems between his nephew Richie and myself. I loved having a good time, but Richie was a fully committed hedonist. Whenever we were shooting a commercial together and I had to confer with Richie about some detail, I always knew where he'd be. He was never next to the camera, but around some corner, sitting back in a chair and taking it in with a smile on his face. This commitment to pleasure was fine with me most of the time. It was even kind of cute.

But he allowed himself to get out of hand. When we were casting for commercials, we would set ourselves up in a small conference room and interview the actors one at a time. If a beautiful woman caught Richie's eye, he would start asking sexually insinuating questions. Sometimes he would ask her to stand up on the conference table and dance, or even take off some of her clothes. I would stand back for a while, but when I considered that he had crossed some invisible line, I would have to step in and put a stop to his antics, sometimes pulling him out of the room to lecture him about professionalism. He always seemed annoyed when this happened. He couldn't understand why I would care enough to stop him from enjoying himself. I realized that Richie had to be controlled, and also that he was beginning to offend some undefined moral sensibility of mine.

I was staying home on this particular weekend, not having or wanting a woman to go up to my country house with and not wanting to spend the weekend by myself up there. I had just settled in with a two-hour reel of jazz, Latin, and bossa nova on my tape deck; a bottle of Nuits-Saint-Georges; a hunk of Kasseri cheese; a block of halvah; and a big bowl of Acapulco Gold, when the phone rang. I figured it to be a friend or a lady wanting to come around, but it turned out to be Richie's wife, Susan. She sounded distraught, saying that she had to talk to me about something urgent. She was already in the city, and she could come up in five minutes. How could I say no?

An hour later, we were lying naked on my leather couch, sweat pouring off our bodies, struggling to catch our breath after the intensity of our sex. When Susan came up, she had told me about discovering that Richie was having an affair with their babysitter. This had been one indiscretion too much for her to bear.

"I always knew that Richie was selfish, but I thought that would be good for me and the kids. Obviously, I was wrong."

She told me her story as we smoked the good weed and drank the good wine, and I became angry with Richie for screwing up such a great family and such a fabulous and beautiful little woman. And as my heart went out to her, my penis did as well.

Reflecting back, I realize that I was the perfect tool for Susan's revenge. I was Richie's friend, sometimes partner in crime, boss, and creative partner, and I was available and, as it turned out, willing. She told me that she was filing for divorce and moving to San Francisco to study law. Obviously, Susan wasn't looking for a long-term commitment on my part.

The following weekend I was buzzed from downstairs again. This time it was the babysitter, Aileen. She had come to tell me that she thought it was wrong for me to be having sex with Susan. It seemed a little strange to me for the "other woman" to be protecting the woman she had just betrayed, but it wasn't that much stranger than anything else going on in my life, so I took it at face value.

In a very short time, this visit followed the course of Susan's visit. Same story, same couch.

A few days later, I was sitting in my office, and Richie called me to his office. I walked over there, wondering if he knew what mischief I had been up to behind his back.

His office door was closed, so I knocked. "Come on in," he said. As I entered, he told me to keep the door closed. Then he picked up a baseball bat that was standing in the corner.

"What would you do if I smashed you over the head with this?"

"Nothing much I could do, except fall down and bleed a lot."

"Maybe I should do just that?"

"I'd understand it if you did."

At that point, I knew that he wasn't going to do anything of the kind, but I was still far out in the wrong, and I had to cop to it. I couldn't very well apologize about what I had done, because I wasn't sorry that I had done those things. I was sorry, however, about the pain that I had caused him, and I told him so. Then I left.

Richie and I didn't have too much to do with each other after that. We didn't hang out anymore, and we stopped working together. Then, about a year later, after Susan and her two girls had moved out to San Francisco, Richie came to see me. He asked if I could help him get a transfer to the San Francisco office. I was more than happy to help him out. It relieved some of my guilty feelings to be able to do this favor for him, and to not have to see him in the office every day.

I heard from him from time to time. He liked it out on the West Coast. The warmer weather suited him. He had bought a little Alfa Romeo convertible, and he loved driving his little girls around with the top down. He enjoyed driving some not-so-little girls around as well.

A few years later, I was out of Young & Rubicam and working at McCann Erickson, heading up a group that worked on Sony, Miller High Life, the Bahamas, and some other accounts. I got a call from Richie. He wanted to come back to New York. He had been a New Yorker all his life, and as much as he liked San Francisco, he missed the bigger city. I had an opening in my group for a senior writer, and I hired him over the phone. He gave his current job a two-week notice, and he came over.

He fit in just fine with the other people in my group. A lot of them already knew him, and the others immediately liked his wry sense of humor. He asked if he could team up with me again, but I already had a partner and didn't want to get that close to Richie again that quickly.

We did spend some time hanging out together, and it got to be more and more comfortable. One day, a few months after he had started working for me, I asked Richie about his uncle.

"Solly's dead," he said. "His wife divorced him, he moved back to Brooklyn, and he got run over by a garbage truck."

I thought about the last time I had seen Solly, and those wise guys at the movie meeting. I remembered the desperate look on his face that losing afternoon in Las Vegas. Then I thought about how someone would come to be run over by a garbage truck, and I was so happy I had walked out of that meeting that day—happy and frightened.

21

LOOSE ENDS

1973

Everything changes; the transfer of energy is the one rule of the universe that we can understand. Everything has its own natural life cycle. Sometimes the cycle is cut short by circumstance or predator, but whatever the cause or the effect, it's still just the transfer of energy.

I remember, a couple of years back, walking down the hallway of the eighth floor at Young & Rubicam, where my Eastern Airlines creative group had their offices, feeling the exuberant glow of success and then thinking that it would inevitably come to an end.

Soon enough, a recession hit the country. Corporate belts were being tightened. People were losing their jobs. I had to change Eastern Airlines' battle cry from "The Wings of Man" to "We're Working Harder for Your Hard Earned Buck." While it addressed the new issues in a direct and hard-hitting manner, and won the approval of the client, it became apparent that the good old days of poetic visions and creative freedom were coming to an end.

The changes in the economy also caused management to be much less inclined to indulge the creative staff or to allow our more outlandish excesses. The business was now back where they understood it, and they felt entitled to take the reins back. One day, Andy Schmidt, the manager of the Art Department, and Carl Sturgis, who was Alex Kroll's hatchet man, decided to take a tour of the eighth floor, where my Eastern group was located. Walking through the hall, they couldn't possibly miss the pervasive scent of marijuana, which constantly hung in the air, but the thing that stopped them in their tracks was the sound of the Ping-Pong match coming from behind the closed door of the conference room. About ten of us were gathered there for a little tournament, when the door opened and Andy and Carl poked their heads in.

The next day the Ping-Pong table was gone. Everyone but I was moved off the eighth floor, and the Research Department was moved in around me. I was assigned to other accounts, accounts whose clients were suspicious of creative people and their ideas, clients who rigidly stuck to a formula that they understood. What I understood was that I was being punished.

A couple of months later, Alex called me up to his office. He told me that they were opening a new office in Hong Kong, and offered me the job of creative director there. In fact, he offered me the job of creative director of Asia. The offer was flattering and exciting, but there was something else that I wanted to do.

Dennis and I had been proposing the idea of an in-house production company that would write and produce corporate films for our clients. We felt that this would give us more creative freedom, more corporate independence, and more income than we had in our current positions. Moreover, it was closer to what we really wanted to do, which was to make films.

When I reminded Alex of this proposal, he replied that the production company idea was far from a sure thing, whereas this job was definite. I felt as if I were caught in the middle of a fast-running river, not knowing whether I should choose a bank to swim for or ride the current. I asked him if I could go to Hong Kong to see what it was like, so I could make an informed decision. He told me that there wasn't time for that. I had to be in place in seven weeks' time for an important meeting with an international tobacco company.

Alex wanted an immediate answer. It didn't seem fair, and I told him so. I said, "Yes, but I'm also going to think about it." I felt that my answer was equal to his proposal.

He sent me directly upstairs to the International Division. The president of International was another Alex, Alex Brody. He welcomed me aboard and proceeded to tell me what I was going to be doing and how I would be doing it. Operating from a base of total ignorance, I didn't argue with him, but I made a mental note that if I was going to do this job, I would do it my own way.

A few days later, I asked Brody what my salary would be, imagining a hefty raise. I was shocked to learn that I'd be taking a cut in pay. He said that there were big tax advantages to working in Hong Kong, plus the cost of living was considerably less, so I'd be taking away more money and living better. That may have made sense to the corporation, but it didn't work for me.

It was time for me to get a visa and working papers from the Hong Kong Consulate. There were lots of papers for me to pick up, fill out, and return. I went up to Brody's office to see if I could get some secretarial help with all of that, but there was none forthcoming. I would have to do all the work myself.

Now, it occurred to me that the International Division worked very differently than in the United States, where I was valued because of my talent. In the International Division, it seemed that I was an interchangeable piece whose value was determined by a title, more like a chess piece than a person.

Other things were bothering me as well. I had the impression that the expatriate business community in Hong Kong was strictly the country-club set, a group I had never been comfortable with.

Also, I was in the process of cleaning up my act. I was stoned almost all the time, and I had come to the realization that it was getting to be a problem. The haze of smoke was making it difficult for me to see ahead into a future. I was at some kind of crossroads that was, as yet, undefined, and I needed clarity to sort things out. Clarity was hard to come by when I was flying in a cloud of ganja all day.

I started to picture myself in Hong Kong, hanging out with Chinese opium smokers. It didn't look like a formula for a successful future. Given that, and the modus operandi of the International Division, I decided that I didn't want the job. I went to Alex's office and told him the news. He looked at me in disbelief; the meeting with the tobacco firm was less than four weeks away. Then he told me to get out of his office.

After that, I was blackballed. I didn't receive any work. The in-house production idea went through, but with only Dennis on board. I was in a weird limbo. I decided to tough it out. "Fuck 'em," I thought. "If they won't give me any work, I'll take their money and coast." I figured that my portfolio was so good that I could do nothing for a year and still maintain my current value on the job market.

I was tired. Tired of not having a clear goal. Tired of knowing that Alex manipulated my creative efforts to further his ambition. Tired of seeing him treating people cruelly and ruthlessly without any regard for their individual talents or sensibilities. He was running the agency like a football team, with him calling all the plays, making all the substitutions, and taking all the credit.

I was embarrassed as well. Embarrassed by the clumsy and stupid way I had handled the Hong Kong situation. Embarrassed by the way I had let my position slip away. Embarrassed because I wasn't doing the creative work that I thrived on, that had fed my pride and given me stature.

Also, I had come to understand the obvious: the business of advertising was all about making money. Hadn't I gone into advertising in order to make money? Yes and no. Actually, I had gone into advertising for the purpose of survival, to pull me out of the dead end that was Brownsville. Advertising had given me the money and exposure to accomplish that. I had sold my soul for a get-out-of-jail card. Now that I was out of jail, what was I going to do?

I occupied my time with reading, writing, painting, and chasing women, none of which eased my feelings of ennui. After about a year of sitting around, I made myself available for the job market. The following week, I was up for three good jobs, and I took a position at Wells Rich Greene. When I went to tell Alex that I was leaving, he was shocked.

"I don't want you to leave!" he said.

"But I haven't had any work to do here for a year."

"But the year is up now!"

His reply was too bizarre to digest. I said good-bye and walked out.

The next bump in my road was also work related. Wells Rich Greene was turning out to be a huge mistake. I was part of a great creative department there, my salary was much higher than it had been at Young & Rubicam, and I had an immense office overlooking Central Park. But the place operated more like a meat-packing plant than an advertising agency.

Almost all the work was done in a clusterfuck. There was no sense of creative ownership to any of it. New campaigns were assigned to at least seven teams of the highly paid creative staff. Each of those teams churned out about seven campaign ideas a day for two weeks or so. Then they were summoned to the office of Charlie Moss, the creative director.

After all the teams had presented their best work, Charlie would inevitably pull a piece of paper out of his pocket and tell everyone that he had an idea. It was never a full-blown idea per se, but a campaign line that he had probably come up with while on the toilet that morning. It was always clever, never great, and it never had the depth of a real advertising concept. Be that as it may, each of the teams was told to adapt Charlie's line to one of their campaign ideas.

If the client ended up buying any of this work, the responsible team would be rewarded with either a cash bonus or a present, such as a large television set or a case of champagne. The major credit, of course, would go to Charlie the Genius.

There was no profit sharing or stock given out at WRG, so there was never any sense of being part of something. Instead it was purely mercenary—cash on the barrelhead. It made me feel like a high-priced hooker.

Then something happened that led me to believe I had a shot of breaking through and becoming one of the very few creative people who were valued as individual talents.

There was a big push to create a new campaign for Multifilter Cigarettes, a small Philip Morris brand that did hardly any advertising. WRG also did very fine advertising for Benson and Hedges, another Philip Morris brand.

More teams than usual were assigned to the Multifilter push. I couldn't understand why, given the size of their budget. However, mine was not to reason why but to turn out my seven campaigns a day.

Somehow, one of my campaigns was chosen as a finalist to be presented to Mary Wells herself. Mary was one of the three founders of WRG, and the only one still there. She was the chairman of the company, although hardly ever in the office. She was usually in the South of France, where she lived with her husband, the CEO of Braniff Airways, coincidentally WRG's first major account. She came to New York from time to time to attend important client meetings or to make decisions about important presentations. This, apparently, was one of those times.

Mary occupied three offices; the first housed her assistant, and the second was where we had our meeting. Mary had her desk in a third office, and I guessed that was where she had more intimate meetings with important people.

I was introduced, and she gave me a quick handshake and a grunt of hello. Then the work was presented. There was a palpable tension in the air as Mary quickly and dismissively went through it all. She came directly to the point.

"I'll fire everybody in the agency if I can't get good work."

At this point I realized why Charlie had not been part of these proceedings. He must have sensed Mary's mood and wanted to distance himself as much as possible.

"Listen," she went on, "Philip Morris is going to give Leo Burnett eighty million dollars to introduce a new cigarette. I want to get that money for Multifilter, and I need a great campaign to beat out Burnett." Leo Burnett was a very large agency in Chicago that had been doing a great job for Philip Morris's Marlboro brand.

Mary paced the floor like a tiger picking up the scent of prey.

"Look, it's just a stupid little brand. People either love it or hate it. We've just got to get them to try it."

"That's it!" I exclaimed. Everyone turned to look at me.

"That's it: 'Multifilter. You'll Love It or You'll Hate It.' It's guaranteed to get trials."

It was the old corny saw of playing the boss's own words back to her. The account guys were already celebrating, jumping up and down in delight, sure that they had a winner, or at least that Mary would be appeased. For her part, Mary wasn't so sure, but she told me to work it up, saying that it just might do the trick.

"We'll see." Those were her parting words as we filed out of her office.

I felt as if I had just grabbed the golden ring. I would no longer be a well-paid assembly-line worker, but a creative star. Now I would see just what Wells Rich Greene had to offer. I decided that a good lunch was in order, and a good cigar as well. I stepped out of the elevator into the lobby, lit up the Havana that I'd been keeping in my desk for such an occasion, and strode toward the street.

Ahead of me in the lobby, I spotted Mary walking to the elevators, coming straight toward me. What a golden opportunity, I thought, to maybe engage her in at least a short how-do-you-do. I cautioned myself not to overplay my hand. I put a friendly smile on my face and kept my face pointed at Mary as we approached each other. I had a nice, casual greeting ready to roll off my tongue as we got closer and closer, and then she passed me without even a glance of recognition, and I then knew everything I had to know about Wells Rich Greene.

I decided that I had to find another place to work. McCann Erickson had been doing some excellent advertising for its three beer brands, Miller High Life, Miller Lite, and Löwenbräu. Nora was working there as a producer, so I had an introduction. She set up a lunch for me with Bob Lenz, the man in charge of the beer brands. We liked each other instantly, and we talked about what I'd be working on if I went over there. He mentioned Miller High Life and the Bahamas Tourism accounts. He also said that the Bahamas account might be in trouble. I answered that I had experience with accounts in trouble and that I was usually successful in saving them. After lunch, we shook hands warmly and went our separate ways.

Soon afterward, I was having lunch with the creative director, Bill Backer, at the Princeton Club. Bill had the soft drawl of his southern upbringing. He had the round head and cherubic features of a young Orson Welles. He was an extremely talented jingle writer, having written many award-winning jingles for Coca-Cola, the agency's largest account, and he considered himself to be a genius.

I had heard that he was wealthy, that the family manse was on Legare Street in Charleston, and that an ancestor, albeit with the name changed for some literary reason, was the infamous slaveholder Simon Legree from *Uncle Tom's Cabin*. He had apparently done some research on me.

"Wait until I tell everyone back at the agency that I got Henry Holtzman to wear a suit and tie," he crowed.

As our lunch wound down, I discovered that Bill was also a tightwad. "Well, I'm not going to pay you what Mary Wells pays you," he drawled. He offered me considerably less but agreed that we could renegotiate in one year's time. That was good enough for me. I was desperate to get out of the clutches of Mary Wells and back to doing good work again. Good work was the only way I had to advance myself financially, and now that was more important than ever.

About six months earlier, I had met Cheryl, and it had been love at first sight. We were now living together and planning to get married, and I could see children in our future. Children meant lots of responsibilities, and lots of money.

Two weeks later, I was working at McCann Erickson, and sure enough, no sooner was I given an office than I was given the Bahamas Account and told that the agency had been put on ninety-day notice by the Bahamas Tourist Board. I was assigned a writer named Dick Fitzhugh. I knew Dick from Young & Rubicam. We'd never worked together, but he had a reputation as a good and intelligent writer, and a good guy as well.

Dick was all those things, but for some reason we couldn't come up with an idea that rang the bell. We worked out ads that were looked good and sounded smart, but they lacked that necessary explosive dynamic that grabbed people by the throats. This went on for weeks. From time to time, we'd present our stuff to Bob Lenz and his partner, Bob Meury, and their response was always, "Pretty good. Keep working."

I was beginning to worry that I had lost my touch. At the same time, I was getting the feeling that I had a great idea rolling around beneath the surface, but I just couldn't pull it out into the open. This feeling nagged at me more and more. Eventually, we were out of time, and we had to present our best ideas to Lenz, Meury, and Backer.

Dick and I sat in my office polishing up the best of what we had, none of which was great. Meanwhile, I continued to feel that a great idea was just out of reach. I was spinning my mind around and around, hoping that the idea would jump out at me, but Dick was yapping nonstop about ideas that had nowhere to go, while I was desperately searching my mind for something I could be proud of. Finally, I told him that I needed a half hour alone with my thoughts, and he gracefully left.

What happened next was improbable but true. I sat down, closed my eyes, and let my thoughts sink down into my subconscious, where I was sure the idea was buried. I only had half an hour, but I knew it was in there.

Ten minutes later, I pulled it out: "It's Better in the Bahamas." It was simplistic, but it was also all-inclusive. Everything was better in the Bahamas: beaches, food, gambling, sex, fishing, diving. Everything you wanted in a tropical vacation was better in the Bahamas. Plus, the line had great alliteration, which made it catchy and easy to remember. The line was so good that, forty years later, it's still being used.

Actually, I'm being too polite here. The truth be told, I felt as if I was giving birth to this idea that had been living inside me. But not having the necessary equipment or the required plumbing, I had to reach way in and pull it out of my ass. Which is probably why I had to ask Dick to leave the room.

Along with the line, I came up with two poster-like visuals. The first was a beautiful American woman, in a light top and billowing skirt, standing in the emerald-green water, hundreds of yards away from the shore. The second was a Bahamian man, also way out in the water, holding a tray filled with tropical treats: fruits, fish, and seafood.

I ran into Dick's office shouting, "I've got it! I've got it!" Dick knew a winner when he saw it, and he immediately sat down to write some copy to go along with my headline and visuals. Immediately after that, we rounded up the bosses to show them what we had, and just a few days later, we were all down in the Bahamas presenting to the tourist board. When the presentation was over, the minister of tourism announced that, for the first time, he was proud of the advertising for his country. Yay me!

Ten months later, I'd been at McCann for a year, and it was time for me to meet with Bill Backer to talk about my compensation.

Bill seemed happy to meet with me. I reminded him about the things I had accomplished over the past year. They included saving the Bahamas account and running the advertising for Miller High Life, although, as Bill was quick to point out, Bob Lenz was still the creative head of that business. Lastly, I pointed out that I had been instrumental in our successful pitch for the Sony business. We'd beaten out Young & Rubicam for that account, which gave me some added satisfaction. I had created a print campaign for our presentation and had written the tagline "Sony the One and Only." Bill had no rejoinder to that last, although he did point out that McCann's work on Miller and Coke had played a major part in our getting the Sony business.

I went on to tell Bill that I would like a significant raise, some stock in the company, and the title of vice president.

"Why would you want to be a vice president?" he asked. "The title doesn't mean anything."

"Maybe you don't have to worry about things like this, but when I go to a bank for a loan or a mortgage, the title means something to them."

"I see what you mean, but you've only been here a year. That's too soon to make you a vice president."

"And what about the rest?"

"Nobody in the Creative Department has any stock."

My blood was starting to pump against the top of my head. "And the raise?"

"I'll have to think about that."

How clever of him to leave our conversation on a hopeful note. I was livid. Who did he think he was, with that smug drawl of his? Did he think he was talking to one of the field hands down on his plantation? But I kept my feelings and plans to myself, and left him with a handshake.

I went back to my office and made a quick phone call. It took me less than five minutes to get an offer for an excellent job at Ogilvy, a competing agency. Then I marched over to Bob Lenz's office, where he was working with Meury, and calmly told them that I was leaving. They were stunned to hear my news. Unbeknownst to me, they had been making big plans for themselves, and they were counting on me to hold down the Sony account while they were busy with other things.

I explained to them what had gone down between Bill and myself, and said that I was going to Ogilvy. They asked me to give them twenty-four hours to fix the situation, and I agreed. I liked the atmosphere and the level of work at McCann, and I liked the two Bobs, but I wouldn't stand still for being played for a patsy by some southern fancy-pants.

The next morning, Bill came to my office and asked me to join him in his. The first thing he did was to apologize. That's when I realized that something serious was going on and that I was somehow involved. Then he offered me everything I had asked for, even more. I didn't doubt for a second that I was worth what he was offering, but I had plenty of doubt about his sincerity. I intuitively knew that I had just made a powerful enemy.

Six months later everything became clear to me. Bill Backer was leaving McCann to open a new agency with Carl Spielvogel, the vice-chairman of Interpublic, the holding company that owned McCann. The word was that Spielvogel had been in line to become the chairman of Interpublic but was being passed over, possibly because he was the only Jew in an Irish corporation. Carl was pissed off, to put it mildly. It was reported that he said, "If they won't let me into their club, I'll make my own."

Backer was leaving, and Bob Lenz was going to be the new creative director of McCann, except that Bob was going to join Bill and Carl in the new agency, as were Bob Meury and a group of the top account guys on the Miller Brewing business. It was apparent that Miller would soon be taking a walk as well.

Interpublic rushed to stop the bleeding. All the remaining top creatives were given big raises and promotions. I was now one of four deputy creative directors, and I was given Backer's old office. I was in a good spot, and it was at the right time; Cheryl and I were now married, and we had our daughter Anna as the center of our universe.

But if I was in a good place, I was going to have to fight to keep it. A free-for-all began among the remaining creative executives to see who would become the next creative director of the agency. Suddenly, all these dreamy, artistic souls developed sharp elbows, hard edges, and shifty moves, all undoubtedly fueled by the cocaine that had replaced marijuana as the drug of choice among our set. That the coke also instilled a sense of power and invincibility certainly added to the aggressiveness of the participants in this contest.

Cocaine had taken a hold on a large portion of society and wasn't letting go. It was an aggressive and insisting mistress, always demanding more attention and always wanting to be flaunted. At work cocaine wanted to be taken out for lunch or sneaked in for a quickie behind closed office doors. It came out to celebrate at parties, dinners, airplane flights, and any place out of sight of authority.

Cocaine proved to be an expensive mistress, and the price was often too high to deal with. Marriages were broken, businesses busted, careers ruined. Luckily, I sensed the danger in time to quit without too much damage. I quit cold turkey, the same way I had given up cigarettes years earlier.

But many of my friends and associates weren't lucky. The ones who got off easiest just wound up spending more money than they could afford, but one guy I worked with had to have an operation for a hole in his nose, and a photographer friend lost most of his clients and his studio as well.

Meanwhile, the infighting at the agency was reaching a fever pitch. Creative executives began to criticize the work of other creative executives, tried to pry away the accounts of their peers, and attempted to recruit talented art directors and writers from their competitors' camps—all supposedly "for the good of the agency."

I was no exception to this skulduggery. I was never hungry for power, and I wasn't crazy about being responsible for other people's work, but I now had a family to support, and I was horrified at the thought of others having power over me. If I had to battle to prevent that, I could handle myself as well as anyone.

But the simple fact of the matter was that I detested politics, and I hated rancor, especially among people who were supposed to be striving for the same goal. I wasn't naive. I'd known from early on in my career that the only way to make more money was to move up, and moving up meant taking on responsibilities and the envy of peers.

Early one workday morning, I stood in front of a full-length mirror in our bedroom, checking myself out in a double-breasted suit cut from a beautifully patterned and expensive Italian wool, deciding which tie to wear to a breakfast in McCann's executive dining room with some guys from DuPont whom I was supposed to impress but had nothing whatsoever to talk to about. When I took a longer and harder look at the man inside the suit, my depression almost sent me back to bed. I was looking at someone I didn't know, someone I didn't even want to know.

The world had changed considerably since the time that I started out in the advertising business. It was more cynical, selfish, hard-bitten. The optimism of the Kennedy years had been crushed by assassinations, by the frustration of trying to end the senseless war in Vietnam, by the rise of Nixon and his criminal regime, and by Reagan and his me-first philosophy.

Those changes were amply reflected in the advertising industry. At Young & Rubicam I had started out working for King Arthur and wound up working for King Kong. From there I moved on to Lucrezia Borgia and finally to Simon Legree. Things had changed in a big way. An era had ended. The suits were back in charge—maybe deservedly so, because everything had gone too far over the top.

Socially and sexually, the time of free love had developed into an obscene promiscuity; romance, it seems, was dead. The cold bite of cocaine replaced the psychedelic pipe dreams of marijuana and mushrooms. The sunsets were tinged with the acid colors of pollution; herpes and AIDS were on the horizon.

At work I was trapped in some cockeyed version of the Peter principle: promoted to a job that I could do but that I hated. I was spending 90 percent of my time on guiding and pitching other people's work and only 10 percent on what I really loved to do: creating. It was the only way to earn more money, and the only way not to have someone looking over my shoulder, telling me what to do and how to do it.

I now had to cozy up to people I couldn't relate to, to get them not only to respect my judgment but to like me as a person. That's what being a salesman was about, but I wasn't a salesman. I was an artist.

Now I had to constantly watch my back. What once had been collegial creative competition had now turned seriously cutthroat, and it could cost me my job. Now I was a salesman and a politician as well. I was the last thing I'd ever wanted to be: a phony.

A phony? A phony what? I was a real person, a real male human being. I did real things. I'd had real successes. I had a real wife and a real daughter.

But I was a phony because I wasn't the man I wanted to be. I wasn't the combination of Picasso and Einstein that I thought I was when I was four years old and considered myself much too good for Sheila Feldman.

I felt trapped by the life that I had created for myself. I could see only unhappiness and disaster down the road. But I was lucky—again. I had another card to play; I could become a film director of television commercials. I had directed some of my own commercials when I was at Young & Rubicam, and I had started doing that again at McCann. Now I had a sample reel that I could show to prospective clients. Those clients would be creative people at the agencies, people like myself. Dealing with them as clients seemed like a much more pleasant task than dealing with the suits. Plus, I would be dealing only with the creative aspect of the commercials. I wouldn't have anything to do with marketing strategies or corporate politics. What a relief that would be!

After twenty years in the advertising business, I knew a lot of people, and I had a stellar reputation as a talent. Those things would help a lot. Still, there was a huge learning curve and an entirely different set of skills, and there wasn't the safety net of a major international advertising conglomerate. I also knew that if I screwed up badly, the word would quickly spread throughout the industry, and no one would take the chance to work with me. I'd be dead in the water.

I had the responsibility of a family now. Was it fair to them for me to take this kind of risk? The answer was easy. If I didn't like who I was becoming as an agency executive, what would my wife and daughter think of me? I had to take this chance. Once again, I had squirmed out of the box I'd been placed in, so I could go on.

22

AT LAST

1973

I came of age along with the sexual revolution. Wasn't I the lucky one? Especially given my innate shyness and my sexual insecurity. It seemed as if everyone wanted to run wild in the sexual playground, and I was usually available to play. Neighbors, coworkers, models, saleswomen working in shops or passing through the office, the English girl who cut my hair, the girl who sold me dope, girls I passed on the street or met at parties, girls from Fire Island weekends. Sometimes I couldn't even figure out how I had met the young woman in my bed. There were young women who lived in penthouses, young women with roommates, and women who lived with other men. There were women of every nationality, race, and ethnicity. It seemed as if the whole world was out to have a good time, and my raging libido was intent on making the most of it.

In truth, I was anything but a ladies' man. I was much too self-conscious for that kind of enterprise. I did very little chasing, partly because I didn't have to, mostly because I wasn't very good at it. If I had to say more than hello, I was at a loss for words. I mean, what was I going to say? "Do you want to fuck?" Because when you got right down to it, that's what it was all about. It was the primal biological imperative pounding away, releasing furious legions of hormones, reducing me to an instrument of base desire.

Sure, I had friendships with women. There were women I liked to hang around and talk with, but when it came time to getting close to a woman because of sexual attraction, it was the "sexual" part that I was after. I wasn't looking for a partner in a relationship because I didn't think that I was capable of holding up my part of one. I had already failed twice, with Dorothy and Nora, and I wasn't ready to put myself to the test again.

In fact, after my breakup with Nora, I was happy to have my independence. Happy, that is, in a lonely kind of way. I moved down to the Village, to a light-filled one-bedroom on the top floor of a five-story walk-up. The rooms were large and well proportioned. There was a small working fireplace and a huge skylight in the living room, which overlooked Greenwich Avenue and a schoolyard filled with grade-school kids who sounded like chirping birds. The bedroom faced tree-filled backyards; it was a peaceful place where I could string up a hammock. The five flights of stairs provided a good memory aid, as I never wanted to climb up to my apartment with a load of groceries only to realize that I had forgotten something.

I became a flaneur in my new neighborhood, taking long, aimless walks through the leafy streets filled with odd and interesting shops and people. Or I'd spend the day in my living room, with a bowl of marijuana, a bottle of wine, and a brick of halvah; listening to music, reading a book, and watching the light change through the skylight.

Of course, I wasn't always alone. Women were everywhere, and often they were just as aggressive as any man. Many women seemed to have gotten it into their minds to choose me. It made perfect biological and Darwinian sense. The best provider was no longer the fleetest of foot and strongest of arm, at least not in our urbane society. For us, it was the ones with the intelligence, cunning, and skills to advance and take advantage of the capitalist system that we'd engineered for ourselves. I had already proved myself adept at that. I was reasonably good looking, for a dark, wiry, ethnic type, and I had the added incentive, for some, of being artistic and rebellious—two traits that had gained great currency in recent times. To some women I was probably some sort of trophy, to others an aspiration of sorts, and of course for others I was just the focus of a sexual urge.

For my part, I just sort of let things happen. I kept moving forward if I felt nudged by my libido or my loneliness.

I lived alone for four years. By that time, I had three regular women friends whom I saw about once every two weeks. One happened to be my dope dealer, which made those playdates wildly psychedelic. A second was a former Miss Tokyo who used me as a sex toy and told me not to fall in love, a request that I was happy to go along with. The third was a young Indian woman who wore ankle bracelets with tiny bells that jingled as she climbed the five flights of stairs to my apartment.

By the time I was approaching my thirty-fourth birthday, I had myself figured as a confirmed bachelor. I was content, but there was a constant mood of ennui about me. That was the state of my life at that point—that and my anger. Anger was my constant companion. All my progress in life had been propelled by anger. All the moves backward had been fueled by anger as well.

What was I angry about? Everything and everybody. I was angry with my parents for sending me out into the world without a roadmap. I was angry with myself for not being the combination of Einstein and Picasso that I thought I should be. I was angry with everyone who had tried to manipulate me for his or her own ends, from my parents and Mrs. Feldman, to Alex Kroll and Bill Backer, and everyone in between.

I was also angry because there was a sharp edged change in the air. The years of rebellion were coming to an end. Creativity was being superseded by productivity. Glamour was overwhelming taste. The utopian ideal was being drowned by a tidal wave of materialism. The tide was changing, as it always does, and it depressed me.

Two days after my thirty-fourth birthday, I sauntered over to the Buffalo Roadhouse to meet Maurice and another friend, Clark, for brunch. The Buffalo Roadhouse was a Greenwich Village standby—a good-sized saloon and restaurant on Seventh Avenue South with a large patio out front.

It was a warm and sunny September day. A day sure to pull everyone out of bed and out into the streets. All the good brunch places were going to be jammed, so I got there early in order to get a good table outside.

The hostess showed me to a large round table smack in the center of the patio. As I sat down, I noticed a young woman sitting at a small table directly across from me. My heart stopped when I saw her. She sat up straight in her chair, intently reading a book. Her face was beautiful—thoughtful, knowing, interesting, and kind. Her tightly curled honey-colored hair was cut short. Her slim yet shapely torso was wrapped tightly in a short silk jacket, blue and white with a Japanese motif.

The sight of this young woman made me gasp. I couldn't avoid looking at her even if I wanted to, as she was directly in my field of vision. I tried not to stare, but I found my gaze constantly drawn to her.

I watched as she gave a waiter her order. Then I made a concerted effort to study everyone else sitting out on the patio. "What am I going to do about this?" I started to talk to myself. "Here's this beautiful, interesting-looking woman that you're definitely attracted to. Are you going to make a move, or are you going to do your usual 'I'm too shy' thing?"

I checked the time. I had at least ten minutes before Maurice and Clark would arrive. I didn't want to have to compete with Maurice for this woman's attention. Besides, I thought that his usual antics would be off-putting if she was as thoughtful as she looked. "Come on, Henry! Are you going to live your whole life afraid to put yourself out there?"

She looked up, and I caught her eye. She smiled politely, and I waved. She smiled again and returned to her book. I thought that I had better find something to occupy myself with so that I wouldn't just be nakedly staring at her. When the waiter passed by, I ordered some eggs Benedict and a bloody mary.

"Okay, stupid," I said to myself. "What are you going to do about this? Are you just going to sit here like a piece of furniture, or are you going to get up and do something? Here's this woman; you're obviously attracted to her. She's beautiful, she looks interesting, she's reading a book, and she seems to be self-contained. So what are you waiting for? Who's the boss here: you or your shyness?"

Our eyes met again, and I took a chance.

"Would you like to join me? I have a nice big table." What a clumsy remark! But it was all I could think of.

This time there was a hint of annoyance in her smile. "No, thanks."

A few minutes later my drink and the eggs Benedict came to my table. I noticed that while she had ordered before I had, I was served first. I caught her attention once more.

"Are you sure you won't join me? It looks like I get better service over here." That was even stupider than my first try! And she refused my offer again.

By now I was committed to making this happen. Time was running out; Maurice and Clark would be here any minute. Nothing was coming into my mind, but I had to make a move. I stood up and walked over to her table. She looked up.

"I really think you should join me," I said. "I won't bother you. You can just sit there and read your book." A look of exasperation came across her face. I had to give it one last shot.

"I really think that we have a lot in common."

"Really? Like what?"

Uh-oh, now I was on the spot. Think fast, Henry!

"Well, I was born in Brooklyn."

"So was I," she responded. "What neighborhood did you grow up in?"

"Brownsville."

"Me too."

Whew! Now we were getting somewhere.

"And what hospital?"

"Brooklyn Women's Jewish Hospital."

"That's where I was born also."

Bingo!

Five minutes later the four of us were sitting at the large round table, the young woman, whose name I then knew was Cheryl, Maurice, Clark, and myself. Maurice was pretending that he was a hair stylist, and he was telling Cheryl how he would completely restyle her. I sat quietly, thinking that his bizarre behavior would make me look better by comparison. I found out later that when I went to the bathroom, Clark asked Cheryl for her number.

When we paid the bill, I asked Cheryl if she wanted to take a walk, and she did. I said my good-byes to my two shit-bum friends and made sure that Cheryl and I took off in the opposite direction from them.

I had no plan. I just wanted to see how the pieces fit together. Somehow, as we walked and talked, we wound up standing in front of the building where I lived. What a coincidence! I asked Cheryl if she wanted to come up, and she did.

Upstairs I put on some music, poured some wine, and lit up a joint. We sat on my couch and talked for hours. I was totally enchanted by this young woman. She was studying acting; she had been married and divorced; she had lived in Israel; she was making her life up as it went along and didn't seem the least bit afraid of what a huge undertaking that was.

I couldn't stop myself from leaning over and planting a quiet kiss on her soft lips. She quickly got to her feet.

"How dare you! Who do you think you are?"

I didn't know what to say, other than "I'm sorry."

"Well, I'm going home." She walked to the door.

"I'm sorry," I offered again as I opened the door for her. She handed me a slip of paper.

"Here's my number." And she was gone.

The Brooklyn Women's Jewish Hospital! Brownsville! It was full circle back to the old neighborhood, the place I had worked so hard to escape. But wasn't she an escapee as well? Yet one more thing we had in common!

From my first day on Earth I've felt like a stranger in an alien world. Maybe having your mother cry upon your arrival will do that to you. I was in over my head, in water too murky to see, not knowing what was on the surface. I longed for someone's hand to hold, someone who could shine a light into the unknown while standing by my side.

The next day I sent her two-dozen yellow roses. Ten months later we were married. Seven months after that, our daughter was born. My life changed forever. I was saved. Again.

95901666R00153

Made in the USA
Columbia, SC
17 May 2018